HATELAND

HATELAND

Bernard O'Mahoney

MAINSTREAM
PUBLISHING
EDINBURGH AND LONDON

First published in Great Britain in 2005 by
MAINSTREAM PUBLISHING COMPANY (EDINBURGH) LTD
7 Albany Street
Edinburgh EH1 3UG

ISBN 1 84018 796 4

The publishers will be glad to make good any omissions
brought to their attention

A catalogue record for this book is available
from the British Library

Typeset in Badhouse and Galliard

Printed in Great Britain by
Antony Rowe Ltd, Chippenham, Wiltshire

I dedicate this book to a man I was proud
to call my friend:
Ray Cartland
Born 1 July 1964
Died 10 April 2002

ODE TO SNAP

The fools, the fools, the green-eyed fools, they could never see what we could see.

From that bench upon that hill, we gazed through innocent eyes at an imaginary ocean that kissed the distant shore beneath the flickering mainland lights.

We sat in silence, immersed in our own perfect world, whilst all around us, the real world was forever threatening to destroy us.

Cast asunder by falsehoods and smears, we drifted away into that ocean, tied by memories, torn by pain.

But fear not, our friendship cannot die, the fools cannot destroy us.

Someday, we will be reunited by the bond their lies, ill-will and jealousy could not destroy.

ACKNOWLEDGEMENTS

Thanks to The Who for their album *Quadrophenia* (released 16 November 1973): lyrics that raced around my brain and made me question everything I was ever told; rhythms that tore through my veins as I rampaged through dance-halls and streets; simply great tunes that set me free and made me feel alive!

Special thanks to Ljuba Hantke, Sheila and Frank Proud, Brian and May McGovern, and editor Kevin O'Brien at Mainstream.

Last but by no means least, thanks also to Liverpool's favourite sons, Vinny Bingham and Lenny Higson (Do They Know It's Christmas?), Devon's own Martin 'Whizz Kid' Moore, everyone in sarf London, Glen, Ebony, Lauren, Emma's sister Siobhan, Hughie, 'The Angel of Manchester' Chemane Thomas, Steve and Lyn Daley and family, the Legion clique, Sean and Kerry Riley, Patricia and Paul Scanlon, Michael and Carol, my mother, my children Adrian, Vinney and Karis, Fr. Philip, and the Posh and Deeping boys – you know who you are!

www.bernardomahoney.com

CONTENTS

CHAPTER 1

GETTING A GRIP

'ADOLF' WANTED ME TO MEET 'THE FÜHRER', SO WE HOPPED ON A TUBE TO ARNOS Grove and looked for a pub full of gardeners. Not real gardeners. Nazis posing as gardeners. In those days, the British National Party (BNP) couldn't use their own name to hire a venue. To book somewhere, even the mouldy upstairs room of a derelict pub, they'd use a pseudonym, like 'The Gardeners' Club' – something I'd always considered somewhat weak.

I used to sneer about it to Adolf. If you believe in something so strongly, why pretend you're someone else? Why the secrecy? Why the deception? If this was the party that was going to march to power and save the Aryan nation from the blacks and the reds and the race traitors, how was the message going to be spread? Preaching to the converted in the locked back-room of a secret location seemed pretty pointless. To me, at least. Not so much to Adolf, who regarded my criticisms as unhelpful, even treacherous, a contemptible flirtation with the forces of ZOG – the Jew-run Zionist Occupation Government, which apparently ruled our land and most of the world.

Adolf traced to my supposed 'northern' roots what he saw as my shallow commitment to the Nazi cause. A south Londoner, he regarded 'northerners' as merely borderline Aryans. He also seemed to think 'the north' began just beyond north London. In fact, I'd been dragged up in Wolverhampton, which geographers, so far as I knew, had always located in the West Midlands.

I'd become friends with Adolf after leaving the army. We were

11

both in our early 20s when we met. He was a friend of my older brother Paul. They had a lot in common – boozing, psychotic violence and Nazism. I could connect with the booze and the violence, but for a long time I remained unsure about what to make of the Nazism. Even at the height of my Nazi involvement, I had little understanding of the politics. Mainly, I just endorsed the far-right's anti-black racism, because I didn't really like blacks and Asians. Of course, I hardly knew any.

I wasn't really politically minded. Since my teens, I'd had a weakness for gang warfare and a desire to be the baddest of the bad. Hanging around with Nazis helped me keep in touch with my real self. They were – so it seemed to me then – the baddest gang on the block.

I'd met Adolf for the first time at the first of Paul's two illegal weddings. He immediately poured scorn on my 'northern' accent, but, perhaps because of our shared council-estate heritage, we got on well. Since then, although Adolf and I had spent quite a lot of time together on and off, I didn't know much about his background. If you asked him what he regarded as a personal question, he'd look at you, disgust forming on his face, and say, 'Are you a homosexual? Are you hoping to sleep with me?'

I assumed he'd had the usual shit childhood, like mine, with some sort of father-figure stomping on his head between bouts of suicide drinking and venomous verbal abuse. But I didn't know for sure. I'd never met his father and he never spoke about him. His mother was a lovely woman. I really liked her. She hadn't held my brother Paul's behaviour against me. Some months after the wedding, Paul had stabbed Adolf in the stomach with a bayonet in front of her in her living room. Adolf recovered but, understandably, his friendship with Paul didn't.

I'd known Adolf for around five years when we set off that evening some time in the late '80s for Arnos Grove in north London to hear a speech by Britain's would-be Führer, John Tyndall, leader of the BNP. We headed off from Adolf's flat in Stockwell, south London. I'd often suggested Adolf move away from the area, because the large number of people there from ethnic minorities (not the term Adolf used) incited him constantly to rage. He was the sort of person who wouldn't buy even a packet of mints from an Asian-owned shop ('I ain't putting money in that cunt's pocket'). If he saw a white woman on the street with a pushchair containing a non-white child he'd mutter, 'White-trash slut.' Sometimes on the street, he'd hold out his hands in theatrical despair and say, 'If I could see just one person here with Aryan blood flowing through their veins . . .'

But his raging could be extremely funny. For Nazis, anyway. He tortured himself with conspiracy theories, making unlikely connections between them and current events. He'd work things out aloud: less stream of consciousness, more stream of fury. He was like a young Alf Garnett (the elderly ranting racist from the '60s television sitcom, *Till Death Us Do Part*, whose catchphrase was 'The wogs start at Calais').

Adolf was about 5 ft 10 in., not particularly well built, but not a sparrow. Wiry – and wired. When he spoke, it was usually through clenched teeth and flecks of phlegm. The veins on his neck would protrude and pulse, and every other visible muscle would bulge and twitch. He oozed violence.

He wasn't without contradictions. His first serious girlfriend came from Liverpool. This surprised me because, like the original Alf Garnett, he reserved special contempt and loathing for 'Scousers'. He said she was 'all right', because her grandparents had been born in London. On his first trip to Liverpool to meet her parents, he told me – seriously – he'd brought up his own supply of bottled water. He'd wanted to minimise the risk of catching typhoid, cholera and other water-borne diseases he believed rife in that part of 'the Third World'.

'Adolf', of course, wasn't his real name, just the unsubtle nickname he'd earned for his dedication to the National Socialist cause. Unlike most so-called Nazis (including me at the time), Adolf had a good grasp of the ideology and politics of fascism. He could rant for hours (and often did) on the differences between the various Nazi and far-right groupings, as well as on the workings of ZOG. He seemed to know everyone who was anyone in 'the Movement', but he always avoided officially joining any group, largely because of his conviction that spies and informers skulked in all of them.

In 1985, around three years after I'd first met him, Adolf had almost been blown to bits. In a south London street, which happened to contain the headquarters of the far-left Workers' Revolutionary Party (WRP), a bomb had exploded in the back of a car that Adolf had been travelling in with a fellow Nazi. The bomb had been hidden in a biscuit-tin packed with nails. Adolf hadn't been in the car at the time – he'd just got out to buy a takeaway from a nearby Kentucky Fried Chicken shop – so he escaped with minor burns, unlike the driver, who took the full impact and was badly injured.

The driver had been charged with making an explosive device intended to endanger life. At his trial, the prosecution claimed he'd been planning to plant the bomb at the WRP's headquarters. However, the jury believed his defence that he'd only been 'experimenting' with bomb-making as a hobby and had not built the bomb for any political use. The judge could only sentence him on the lesser charges. He got three years' imprisonment for possessing the contents of the biscuit-tin (and ten home-made grenades, seven detonators and two petrol bombs).

Adolf escaped prosecution. The police accepted his claim he'd known nothing about the bomb on the back seat. They believed him when he said he'd just accepted a lift from a friend. Adolf told me later that his claim of innocence had been aided by the fact that, when the bomb exploded, he'd been in possession of two pieces of chicken, a large portion of chips and a milkshake. But the fact he'd never officially joined any Nazi group may also have convinced the police they were dealing with an innocent fellow-traveller.

I'd been living in apartheid South Africa at the time of the explosion. I'd gone there to escape prosecution for wounding someone. In the end, I fled the country before the Afrikaners could jail and deport me. This had boosted my status in Adolf's eyes. He chose to believe that South Africa – the beacon of white light in the dark continent – had sent me into exile. He praised me as the only person to be expelled by the apartheid regime for being too right-wing. In fact, my forced departure from white man's heaven resulted from crimes of violence and a general disrespect for the little law that then existed there, rather than anything political.

Adolf and I arrived at Arnos Grove and set about looking for the pub where the BNP meeting was to be held. We half-expected to encounter a crowd of shrieking leftists outside the pub. No matter what precautions were taken to keep secret a Nazi meeting's location, the anti-Nazis usually swung an invitation.

The police tended to prevent major battles, although Adolf told me he'd sometimes been hit by a 'carrot-juice' bottle, a Socialist Worker placard or 'a lesbian'. Adolf assumed all women at anti-Nazi demos were lesbians, partly because they didn't tend to wear miniskirts, high-heels and crop-tops, and partly because he thought lesbians searched unconsciously for 'a good man' to set them right and therefore felt drawn to demos where they could encounter good men like us. It was one of his numerous theories.

Eventually, we found the pub. All was quiet outside. Inside, we knew instantly we'd come to the right place, because the bar was dotted with pairs of skinheads sitting at different tables, all trying to pretend they didn't know each other. They remained deep under cover, observing the secret-society rule, 'Don't all sit together or the guv'nor will suss.' Around 15 pairs of men wearing boots, braces and Union Jack T-shirts suddenly descend on a pub – and it's just a coincidence. No one will ever guess.

Then, almost as one, these unconnected people suddenly got up and made their way upstairs to the meeting. I looked at the landlord standing at the bar. He was a thick-set Irishman. I could tell he'd twigged that the members of this gardening club weren't about to discuss the pros and cons of paraffin-fuelled lawnmowers.

Adolf and I entered the meeting room – and I wondered what I was doing there. I didn't really need another Nazi lecture. Listening to Adolf on the long tube journey up had been enough for one day. I'd already received a verbal top-up about our race, our nation's destiny and our need to be fit and ready when the call came.

Union flags draped a table on a raised platform at the front of the room. 'The Führer' John Tyndall sat there, flanked by lieutenants. Tyndall looked like an old-fashioned schoolmaster. I could imagine kids flicking snot at his balding head when he turned to face the blackboard. I'd heard one of his speeches before. It was all about 'war on the streets', 'direct action' and 'the bulldog spirit'. Tyndall stood up, cleared his throat and began to speak. Suddenly, the pub landlord burst into the room. 'Hey, hey,' he said. 'What the fuck's going on here? I'm not having any National Front meetings in my pub. You'll all have to leave now. Come on, or I'll call the police.'

He said he'd give us five minutes to piss off. He left the room. There was silence. People began to get up meekly from their seats. Tyndall asked sheepishly if we could continue the meeting somewhere nearby. I didn't particularly want to hear his speech, though he wasn't a bad speaker, but I'd just travelled all the way across London, and I didn't think the hardened foot-soldiers of fascism ought to be sent packing by a few mildly threatening words from a single, unarmed Irishman. It wasn't quite 'the bulldog spirit'.

I turned to Adolf. I could tell he was thinking the same.

Adolf said, 'Fuck this. Let's lock the door.'

We walked towards the door, and I bolted it shut. I said loudly, 'Carry on with the meeting in here. You're not going to let some fucking paddy tell you what to do, are you?'

Tyndall, who'd already packed his lunchbox into his briefcase and was heading for the exit, stood about five yards from me. He ordered me to open the door. I told him to fuck off. He shouted, 'Open it.' Again, I told him to fuck off. He stormed towards me and tried to bustle past to open the door. I grabbed hold of him. He tried pushing me off, so I put him in a head-lock and stood there with his head under my arm. We had a little dance as he struggled to break free. I looked down at his bald patch. Our struggle was shaking the dandruff from his remaining hair. I had his neck in a very firm grasp. He gurgled something at me, and a bit of his spit dribbled onto my arm. He kept struggling, but the more he struggled, the more I squeezed. Adolf was laughing. He kept saying, 'Fucking let go of him, Bernie.' So I did.

Tyndall regained his erect posture. His features flashed with outrage. Flushed and sweating, he turned towards his minder, presumably because a minder should normally be mindful of such assaults on the mindee's person and dignity. The minder looked as if he was going to do or say something, so I moved towards him as if about to bash him. The minder stepped back and cowered behind his friends.

I began shouting at Tyndall, 'Some fucking nationalist you are. One paddy tells 30 of you to leave and you scuttle off.' Tyndall began addressing his followers as if I were invisible. I kept shouting, 'You fucking wanker.'

Tyndall ignored me and, with the little of his dignity that remained, said they'd finish their meeting elsewhere. I let him unbolt the door. Everyone trooped out after him.

I wanted to go home, but Adolf said, 'We might as well hear what he's got to say.'

The group walked to a nearby park. There, in darkness, Tyndall stood on a low wall and addressed his disciples. I didn't stay to the end. I'd had enough of the bulldog spirit. I said to Adolf, 'Come on. Let's go.'

On the way back to the tube, I began raging about Tyndall and the Nazis. Adolf wouldn't stop laughing. I said, 'You can fucking laugh, Adolf, but I'm not going to another one of their fucking meetings.'

This made him laugh even more. He said, 'Do you really think they're going to invite you?' We both started laughing. We agreed that another invitation seemed unlikely.

I suppose this meeting was a sort of turning point for me. It wasn't that I suddenly saw the British Nazis in a new light, scales falling from my eyes. It was more a confirmation of every negative thought I'd ever had about them. I'd been chewing their shit for several years, but thankfully I'd never got round to swallowing it. And now I knew I never would. There had always been something ridiculous about my involvement with the British Nazis. For one thing, my parents were Irish Catholics – a group that hasn't always contained the most loyal defenders of the English nation. Even Adolf's blood wasn't pure St George – his dad was Irish too. In fact, almost every one of the small group of south London 'Nazis' I hung around with had either Irish, or mixed, blood.

CHAPTER 2

RIVERS OF BLOOD

I'M STANDING IN A FIELD PICKING POTATOES WITH MY MOTHER. I'M ABOUT EIGHT years old. Around us are other pickers, all white and mostly women. On the other side of the field, a group of Asians are working. Occasionally, a white woman throws a potato in their direction. A few of her friends laugh. The Asians, mostly women and children, don't respond. They get on quietly with their work.

We're on the outskirts of Wolverhampton at Bradshaw's, one of the largest fruit and vegetable farms in Europe. My father needs all his money for his beer, so to support me and my three brothers, my mother must work here at the weekends and in a factory during the week. Somehow, she manages to squeeze in a few cleaning jobs as well.

The roar of motorbike engines makes me look up. A gang of Hell's Angels on perhaps 20 bikes has stopped on the A5 overlooking our field. I can see them looking down at us and the Asians. Then they rev up their engines and peel around, heading back down the A5 to the farm entrance. As soon as the first bike passes the gate, the Asians begin to run. In our white group, no one moves or seems to feel threatened.

I realise the bikers want to get at the Asians. No real surprise registers in my childish mind, because everyone, apart from my mother, seems to dislike them. Every day, I hear the words, 'dirty Indians'. Perhaps their skin is brown because they're dirty, I think.

Because of the furrows, the bikers can't drive over the field to reach the Asians. Instead, they roar up and down the two dirt tracks on either side. The Asians run from one corner to another, pursued by jeering Angels. The white pickers have stopped work to watch. Some are laughing. After five minutes or so, the Angels tire of their game and roar off. For a few minutes, the terrified Asians stay huddled together in the middle of the field. Some of the women are shaking. Others are crying. After a short while, everyone, white and Asian, goes back to picking potatoes, as if nothing's happened.

I'm pretty sure this incident took place in 1968, but maybe it was six months earlier or later. It was certainly around the time of local MP Enoch Powell's infamous 'Rivers of Blood' speech.

In April 1968 – one month after my eighth birthday – Powell (then Conservative MP for Wolverhampton South-West and a member of the Shadow Cabinet) said Britain had to act to halt immigration (especially black and Asian immigration from Commonwealth countries). He feared that, unless the government took urgent counter-measures, by the year 2000, 'whole areas, towns and parts of towns across England will be occupied by different sections of the immigrant and immigrant-descended population'. He said this was 'like watching a nation busily engaged in heaping up its own funeral pyre'. He proposed that the next Conservative government should refuse to let in more immigrants – and send back as many as possible of those already here. The absence of such measures could provoke serious civil strife. He said, 'As I look ahead, I am filled with foreboding. Like the Roman, I seem to see "the River Tiber foaming with much blood".'

The speech went down well at my Wolverhampton primary school, which didn't contain many 'Commonwealth' pupils. I remember the older children chanting in the playground, 'Enoch, Enoch, Enoch Powell, Enoch Powell, Enoch Powell.' I doubt whether the chanters could have explained much about the speech's content, but they'd certainly picked up something from their parents.

Four national opinion polls recorded an average of 75 per cent support for Powell's views. If the parents outside my school's gates were anything to judge by, I suspect support for him may have been even higher among the whites of Wolverhampton, many of whom embraced the MP as a folk hero.

I'd often hear parents talking about 'jungle bunnies', 'dirty Indians', 'nigger bus drivers' and 'the fucking Irish'. The older children at my school started calling everyone who displeased them 'Paki', 'wog' or 'coon', regardless of their colour. These were the 'in' insults. I don't really know what I made of it all. I was myself the son of Irish immigrants, and I had a vague sense of not being English, but I absorbed a lot of the anti-black prejudice of my peers. Perhaps I hoped that, if I joined them in hating blacks, they'd overlook my 'fucking Irish' background. I don't know. I only know that this prejudice couldn't have come from anywhere else, because my parents never said a word against black people. When my mother and father first came to England in the '50s, I think they encountered similar hostility ('dirty Irish' and the like).

To be honest, the questions of immigration and national identity weren't uppermost in my mind at that age. I was more preoccupied with the hostile environment in my own home. My mother came from Sligo in the Irish Republic, one of thirteen children raised in a four-bedroom council house. I was her third child. There were two boys before me, Jerry and Paul. A fourth, Michael, came later. I was christened Patrick Bernard, taking the first name from my father and the second from a favourite uncle. As soon as I could exercise any choice in the matter, I stopped using my father's name.

My father came from County Waterford in the Irish Republic, but never told me anything about his background. In fact, he never told me anything about anything. Normal conversation didn't take place in our home. Over the years, I've pieced together fragments of his story. They've helped me understand better why he became such a vicious bastard. Born illegitimate in the 'county home' (otherwise known as 'the workhouse') and abandoned by his young mother, the experiences of his childhood must have killed any decency within him. They certainly convinced him he could survive only by suppressing his softer emotions. That was what life had taught him and it was the only lesson he wanted to pass on to his children. He hated to see us crying or showing 'weakness'. Even as infants, he expected us to behave like grown men, or, rather, like the man he'd grown into – cold, hard and ruthless.

I'd been born in Dunstable, but when I was four my father, who worked at the Vauxhall car plant, decided we should move to Wolverhampton. He began to drink a lot and also became extremely violent towards all of us, my mother especially. He'd come home barely able to stand, spitting obscenities at my mother before beating her and slouching off to bed. Memories of my mother screaming as she was beaten still haunt me. She'd be screaming for him to stop and we the children would be screaming with fear. Other nights, even without much drink taken, he'd just turn off the television and sit there slandering her family, humiliating her, degrading her, even questioning the point of her existence. His most decent act would be to send us to bed. Then I'd lie awake in the darkness listening to her sobbing downstairs, pleading with him in my head to stop. As I got older, I'd sometimes overcome my fear and shout out, 'Leave her alone, you bastard.' And he'd come running up the stairs to beat me.

My father had another notion to move, this time to Codsall, a village close to Wolverhampton. He'd found us a three-bedroom terraced house which backed on to the main railway line. At night, I felt the house was going to fall in on us as coal trains thundered past at the end of the garden.

As I grew older, I didn't try to hide my hatred for my father. I forced myself to endure his violence stoically. I didn't want him to know he was hurting me. His dislike for me seemed to grow in response to my defiance. His physical violence only ended up hardening me, but his verbal violence had a more disturbing effect. He'd grip me by the throat or hair, shouting obscenities in my face while prodding or punching me in the head or body. His favourite insult was a reference to the circumstances of my birth (when my mother had almost delivered me in the street). 'You were born in the gutter,' he'd say, 'and you'll die in the gutter.' He'd tell my brother Paul that our mother had tried to kill him by pushing him in front of a bus when he was in his pushchair. He'd scream, 'She didn't want you, son. She didn't fucking want you.'

But this was nothing compared to what he saved for our mother. He treated her like a dog. In fact, if she'd been a dog, he'd probably have been arrested for cruelty, but because she was his wife the police and others felt they could do nothing. It was, they said, a domestic.

One Mother's Day, I brought her home a card I'd made at school. She put it on the sill above the kitchen sink. I was still sitting at the table eating my dinner when my father came home smelling of drink. He saw the card and picked it up. 'Is this what your little pet got you, is it? Mother's little fucking pet.' My mother asked him to stop, but that only made him worse. He turned to her and said, 'Shall I give you something for Mother's Day, shall I?' He picked up a plate off the draining board and went to smash it over her head. She raised her arm to protect herself and the plate broke across it, cutting it wide open. She spent the rest of the day in casualty getting it stitched.

Another evening, he came home and complained his dinner wasn't freshly cooked, just heated up. Presumably, he expected my mother to guess what time he'd stagger back from the pub. He threw the dinner and the plate against the wall, grabbed my mother by the hair and started punching her. She was bleeding from the nose and mouth, but he kept punching her until she collapsed on the floor. He stood over her as she lay there, his hands and shirt smeared with her blood. My mother raised her head slightly, coughed up some blood and asked me to get her some water. My father said he'd get it. He walked out of the room and I helped my mother sit up. He came back holding a mug of water, 'Here, Anna. You wanted fucking water – take it.' And with that he dashed the mug into her face.

I used to go to school in the mornings like a bomb waiting to explode. I loathed the other children's happiness: Daddy did this for me, Daddy did that for me. I needed to shut them up. I used to fight them with a ferocity fuelled by a hatred of their normality and happiness. Even at that young age, I was developing a fearsome reputation for violence. I must have spent more time in front of the headmaster than in lessons. I wasn't invited to another child's house until I was ten, when I went to the birthday party of my next-door neighbour, Nicky. There were about 12 children there, as well as adults, and everyone was laughing and joking. Their joy made me feel angry and down.

One of Nicky's presents was a model of an American Flying

Fortress bomber. When all the other children went out to play football, I stayed behind and smashed the plane to pieces, dropping the remains behind the television. I wasn't invited back.

In 1971, just before I went to secondary school, my father decided to show me how to do up a tie. He made me stand still with my hands by my side. This meant I could only see his hands and not what he was doing with the tie. Then he undid the tie and told me to do it. I got it wrong. He grabbed the tie, which was round my neck, and began pulling me about with it, slapping me round the head and saying I was fucking stupid. Finally, I could take no more. I shouted at him, 'I wish you were fucking dead,' then I punched him on the side of the head before running out of the room and up the stairs.

He ran out and caught me halfway up. He laid into me with a vicious fury. I ended up at the foot of the stairs curled into a ball to protect myself from his kicks, which were aimed at the small of my back. I thought he was going to kill me. My mother screamed at him to stop. Suddenly, I felt a sharp pain and my legs went numb. I began shouting, 'I can't feel my legs! I can't feel my legs!' Only then did he stop. He tried to get me to my feet, but I kept collapsing. My mother ran out to call an ambulance.

As I lay on the floor waiting for the ambulance, my father knelt down beside me. He pulled my head up by the hair and said, 'Say you were playing and you fell down the stairs on your own or I'll fuckin' kill ye.' And that's what I told anyone who asked. Fortunately, nothing was broken, but the discs in my spine were damaged in a way that even today causes me pain.

I started going to Codsall Comprehensive, a school of around 1,200 pupils. I'd have fights with other boys almost every day of the week. If I came home with a black eye or another mark on me my father would beat me and offer me the only bit of fatherly advice he ever gave any of us: 'Don't let people get away with hitting you. If they're bigger than you, hit them with something.'

We all started following his advice. My brother Paul got into a fight in a pub car park with a gang from another part of town. He ran at them with two screwdrivers, one in each hand. He stabbed three people before being beaten to a mess. He served two years in Borstal. The eldest, Jerry, took on a group of men in a pub.

He'd armed himself with a pair of large mechanic's spanners and started clubbing all round him. The police arrived and he clubbed one of them too before being overpowered. He'd given one of the men a fractured skull; a policeman had a shattered knee. Jerry was sent to prison. All of us, under my father's tutoring, had developed a capacity for extreme and awful violence. It set us apart – and set us against the world, especially the world of authority.

I never felt English growing up, although I suppose I never felt properly Irish either. With everything else that was going on, I didn't spend much time agonising about that aspect of my identity. I knew my roots were in Ireland and I felt comfortable around Irish people. In a sense, I lived in an Irish-Catholic world, although there was no flag-waving paddiness. I was a so-called 'plastic paddy' (the less-than-welcoming Irish term for people born in England of Irish parents).

At school at first, I encountered some anti-Irish abuse – 'thick paddy', 'Irish drunks' and that sort of stuff. It didn't last long. A good punch in the head tended to discourage repeat offences. I used to hate the superior attitude of some English people and their nauseatingly deluded belief that the whole of the world somehow looked to England. They'd try to make me feel inferior, which infuriated me, because I knew I wasn't inferior to them. I also hated posh English professionals who'd talk down to my mother as if she were stupid.

'The Troubles' in Northern Ireland began to float on the margins of my awareness. I remember 'Bloody Sunday', the day in January 1972 when paratroopers shot dead 13 unarmed Catholic men and boys on a civil rights march in Derry. My one clear memory comes from watching television and seeing a priest crouching over one of the victims, waving a blood-stained handkerchief. I can recall this event being met with jubilation by some people in Wolverhampton.

Around this time, while on holiday in Ireland with my family, an Irish teenager broke my nose with a punch at a youth-club disco, calling me an 'English bastard'. I didn't take his attack personally. I seem to remember thinking it was natural for an Irishman to want to punch an Englishman. Despite my 'empathy' for my attacker's motivation, I returned to the disco with a mob of my Irish cousins and we gave him and his mates a good beating outside.

The first time 'the Troubles' really registered, though, was when the soldier son of a family in our street was shot and wounded by the IRA in Derry. The news caused great shock and excitement in the village, and I remember a ripple of anti-Irish feeling. Around this time, I had a slanging match with some of the wounded soldier's family. I started shouting, 'Up the IRA!', presumably to wind them up, because I can't remember being especially supportive of the Provos or even very aware of what they stood for.

However, I met the wounded soldier in a pub a few years ago and he remembered me as far more pro-IRA than I remember myself. He told me I'd also thrown stones at him as he recovered and shouted, 'You British Army bastard!'

I suppose my gut instincts were certainly pro-republican, and I did have a sense of northern Irish Catholics being underdogs, though I can't say I had any real political consciousness. I tended to sympathise with anyone who fought authority, so people who threw petrol bombs at the police and army seemed like my sort of people. I was constantly in conflict with teachers. Whenever anything punishable happened, I was rounded up as the usual suspect. I did get up to a lot of mischief, but I also found myself blamed for things I hadn't done.

After the window of the school coach was smashed, I was unjustly fined for the offence. I had to pay the fine over three months in weekly instalments. The money came from my part-time job killing turkeys at a local farm. I despised the teachers and I despised their justice, just as I despised the woman who'd slide back the hatch at the school office and take my hard-earned money. For the first six weeks, she said the same thing: 'Oh, you ought to be putting this in the bank, O'Mahoney. Maybe next time you'll think before you act. Do you want a receipt?' I hated the bitch.

One night, I crept into the school grounds and hurled a crate of empty milk bottles through the headmaster's window. Then I sprayed blue paint over the school coach. I wasn't caught. For the next eight weeks as I handed over my money I used to smirk at the woman and ask, 'Have they caught anyone yet?'

I soon started coming to the attention of the police. They began arresting me for, and charging me with, various petty offences. A conviction for using 'obscene language in a public place' got the ball rolling. I was charged by a desk sergeant who, calling me 'a little fucker', accused me of causing 'fucking trouble'. I was subsequently fined five pounds by a magistrate who lectured me about bad language.

My second criminal conviction was for an even more laughable offence. At the farm where I worked part-time, breaking turkeys' necks in a cone-shaped metal bucket with squeeze bars, I found a broken wristwatch on the floor in the yard. It only had one hand. I was subsequently arrested by a policeman who assaulted me and charged me with 'theft by finding'. A magistrate later fined me thirty-five pounds and gave me a lecture on morality.

In my adolescent mind, all I could see was that the forces of law and order could hound a boy for petty irrelevancies, but couldn't intervene to prevent a man battering his wife and children half to death. Rage and resentment stewed inside me. School was a farce, the law was a farce, 'normal' life was a farce. But I wasn't going to take their shit for long. I planned to hit back.

I carried out my first street robbery when I was around 13. It became a regular pastime of mine. Our targets were usually teenagers our age or thereabouts, but we weren't averse to robbing adults. Life became a non-stop cycle of violence. One Saturday afternoon in 1973, I was on my own in Wolverhampton town centre when I saw a group of around 20 skinheads on a sinister stroll. They wore high-leg, cherry-red Dr Marten boots, white Skinner jeans and Ben Sherman checked shirts. Tattoos decorated their arms, heads and, in some cases, faces. Chanting 'There ain't no black in the Union Jack. Wogs out! Wogs out!', they jostled blacks and Asians on the street. The occasional young man who offered resistance would be punched and kicked to the ground, then steamed by the entire mob.

I was shocked. I'd never before witnessed such mayhem. I followed the skins, mesmerised by the effect they were having. Shops closed rapidly, taxi ranks emptied and six or so policemen just looked on helplessly. More teenagers, middle-aged men, bikers and even a postman joined the lawless procession. The group of 20 swelled to 50. Their bravado swelled too. Someone kicked in an Asian shopkeeper's window. The sound of smashing glass seemed to act as a signal for the mob to go on the rampage.

Everyone started running. Shoppers were knocked flying, more blacks and Asians were beaten up, small shops were swiftly ransacked. I saw one black youth run into a shop doorway in a bid to escape. He tried to open the shop door, but the terrified female assistant had already locked it. She stared out the window in horror as four skins and a middle-aged man attacked the youth. They kicked and stamped on him as others looked on, chanting, 'Pull, pull, pull that trigger. Pull that trigger and shoot that nigger.'

I hadn't hit anyone or smashed anything, but when a couple of police vans pulled up, sirens wailing, I ran with the mob. Officers leapt from the vans and gave chase. I ran into a large department store with six of the skins. Two ran down into the food hall in the basement. I got into the lift with the others. We went up to the top floor. The skins were hyped up. I felt flattered when they talked to me as if I were one of the gang. They asked me if I was 'all right'. I said I was, although I hadn't done anything to make me feel otherwise. They talked excitedly. When one paused for breath, the next would chip in, 'Did you see me do this? Did you see me do that?' They all laughed like hyenas after a feed, revelling in the chaos they'd caused.

We decided to take the stairs back down. As I was dressed in 'normal' clothes and had a 'normal' haircut, they asked me to walk down in front of them to check each floor for police. Once outside, I jumped on a bus home, though not before one of the skins had given me a National Front sticker. It was decorated with a Union flag and contained a slogan about hanging IRA terrorists and muggers (black muggers, of course, which was a relief as I was active in that field myself). As I looked out of the bus's upstairs window at the aftermath of the chaos, my whole body buzzed. I felt like a fugitive, but I'd done no wrong. The skins' sheer lawlessness shocked and delighted me. They'd strolled down the street in broad daylight, assaulting people and destroying property, and the police hadn't dared take them on till they'd had plenty of back-up. I knew little or nothing about their politics, although obviously I'd gathered they might be anti-black. I just loved their utter contempt for authority and normal society.

Later, I rang the London telephone number on the sticker. An answering machine informed me I'd telephoned the headquarters of the National Front. The man's voice asked me to leave my name, address and telephone number, which I did. Thereafter, I received newspapers, magazines, stickers and leaflets urging me to write to 'other nationalists', join other groups, go on marches and generally support the struggle to rid the land of 'foreign invaders'.

The angry, hate-spitting tone of these publications struck a chord with me. I liked the way they seemed to defend my right to behave in an anti-authority way. However, most of the writing about political issues such as repatriation came across as gobbledegook and I lost interest. Politics weren't really for me. I couldn't be doing with that shit. I had more than enough shit in my life already.

My mother had told me after junior school that I should make a fresh start when I started at secondary school, but I was fighting the other pupils within hours of getting there. Thereafter, I fought daily, at least for the first few years when there remained people willing to take me on. The teachers tried increasingly drastic methods to lessen my disruptive influence, though without much success.

In order to pay my fines and buy some decent clothes, rather than the rags my father occasionally provided, I needed to increase my income. My part-time jobs, legal and illegal, weren't sufficiently remunerative, so at school I branched out into other areas. My money-making scams included selling alcohol from the cloakroom loft. I also had a team of shoplifters who'd steal to order for me – some of the orders having been placed by parents, including one for a lawnmower.

Money and extreme violence gave me an exhilarating sense of power. The kid who'd always been told he was a nobody had become a little somebody. I revelled in my new-found status. Towards the end of my school career, I appointed myself Lord Chief Justice of a kangaroo court designed to bring to trial those fellow pupils who'd committed 'offences', real or imagined, against me and my friends. I wanted to dish out unjust justice to the mummies' and daddies' boys I hated.

These trials would take place several times a week on the school field. Punishments included fines and beatings. If someone displeased me, I'd say, 'Pass me my gown. I feel a fine coming on.' The defendant would usually be dragged to the field with violence. My friend Hughie prosecuted, my friend Stan acted for the defence and I sat in judgment. None were ever acquitted. One boy called Mosley – coincidentally the name of the pre-war leader of the British Union of Fascists – committed some abominable offence, the details of which I've forgotten. Perhaps he'd failed to hand over his dinner money on demand. Maybe he'd failed to show sufficient respect to his betters. Whatever it was, it was a crime so heinous it demanded the ultimate penalty. I sentenced Mosley to hang.

A pulley protruded from the ceiling of the science lab. I tied a rope to the gas taps, ran it through the pulley, then placed a noose round the neck of Mosley, whom Stan had forced to stand on a wooden stool. The condemned boy seemed to accept his fate meekly. I then ordered Hughie to carry out the sentence, but he wouldn't. So I kicked the stool away myself. I thought I'd arranged the rope so that Mosley's feet would hit the floor, and he wouldn't hang, but I miscalculated and he dangled about three inches above the floor, kicking and gurgling. The rope had begun to choke the life out of him.

Fortunately, the teacher came in and swiftly lifted Mosley onto a desk. He had ugly, red rope-burns on his neck. The headmaster caned me and Stan on stage in front of the whole school.

I sentenced another boy to face the firing squad. Hughie, Stan and I all had pellet-firing air pistols. Without even offering the prisoner a last request, we stood him against a shed and shot him. He informed the police, who arrested Hughie and Stan. Thankfully, the victim hadn't grassed me. I think he feared a charge of contempt of court if he snitched on the judge. The police couldn't find the airguns – they'd been hidden in a secret IRA-style arms dump – so no one was charged. I met our former victim recently in the pub. He almost broke down as he told me how the experience had affected his life. The trauma remained fresh in his mind.

Our justice system could also devour its defenders. Stan himself used to find himself on trial at least once a fortnight. We used to bully him a bit because he lived in a private house and would come to school with items like a briefcase.

Our school had only one black pupil. Called Paul, he was two years below us. Fortunately for him, he was the best fighter in his year. So he found himself bullied only by us and not by his own age group. We used to call him 'spade', 'nigger' and 'sooty'. We'd often fine him his dinner money. In truth – and I'm not trying here to mitigate our behaviour as wicked bullies – our treatment of Paul had less to do with his being black than with his being a good fighter. We didn't want him getting above himself.

On one occasion, Paul won a fight against someone we knew. We decided to charge him with assault. We apprehended him and brought him struggling before the court, clearly terrified. He asked me to let him go. He even tried appealing to my better nature. Sadly, I didn't have one. I asked Stan what defence, if any, he wished to offer on behalf of the defendant. As usual, Stan threw his client to the mercy of the court. He said the crime was so grave, the lawbreaking so monstrous, the offence so flagrant, that he could offer neither defence nor mitigation.

I found Paul guilty and sentenced him to an 'altogether'. This involved everyone present piling into the prisoner, kicking him, punching him and generally giving him a good beating, while shouting 'altogether, altogether'. Later, I felt a bit guilty about the 'altogether' dished out to Paul. Not so guilty that I said sorry, but I did later befriend him. He then started hanging about with us now and again as a semi-detached part of the gang. That was also better for him financially.

No one ever seemed to question why I was so unruly. No one witnessed the physical and mental torture I endured at my father's hands. I was just 'bad' and had to be punished. But the special treatment I received, and my reputation for violence, gained me what I thought was the respect of my peers. In fact, it was only deference based on fear. But I liked it. It made me feel powerful – an enjoyable sensation for someone who'd felt powerless for so long. People could only see this aggressive, couldn't-care-less delinquent. They couldn't see the confused and frightened child I knew myself to be.

I wish I could have broken and poured everything out to someone. Instead, I continued to act out my bad-boy role, because at least that way I could get a bit of adoration and recognition, which is what I craved. I soaked up the attention of my minions. In my mind, I felt I was beginning to win the fight against those who tried to impose their authority on me. In reality, I was systematically destroying myself and my future.

At home, throughout my early teens, I'd harm myself, gouging my stomach with a craft knife or broken glass. I still bear the scars of this self-mutilation. I didn't want to feel I was being hurt by my father and, when I realised I was, I hated my weakness and wanted to harm myself. Emotion and pain were for weak people. I'd learnt that from my father.

In November 1974, 4 months before my 15th birthday, the IRA blew up 2 pubs in nearby Birmingham, killing 21 people and injuring 182. The bombing caused an outpouring of anti-Irish feeling throughout the country, but especially in the West Midlands. My father was attacked at the Goodyear tyre factory in Wolverhampton where he worked. Unfortunately, he wasn't badly injured. My mother found people ignoring her in the shops and giving her dirty looks in the street. For years afterwards, she wouldn't leave the house when the IRA committed an atrocity, especially if it had taken place in England.

I wouldn't be intimidated. I even argued with teachers at school that the IRA bombers had more guts than the RAF airmen who bombed unseen German women and children during the war. That's not to say I was supporting the bombing. On the contrary, it turned me completely against the Provos. The main point I was trying to make was that planting a bomb in a pub – where you'd have to look into the eyes of those around you knowing you might kill every one of them – was not the work of 'cowards', as some teachers tried to suggest. In truth, I just wanted to provoke. I wanted to hit back at society, the Brit society that was always putting me down.

By the time I was 15, I'd come to regulate myself by my own rules. Laws enforced by police officers as part of what I saw as the no-justice system had become irrelevant. I started getting involved in huge gang fights against rivals from other areas. Our main rivals were from a suburb of Wolverhampton called Tettenhall. Sometimes, there'd be as many as 200 of us battling in parks and on wasteground. When people began to get seriously hurt, the police became involved and numbers dwindled to a hard core of about 30 on each side.

When I wasn't robbing people, sitting in judgment or waging war with other gangs, I used to enjoy sport, which in particular meant watching Manchester United. My passion for Man U grew to the point where I used to live for Saturdays when I'd follow the team around the country. I loved the football on the pitch, but the hooliganism off the pitch added greatly to my enjoyment.

I loved the sounds of glass smashing, people screaming, sirens wailing. The uncertainty of the outcome when fighting rival fans would keep me alert and pull me violently through the scale of emotions: euphoria as the hunter, panic as the hunted, but all the time with a constant flow of adrenalin. Mayhem and disorder had become the sources of my joy.

As we got older, we used to carry craft knives with us to football matches – but with a vicious twist. We'd put two blades in the holder, place a matchstick between them and tighten up the case. When the victim was slashed, he'd suffer two identical wounds only the thickness of a matchstick apart. This meant surgeons would be unable to stitch the wounds and the victim would be left with a horrible thick scar, usually across his face.

On more than one occasion, we thought we'd beaten or slashed rival football fans to death and we'd switch on the local news praying our worst fears wouldn't be confirmed. Thankfully, they never were.

When I was 15, the police caught me and Hughie after we'd robbed two teenagers at knifepoint in Birmingham's Queensway subway. We received only 'strict' supervision orders, which meant that once a fortnight we had to go for a meaningless chat with a probation officer. At the end of the summer term of 1976, I left school with few qualifications. Aged 16, I had little fear of, or respect for, anything or anyone. Only my father continued to have the power – physical and psychological – to turn me into a frightened little boy.

But that wasn't going to last much longer. He must have

noticed what he'd turned his sons into – and he must have guessed the day of vengeance was on its way. In fact, it came in August 1976.

My father came home, drunk as usual, and started beating my mother in the kitchen. My brother Paul and I were in the front room. We heard the familiar sounds. Paul looked at me and I looked at him and we both just got up and ran into the kitchen. Paul shouted at my father, 'Leave her alone, you fucking bastard!' My father lurched towards Paul and punched him. Paul snapped. He grabbed my father by his hair with one hand and with the other began punching him in the face with an unstoppable ferocity.

I stood and watched as Paul went berserk, punching and kicking until my father lay on the floor, his face a bloody mess. Everything went quiet. The only sound was of Paul breathing heavily from his exertion. I suppose we all expected my father to get to his feet and inflict violent punishment on us for this outrage, but he stayed on the floor. He didn't move for a little while, then slowly pulled himself up. Paul was ready for more, and I was ready to help him, but we could all see something had changed.

The fight had gone out of my father. He didn't say anything. He just slouched off to bed. As he walked past me, I spat at him. He didn't respond. His face gave nothing away, but he had the air of a tyrant who knew his time had come. He left the house the next day – and never came back. It took us 25 years to find out what had happened to him.

CHAPTER 3

PLASTIC PADDY ON TOUR

DESPITE MY CRIMINAL RECORD, ZERO QUALIFICATIONS AND A LESS THAN impeccable school reference, I managed to secure a furiously fought-over apprenticeship as a toolmaker. Like all the other boys, I'd been brainwashed into believing life wasn't worth living if I didn't have a trade. I soon came to realise that life shackled to a lathe didn't represent my dream.

I also found the unions ludicrous. In 1976, they hadn't yet been given the kicking they badly needed. On my first day, I was confronted by a picket line, advised not to cross it and sent home. In the factory, the shop stewards constantly ordered me not to do other people's jobs, such as sweeping up if I dropped something or replacing dirty towels in the washroom. I found this tedious and childish, and said so, which annoyed my adult 'brothers', whose reasons for being seemed to hinge on the existence of clear demarcation lines between them and other 'brothers'. One day, after being called in to head office for a disciplinary hearing, I told the personnel manager he could stuff his poxy job.

I remember this time in the mid-to-late '70s as being highly politicised, shaped by anger and conflict. In the West Midlands, hatred of immigrants, particularly blacks and Asians, seemed part of the air that many white people breathed. A working men's club near the Wolverhampton Wanderers football ground enforced a strict 'whites only' policy.

In 1978, a new Indian restaurant opened in Codsall. My friends and I welcomed it with abuse and vandalism. The owner placed

34

outside the entrance a 7 ft statue of a maharajah, an Indian prince. One night, we kidnapped it, drove it in a van several miles away and dumped it in the middle of a paddling pool. Within days, the maharajah had returned to his position outside the restaurant. This time, we snatched him, ran a little way down the street, threw him in the gutter and chopped off his head with a machete. The waiters heard the commotion and gave chase, but we escaped into the night, screaming with laughter and confident we'd destroyed the statue beyond repair.

To our surprise, the maharajah reappeared a fortnight later, looking like new. We decided to attack again. One of my friends backed his van up to the restaurant. I pushed the statue into the back and we drove away at speed. A few hundred yards down the road, we stopped. We pulled out the prince and, using axes and machetes, chopped off his legs and right arm as the waiters ran towards us, shouting in fury and despair.

As they got near, we picked up the amputated limbs and waved them above our heads tauntingly. Then we threw them down, jumped in the van and drove off. Victory, we thought, was ours.

A week later, the local newspaper, the *Wolverhampton Express and Star*, pictured the owner standing outside the restaurant with his newly repaired statue. The accompanying story, headlined 'Maharajah – no Indian takeaway', read:

> The much-aligned Maharajah of Codsall has regained his usual pride of place as living proof that it takes more than a bunch of yobs to keep a good Indian prince down.
>
> The life-size statue has been subjected to a spate of ordeals since he was bought to stand guard outside the new Indian restaurant in the village near Wolverhampton.
>
> He has been stolen three times since being installed in January – the first time, he was found in the middle of Tettenhall pool.
>
> The second time, he was found with his head chopped off and he has just had to undergo major surgery after he was found a third time with both legs and right arm hacked away.
>
> Now, owners at the Rajput Tandoori restaurant in the

square have decided to keep a closer watch on their
Maharajah and have chained him to the spot.

Chained or otherwise, we decided the maharajah had to go. We
waited a few weeks, then one evening a friend and I struck. I
doused the wire-mesh and fibre-glass statue with petrol and my
accomplice tossed a lighted match. Flames engulfed the prince.
He was taken away, never to return.

The late '70s was also the time of punk rock. I used to pogo
regularly at Wolverhampton's Lafayette club, where I saw all the
major bands of the time, from hard-core punk to the more
melodic New Wave. The Sex Pistols, The Clash, X-Ray Spex, The
Jam and Blondie all played the Lafayette's tiny stage. I never
became a punk – I wasn't one for dressing up, no matter what the
cause – but I loved the scene's chaotic anti-authority, 'destroy,
destroy' mentality.

After their early shows and TV appearances, no council in the
land would grant the Sex Pistols a licence to play. So they toured
a handful of venues undercover as 'The Spots' – the Sex Pistols on
Tour. In Wolverhampton, their first gig was cancelled, supposedly
because of lead singer Johnny Rotten's laryngitis. It was
rearranged for the following week. Rotten's first words to the
audience were, 'Disappointed the other night? They told you I
had a sore throat, didn't they? They were lying. There was fuck all
wrong with my voice. I just couldn't be bothered playing to a load
of wankers like you.' Then the band crashed into an extremely
anarchic version of 'Anarchy in the UK' and the club went wild.

Afterwards, a friend called Roy and I saw Pistols' bassist Sid
Vicious swaying at the bar, pint glass in hand. Although totally
wankered out of his mind, Sid continued slurping down lager, half
of which spilt down his front.

Roy said matily, 'All right, Sid!'

Sid looked at him contemptuously without saying anything.

Roy said, 'Can I have your autograph, mate?'

Sid remained silent, then took a huge slurp of lager and spat it
into Roy's face, adding, 'Fuck off, tosser.'

Roy just stood there, dripping, with his mouth open. I started
laughing and couldn't stop. Sid glared at Roy for a few seconds

more, as if looking at a piece of shit he'd just trodden on, then shook his head and downed the rest of his pint before turning back to the bar to order another beer. To avoid another drenching, Roy walked off swiftly before it arrived. I followed, still laughing.

I started touring the country with a punk band formed by ex-pupils of my school. I travelled in their van and acted as doorman at their gigs in pubs and clubs. Politically, punk could have gone either way. It wasn't instinctively left-wing, although the reds later co-opted it, signing it up for 'Rock Against Racism' and the like. The original punk impulse was very individualistic and anti-social. Many of the early punks wore swastikas to shock. The Sex Pistols themselves released a song called 'Belsen was a Gas' about the Nazi concentration camp Bergen-Belsen, where thousands of mostly Jewish inmates were murdered. A mate of mine called Pete O'Shea formed a punk band with far-right leanings called Stench. They had one single out called 'Raspberry Cripple', which looked inhumanely at the disabled, and another called 'Nonces', which advocated the torture and murder of sex offenders.

By the age of 18, I'd had 13 separate court appearances in which I'd been convicted of more than 20 offences. I'd received almost every one of the legal system's alternatives to incarceration. By the end of 1978, I remained under a supervision order for street robbery, I was carrying out 240 hours' community service for going equipped for theft and I was on bail for assault, theft, threatening behaviour and possessing an offensive weapon.

I should have left it at that, really. But I became part of a criminal conspiracy to steal a blue velvet jacket with huge lapels like those worn by one of my pre-punk pop idols Marc Bolan, lead singer of the group T-Rex. Marc had died two weeks before his 30th birthday in September 1977 when his Mini left the road and smashed into a tree. I was saddened by his death and didn't approve of the tasteless joke that soon did the rounds (Q: What was Marc Bolan's last hit? A: A tree). I think I intended wearing the blue velvet jacket in tribute to my fallen hero. Bad taste isn't a criminal offence. Theft is. Store detectives caught me with the shoplifted jacket in my hand. A prison sentence now seemed inevitable – unless I could think of a dodge.

And that's how I ended up in the army. I've written about this period in detail in my book *Soldier of the Queen* (2000). I signed up at a recruitment office in Wolverhampton town centre, although I had no intention of ever joining the ranks. My plan had been to wave my recruitment papers at the fearsome stipendiary magistrate who'd already said he intended imposing a custodial sentence. I hoped he'd let me off with a suspended sentence. Then I'd 'resign' from the army. At my hearing, the magistrate looked at my army papers suspiciously. I said I'd always wanted to become a soldier. He said, 'You might just be saying that.'

He told me he intended giving me a total of six months' imprisonment, but was prepared to defer sentencing for a little while. If I wasn't in the army on the day he set aside, then I'd be sent to jail. However, if I was a soldier by that date, he'd suspend the sentence for two years.

The army seemed the least unsatisfactory alternative, although my friends laughed hysterically at the idea of me as a soldier. They didn't think I'd last five minutes in an environment where I had to take orders. The British Army was the first extreme right-wing organisation I ever joined. Patriotism, or rather a narrow, arrogant, Rule-Britannia, God-save-the-Queen jingoism, was rammed down our throats at every opportunity. And, like the other far-right groups I later encountered, the forces of the Crown didn't seem to care too much about the presence of criminals in the ranks.

I'd already told the recruitment sergeant I had no criminal record, so at first I feared the promised stringent background checks would unmask me. I needn't have worried. During my three years in the army, I came across many people – at least 20 – with undisclosed criminal records, often involving crimes of violence. And twice during my service, the army sent an officer to speak up for me when I appeared in court for new offences.

The initial selection process took place at St George's Barracks in Sutton Coldfield. I didn't have much time for most of the other recruits. Many of them seemed desperately keen to make the army their life. For the first time I came across the term 'army barmy', used to describe people who adore everything to do with soldiering.

I got on well with only one recruit. Called Alan, he came from Rhodesia. He was bright and amusing and had done some strange things in his life. He hated blacks, especially black Rhodesians, and followed intently the progress of the war in his homeland between the whites and the black 'commie bastard terrorists', as he called them. He couldn't understand why white people in England seemed to treat blacks – he called them 'kaffirs' – as equals. I told him we didn't.

He said that when he'd first arrived in England he'd taken the underground from Heathrow Airport into central London. Further down the line, a black man had got on and sat in the same carriage. Alan couldn't believe the man's cheek. He thought blacks were forbidden to travel in the same compartments as whites – as was the case in his own country. He told the man to get out. Not surprisingly, he refused. So Alan pulled the communication cord. When the guard arrived, Alan told him to remove 'the kaffir' immediately. The guard threatened to call the police.

Alan's father was Scottish, so he had no problem being accepted into the British Army. He intended getting an up-to-date military training before returning home to bayonet some commie kaffirs.

At that time, I hadn't grasped the meaning of regiments. I just thought we were all in the army and that was that. Alan explained the regimental system and told me he wanted to join his father's Scottish regiment. He wanted me to go with him, but I said, 'I ain't going in no fucking jock regiment.'

So he suggested – because of my Irish background – that I join an Irish one. He added, 'Then you can be a war-dodger as well.' I didn't know what he meant. He explained that the army had a policy of not sending so-called 'Irish' regiments to serve in Northern Ireland.

My mind had been so focused on avoiding prison that until that point I hadn't properly considered the most unpleasant implication of joining the army, namely, that I might have to serve in the British-occupied section of Ulster. War-dodging struck me as an excellent idea.

The results of my aptitude tests had indicated I'd make a good tank gunner. I asked Alan if he knew of an Irish tank regiment. He said, 'Yes, the 5th Royal Inniskilling Dragoon Guards.' I said, 'They'll do.'

I was sent to start my seven weeks of basic training with the Royal Armoured Corps in the Yorkshire garrison town of Catterick. A childhood of verbal and physical abuse had prepared me well for the training regime. Indeed, some days I used to feel my childhood was being repeated as pantomime farce. Unlike most of my fellow recruits, I found a lot of the extreme behaviour extremely funny. None of the instructors ever talked normally. They barked, shouted or screamed every instruction and, perhaps through fear you hadn't heard them, would often supplement their words with punches, slaps or kicks.

The training left me physically exhausted all the time. One of the instructors' favourite games – usually played at 3 a.m. – was called 'changing parades'. They'd order us to change into a bizarre combination of clothing which had to be worn in the stipulated order. Then they'd shout 'Go! Go! Go!' and we'd have to run back upstairs to change, before running back down as fast as we could. The first three downstairs would be allowed back to bed. The others had to change into another combination, invariably involving a gas mask.

One recruit lived in fear of 'changing parades', because he always ended up last in bed. He came from south London. Slightly built with short dark hair parted at the side, he sometimes wore glasses. He didn't mix well and rarely spoke, preferring to spend his time sitting alone reading war comics or books about Hitler's elite troops, the Waffen SS. We nicknamed him Rommel. He knew everything you might possibly want to know about Waffen SS panzer divisions, especially their soldiers' clothing and weaponry. He wanted to join the Royal Tank Regiment because their tank crews wore black overalls like his SS panzer heroes. Members of other tank regiments wore green.

He'd also listen to tapes of the 'Speak German in a Fortnight' variety. We used to take the mickey out of him and sometimes he'd play up to us, goose-stepping up and down the room with his right arm outstretched in a Nazi salute. However, though clearly army barmy, his enthusiasm didn't translate into efficiency, which was why he feared 'changing parades'.

One night as we frantically changed, he said, 'Fuck. I'm going to be last again.' I suggested he jump out the window to get downstairs quickly. As we were at least 20 feet up on the third floor, I thought he'd take my suggestion as the joke I'd meant it to be. But in his desperation, it must have seemed like a good idea, because the next second he was clambering out the window.

The image that remains in my mind is of him looking back at me, eyes flickering madly, as he launched himself into the air. I heard a crunch and a piercing 'Aaaaarrrggghhh!' and I ran to look out. Rommel lay writhing on the ground. Instructors stood over him shouting, 'What are you doing, you silly cunt?' Miraculously, he didn't break any bones, although he could hardly walk. They made him crawl back upstairs to continue the game.

Most recruits, especially those from normal loving backgrounds, couldn't overcome the shock of army life. They'd crack under the bombardment of abuse. At night, people would be talking about running away – or even suicide. Around two-thirds of the recruits in my intake didn't finish the course. It seemed to me that the whole selection process was designed to weed out normal people. Only the disturbed or desperate survived.

On 23 April 1979, about 12 weeks into my army career, rioting broke out in Southall, an area of west London containing many Asians. Blair Peach, a 33-year-old white teacher from New Zealand, was killed by a blow to the head as police dispersed thousands of demonstrators protesting against a National Front rally. The talk at the camp was of the National Front, 'spades', 'wogs' and 'fucking foreigners'. It seemed to me that the army was overflowing with potential and actual Nazis. At times, I thought I'd joined the National Front's armed wing.

Ten days later, the election of a Conservative government led by Mrs Thatcher was greeted all round with scenes of jubilation not seen since the Relief of Mafeking. There was, however, widespread disappointment at the poor showing of the National Front.

One day, my Rhodesian friend Alan suddenly started crying. I knew something catastrophic must have happened for him to break down in such a way. I asked him what was wrong. He said the 'kaffirs' had taken over Rhodesia and wanted to rename it Zimbabwe. His family owned a big farm, which he feared the blacks would seize.

The only good news in his life was that he'd got on so well in basic training the army wanted to make him an officer. They felt he had the qualities to become a leader of men. He ended up being sent to the officer-training school at Sandhurst.

Eventually, the training ended and I was posted to my regiment in Germany, where I spent the next two years. Life in Germany was a lot more relaxed, though I kept running up against petty rules. The army thrived on total bullshit. It was smeared on everything.

My time in Germany was spent largely on 'exercises' involving thousands of men and machines causing havoc to the locals. For six weeks each year, we went to the tank-firing ranges at Hohne in northern Germany, just down the road from the former Bergen-Belsen concentration camp mentioned in the Sex Pistols' song.

The NAAFI canteen, which existed to poison and demoralise soldiers, was based in a grand, grey stone building which looked like a Roman palace and was rumoured to be the former headquarters for the SS who'd run the nearby death camp. Eagles clasping Nazi swastikas in their claws had been carved into the stone on either side of the entrance porch.

I visited Belsen one day. It's situated in beautiful woodland, but I couldn't hear any birds singing. Mounds of earth with small plaques marked the graves of thousands. The museum outside the main gate contained photographs, and some possessions, of some of those who'd perished there. The experience troubled and horrified me in a way I hadn't expected.

Social life in Germany mirrored the social life I'd led prior to enlistment – a cocktail of drinking and fighting. The only German word most soldiers learnt was '*Bier*'. The squaddies' world revolved around beer. I made a few good friends, one of whom was called Lofty. He was an even more unlikely recruit than me. Extremely laid-back, he'd smoke dope and strum a guitar in his room, the walls of which were covered in Campaign for Nuclear

Disarmament and anti-war posters, including the one which said, 'Join the army, get a trade, travel to exotic locations, meet interesting people – and kill them.'

He worked as a clerk in the HQ offices, because he didn't like guns. The real soldiers hated him. It must have been one of them who reported his dope-smoking to the Military Police, who raided his room looking for evidence. Fortunately, he'd smoked everything the night before. The redcaps had to be content with confiscating some of his revolutionary posters, including one featuring the Cuban guerrilla leader, Che Guevara, and another advertising the Paul McCartney record 'Give Ireland Back to the Irish'.

No one knew what to make of him. When you asked him why he'd joined the army, he'd say, 'It's something I ask myself every day.' Like a lot of squaddies, he was probably escaping something worse.

On 2 April 1980, rioting took place in the St Paul's district of Bristol following a police raid on a black-run cafe where alcohol was being sold illegally. Squaddies taunted the two mixed-race soldiers in our regiment with the words, 'Oi! Have you paid for that?' every time they returned from the bar with drinks.

The news that we were being posted to Northern Ireland landed like a mortar among us. We'd heard the army intended changing its policy of not posting Irish regiments there, but we'd assumed an infantry unit would have the privilege of being the first to be sent. We were tank soldiers, after all.

The atmosphere of shock and gloom that followed this news made me realise the derogatory nickname 'war-dodgers' had been neither unkind nor inaccurate for many in 'the Skins' (as we were known). A lot of people had genuinely joined in the belief they'd never have to serve in Northern Ireland.

Our four-and-a half-month tour of duty would start on 10 April 1981. What was more, we'd be going to the historical recruitment base of our regiment – Enniskillen in County Fermanagh. The idea of returning to patrol their own streets seemed to appeal greatly to the regiment's staunch Loyalists. Some of them made plain they had scores to settle with the Catholic population. I imagined how I – or indeed the locals – might react if I were sent back to patrol Codsall with a rifle. All the same, I had to wonder why – if they were really so keen to bash republicans – they'd joined a regiment they'd thought would never have to serve in their beloved land of Orange.

Because of my Irish-Catholic background, I was told I didn't have to go if I didn't want to. I said I wanted to, but I didn't explain why. My desire had nothing to do with going to fight for Queen and country; I just wanted to be with my friends. My loyalty was to them – and I had no intention of being the one waving at the gate as they left. To me, it was like they were going out for a fight in the car park and I was going to join them.

On the day we arrived in Ireland, riots broke out in Brixton, south London. The violence lasted two days before order was restored. Lord Scarman later wrote a report into the disturbances. The feeling in the regiment was that we should have been on the streets of Brixton rolling over Rastafarians in our Chieftain tanks, rather than patrolling Northern Ireland on foot.

We arrived in Fermanagh a month after the local MP, the IRA prisoner Bobby Sands, started his hunger strike for political status. Sands, and nine other republican prisoners, starved themselves to death during our tour of duty. Pictures of Sands festooned our camp. Juxtaposed mockingly beside them were adverts for slimming products and headlines from articles celebrating the achievements of Weight Watchers ('I lost four stone in three months'). The most popular headline was 'Slimmer of the Year'. There was also a Hunger Strike Sweepstake: on a board in the operations room were listed the names of all republicans on hunger strike. Soldiers would have to guess the number of days a particular hunger striker would take to die. Each guess cost one pound and the soldier who guessed correctly would get to keep the pot.

We hadn't been properly trained or prepared for Northern Ireland. As tank soldiers, the small arms we'd trained with were sub-machine guns, not the standard infantryman's Self-Loading Rifle (SLR). A week of special training to sharpen up our urban warfare skills had left our instructors almost crying with despair. But what could they expect? We were tankies, not nasty little 'grunts' (the name we used for infantrymen, who had to grunt round the countryside with huge packs on their backs while being showered with mud from the tracks of our regiment's tanks).

I went for a week of extra training to Hollywood barracks outside Belfast, where I found myself in a group of about 20 soldiers from different regiments. On the first day, we sat in a room containing a large television. A major walked in, marched to the front and said, 'If you're going to die, we might as well tell you why.'

He then played a video which condensed Ireland's history into 30 minutes. When the video finished, he began talking to us in a tone of matter-of-fact cynicism. He opened his talk by saying that the film had probably left us more confused than enlightened, but that this didn't really matter. The essential fact, he said, was that as British soldiers we were little more than piggies-in-the-middle in a baffling tribal conflict, the intricacies of which need not concern us too greatly. All we really needed to bear in mind as we went about our duties were the simple equations, 'Catholic = IRA = bad' and 'Protestant = British = good'. He said he didn't mean to give offence to any Catholics in the group, if there were any, as British Catholics were obviously different from Irish Catholics. He said he knew also he was being deeply unfair to the many Irish Catholics who didn't support the IRA. However, his purpose was merely to identify the tribal grouping from which the threat to our lives was most likely to come, and the simple fact of the matter was that we didn't need to be as wary of Protestants.

He rounded off his talk by saying that of course Britain should give Northern Ireland back to the Irish, but the Province was such a good training ground that the army didn't want to let it go. He said that in most years more soldiers were killed on exercises in Germany than died at the hands of terrorists in Northern Ireland.

After he'd left the room, a Liverpudlian recruit turned to me and said, 'Was he taking the piss?'

Before I went out on my first street patrol, the troop sergeant had a chat with us. He said that if, for whatever reason, we had to open fire on anyone, and we wounded him, we had to ensure he didn't live. We had to kill him outright. He said surviving victims might be able to dispute the army's version of events – and the last thing any of us needed was a prolonged investigation and a messy court case in which we had to go back and forward to Ireland to be examined by 'cunts in wigs'.

He said, 'Just shoot the fucker dead and we'll make it up from there.' I saw a few people looking uncomfortable. I wasn't one of them. I thought the sergeant's advice extremely astute. Perhaps to lighten the atmosphere, he finished by saying there'd be a crate of beer for the first one of us to kill a paddy. A real paddy, that is, not a plastic paddy.

You had to remember that everyone you met might be out to kill you. This awareness put a great strain on all our minds. Some soldiers cracked up completely and had to be returned to Germany. Others would cry themselves to sleep at night. More than once, I had to shout out, 'Shut up, you wimp!'

Most of us were in our late teens or early 20s and we all lived in the anticipation of being shot or blown up. I didn't give a toss about the politics of the situation. I just wanted to survive – and was determined to do so in the best way I knew how. I'd survive by dealing ruthlessly with any potential threats. And, as far as I was concerned, anyone I didn't know personally, Catholic or Protestant, was a threat.

Motorists who were nice to me at checkpoints tended to be treated the worst. I had the theory that if someone was being nice then they probably had something to hide. Vehicles would be turned upside down, regardless of who was inside – granddad on crutches, granny in a sling, pregnant wife with birth pangs, husband in a wheelchair. And that was my behaviour with ordinary, innocent civilians. People we identified as republicans could expect a lot worse.

One job I hated was raiding houses. I remember once going into the home of an IRA man on the run. His wife stood in the front room. Her two sons, aged about eight and ten, stood next to her with their arms around her. I could tell they were protecting her, rather than seeking protection. I'd clung to my own mother in the same way in the face of my father's brutality. I recognised the look on their faces, that expressionless gaze of silent hatred. At such times, I felt like a Judas betraying my own kind. I wanted to reach out to them and explain myself: 'Look, I'm not here to oppress you. I just didn't want to go to prison, OK?'

At other times, when Catholic youths would spit or throw stones, I could happily have smashed their heads open with the butt of my British oppressor's rifle.

On republican housing estates, we'd hand out sweets to small children knowing that as they eagerly swarmed around us they'd effectively be shielding us. No IRA sniper would dare fire at a soldier surrounded by children, especially Catholic children.

The regiment soon had its first casualty. While cleaning his General Purpose Machine Gun at a permanent checkpoint, a soldier accidentally shot and wounded another soldier. We'd been taught various code words to use on the radio to cover incidents for which we needed assistance. However, there was no code for shooting a comrade. I could hear the soldiers on the radio asking for help, but not being quite sure what to say. To me, this incident merely underlined that we were the wrong soldiers in the wrong place at the wrong time.

For most of the tour, I stayed at Fermanagh's main military base, St Angelo Barracks, sited on a disused airfield outside Enniskillen. I found myself sharing living space with a few staunch Ulster Loyalists whose hatred of Catholics made them regard me as suspect. The more I got to know them, the more I thought that sending them home to police their own community was not one of the British Empire's most inspired deeds. One of them, I nicknamed Nasty. He was a loudmouth drunk and bully who claimed to relish the idea of going home to persecute 'Fenians'.

Only years later did I discover that 'Fenian' – the favourite Loyalist nickname for Catholics – came from the activities of one of my nineteenth-century near-namesakes. John O'Mahony co-founded and named the IRA's historical forerunner, the Fenian Brotherhood (later notorious for the so-called 'Fenian Rising' of 1867).

Nasty would often say to me, 'Hiya, Fenian!' I'd tell him to fuck off, which would make him laugh. 'Ha! Ha! Ha!' he'd cackle, as if we were best friends joshing. I hated the bastard.

Another Loyalist bigot was nicknamed Charisma (because he didn't have any). He was about 23 but, with his moustache and boring manner, could have passed for 50. He was the non-smoking, non-drinking 'saved' type. His 'da', a locally recruited

Ulster Defence Regiment (UDR) man, was a disciple of the Reverend Ian Paisley – the fanatical Orangeman, Defender of Ulster and hater of popery. Charisma was full of himself and slagged off anyone who didn't share his fundamentalist Protestant beliefs. There were the doomed and the saved, the righteous and the unrighteous, and I knew which category he put me in.

Once, I was lying on my bed trying to sleep while listening to him droning on about God and republicans and loyalty to the Queen. Finally, I snapped and shouted, 'Shut the fuck up, you lemon.' In our regiment, 'lemon' was slang for a yellow (that is, gutless) Orangeman. He was holding his rifle, which he'd been cleaning. He leant over my bed, pointed it at me and said, 'Bang! Bang! You fucking Fenian.' I jumped out of bed and he ran off.

I made the mistake a few times of trying to have an argument with the Orangemen about Northern Ireland. I had no real interest in the politics of the situation – quite frankly, it bored me – but I had the gut feeling, shared by most English, Welsh and even Scottish squaddies, that the six counties belonged to Ireland. When the Loyalists said Northern Ireland was (and always would be) British, my argument was (and still is), 'It's like saying London doesn't belong to the English.' But you couldn't debate things with them, because they wouldn't put forward any reasoned arguments. They'd just bluster and shout and tell you that even to question the link with Great Britain was tantamount to treachery.

One time, when Charisma told me his ancestors, with God's help, had settled the land, I drove him to fury by saying that when I was a thief, I at least had the decency not to walk round saying that God had given me permission to do it and was happy for me to keep the spoils. When Bobby Sands died after 66 days on hunger strike, every nationalist area in Fermanagh seemed covered with black flags and memorial posters. This widespread sympathy for the dead Provo confirmed the prejudices of people like Nasty and Charisma that all Catholics were closet republicans.

The UDR soldiers with whom we shared the camp felt the same. In the canteen and bar, they'd talk as if an uprising were imminent. I often heard UDR people say, 'Kill all Catholics. Let God sort them out.' However, despite their loudmouth displays among their mates, I felt I could see the brown-trousered signs of people shitting themselves in fear that the day of reckoning might finally have arrived for a society built on injustice. As republicans died on hunger strike, a Provo mortar attack tore apart a small outlying base that our regiment shared with the Royal Ulster Constabulary, injuring one of my friends.

One person we harassed into the ground was Owen Carron, the republicans' candidate in the parliamentary by-election following Sands's death. Carron could rarely get a few miles in his car without being stopped. Then we'd turn his car inside out and threaten to shoot him. Half a mile down the road, another patrol would stop him – and repeat the procedure. Some years later, I read that Carron had gone on the run after being found carrying a rifle in the back of his car. He'd probably been looking for me.

On 13 May 1981, a Turkish man shot the Pope in Rome, seriously wounding him. The attempted assassination became the talk of the camp, especially among the fundamentalist Protestants, who were hugely disappointed by the gunman's failure to kill the Antichrist. I heard them debating the attack as they would a vital goal that had been disallowed at a cup final: if only the stupid bastard had shot him in the head or if only he'd used a different weapon. I didn't like the way their hatred seemed to cover every member of the Catholic Church, regardless of nationality. My friend who'd just been wounded in a mortar attack was an English Catholic. And, although religion was an irrelevance to me, I still regarded myself as a Catholic, if only in name.

It was one of those moments when I felt distanced from these people. Although I wore the same uniform, I felt no sense of loyalty to them and certainly didn't see myself as fighting for them. I'd say most English and Welsh soldiers felt the same: they didn't give a toss about the Ulster Protestants – and certainly didn't fancy dying for them.

Hunger strikers died at regular intervals throughout our tour. Two died on the same day. This provoked a whirlwind of violence across Northern Ireland. Around 10,000 petrol bombs were thrown at the Crown forces in the week that followed. None was aimed at me.

In the week of the two hunger strikers' funerals, the Reverend

Ian Paisley, leader of the Democratic Unionist Party and scourge of Fenians everywhere, boosted morale. He suggested during a television interview that shotguns ought to be issued to soldiers for use against street rioters. After the terrible onslaught of 10,000 petrol bombs, he thought that shotguns would be able to clear streets of rioters without risking life in the way a bullet from a rifle might. The packed TV room burst into laughter and cheers. Some people stood on chairs and made Nazi salutes, chanting, '*Sieg Heil! Sieg Heil!*' Outside the television room, there was less bravado. At night at remote permanent checkpoints, animals would often get shot if they triggered tripwires. It was in such an incident around this time that I shot my first sheep. Rabbits, foxes and even, occasionally, cows also fell victim.

One night, I was on a mobile patrol roving through the countryside around Belcoo. It had been raining in that special Irish way since we'd first jumped from the helicopter. Everyone was soaked. We decided to have a false 'contact'. If you encountered terrorists while on patrol and opened fire you were supposed to get on the radio immediately and shout 'Contact! Contact! Contact!' That night's Quick Reaction Force would then be despatched to you swiftly by helicopter as back-up. But, most importantly, as your position had been compromised, you'd be taken back to your nice warm bed and a cup of tea.

We all agreed on our story in case of investigation. Apparently, we'd spotted a figure carrying a rifle near a tree several hundred yards away. I laughed as two flares exploded in the evening sky and we opened fire on the tree and bushes. Meanwhile, the corporal screamed into the radio handset, 'Contact! Contact! Contact!'

Back at base, they must have thought we'd encountered an IRA Flying Column. Within seven minutes, we heard the whirr of the helicopter. Soldiers jumped from it before it had even touched the ground. They ran towards us, hyped up and ready for action. Our corporal pointed in the direction of the tree and the QRF soldiers moved off in defensive zigzags to hunt down the enemy, helped by the helicopter's powerful search beam.

Our regiment soon had its second casualty. A soldier was shot in the foot. Thankfully, he hadn't been shot by other soldiers.

He'd shot himself. He claimed it was an accident, but no one believed him. During our tour of duty, the IRA only caused one casualty among our regiment's soldiers: the friend of mine injured in a mortar attack.

That summer of 1981 saw rioting throughout the United Kingdom. The season kicked off in July with four days of riots in the Toxteth area of Liverpool. At least 70 buildings were burned down and 468 police officers were injured. Smaller riots then took place in Manchester, Leeds, Birmingham, Leicester and just about everywhere else with a significant ethnic minority population.

I started going out with a 'Greenfinch' – a female UDR soldier. She was called Elizabeth. Through her, I got to meet a lot of UDR soldiers. Several of them seemed all right, though none of them left me feeling overwhelmed by the desire to form a lifelong friendship. There were, however, several out-and-out sectarian bigots who made no attempt to hide their hatred of Catholics.

One of the worst bigots was someone I nicknamed Billy Bunter. He was overweight, with a red face, and had the unpleasant habit of sniffing when he finished a sentence. His favourite saying was, 'What would really make me happy is if you gave me a pope on a rope.' He continually made a point of telling me not to be anywhere near him if a gun battle broke out. 'Yer man,' he'd say, 'watch your Fenian back if the bullets start flying.'

I'd reply, 'Why wait till my back's turned, fat boy?'

He'd pretend to laugh.

I wish I could say his views were unusual, but they weren't. That sort of demented anti-Catholicism was widespread among the UDR soldiers. Even Elizabeth told me not to broadcast my Catholic background. She said it didn't bother her, but she thought other UDR people might not be so 'forgiving'. It wouldn't have been hard for any of the UDR people to justify their hatred of republicans, but I didn't like the way they seemed to hate all Catholics.

Most UDR soldiers had lost friends or relatives at the hands of the IRA. And all of them, especially the part-timers, lived with a constant sense of personal threat. Out of uniform, at home and at work, they must have felt vulnerable all the time. Behind their backs, we used to call their unit 'the Utterly Defenceless Regiment'.

Our officers never wore badges of rank on patrol and we were constantly told never to address them as 'Sir' in front of civilians. These precautions were designed to prevent terrorists identifying them as officers. The thinking was that an officer would present a more tempting target than a mere squaddie. I understood the logic of this, but I still resented it, especially when the officers who in camp would put you on a charge for not calling them 'Sir' were the ones who outside camp would be most upset if you called them 'Sir'. At checkpoints, I made a point of calling officers 'Sir' whenever I could, especially in front of Catholics. Some officers would get really freaked, 'O'Mahoney! Don't call me "Sir". How many times do you have to be told?'

It's difficult to describe how I felt about 'the Troubles'. It wasn't exactly a case of being torn between two sides – I knew which side I was on. I was a British soldier, and I had no time for the IRA. Yet I agreed with the republican goal of a united Ireland and I secretly admired the hunger strikers, even though sometimes I could feel elated at their deaths.

The strange thing was that while I could allow myself to feel satisified that a hunger striker had died, I didn't like to see English soldiers, especially middle-class officers, sneering at hunger strikers' deaths. Contradiction was the dominant force in my mind.

Life was full of injustice: everyone behaving unjustly to everyone else. That was the way of the world, it seemed to me. I'd felt this from an early age and, in some ways, I suppose this feeling helped me resolve the contradictions in my mind. I stopped getting bothered about who was right and who was wrong. Everyone was right and everyone was wrong. My only goal was survival.

I was sitting in the canteen one day with a group of soldiers from my regiment. Someone was reading an Irish newspaper containing reports about the Pope's convalescence after his shooting in Rome. A double-page pull-out poster showed him in better days celebrating mass in front of a huge crowd. In the picture, he held his shepherd's crook in one hand. His other hand was raised to give a blessing. Underneath the photo stood the words, 'Pray for His Holiness'. I stuck the poster above the hotplate and sat back down with my mates. We all started giggling.

Around five minutes later, a group of about twelve UDR and police walked in, among them Billy Bunter. Suddenly I heard him shout, 'You Fenian bastard!' I looked up and he was pointing at the poster. What happened next was extraordinary. At least six UDR men ran to the poster and tore it violently from its place. Then, in a group frenzy, they ripped it to pieces, spat on it and finally stamped on it, all the time shouting madly.

My mates and I were laughing. Billy saw us and ran over, his face afire with anger. He looked at me and shouted, 'Who put that up there? Who fucking put that up there?'

I said, 'What are you talking about, you idiot?'

We denied having anything to do with it – and no one outside my group had seen me put it up.

Billy said, 'You saw it up there and you did nothing about it.'

They were all deadly serious. I'm sure they'd have been less offended by a bomb. Elizabeth told me later that two of the UDR people had gone to the ops room to demand an officer launch an inquiry to find the culprit.

The incident created a lot of bad feeling between our regiment and the UDR. It overshadowed the rest of the tour. It seemed to confirm the suspicions of some UDR soldiers that our regiment was a haven for IRA sympathisers. I wasn't aware of many sympathisers, but there were plenty of hooligans. In my mind, hooligans made the best soldiers. On the ground, dealing with real people in real situations, the army barmies were often clueless, whereas natural-born hooligans like me and a few others could deal effectively with whatever trouble came our way.

To escape the tensions of active service – at least that was my excuse – I started drinking a lot more. There was little else to do when you weren't working. A few of us even started bringing alcohol with us on night-time checkpoint shifts. I can't remember us ever being drunk on duty, with our loaded rifles, but four or more pints of lager mixed with adrenalin probably contributed to some of our more loutish behaviour. We used to joke that at least the booze helped us walk in zigzags, thus making us hard targets for snipers.

I started really enjoying myself on patrol or at checkpoints. I really did get into it. The more confident I got, the more enjoyable I found it. Some people should never be put in positions of power. I was certainly one of them. I began to relish the opportunities for confrontation, especially as the people who used to confront us tended to be around my age. I'd experience the same buzz I used to get from gang fights and I'd behave in much the same way as I did formerly. The difference now was that I wore a uniform, carried a gun and acted with lawful authority.

Of course, we knew such incidents bred hatred and helped swell the IRA's ranks, but we didn't care. Our overriding goal was to get back to camp, and ultimately to Germany, alive and intact. The future was someone else's problem.

We used to break into isolated houses. The purpose wasn't to steal stuff, although we did occasionally pinch small items, it was really to have a place to put our feet up for a few hours and watch TV, instead of footslogging through the countryside. If there was any beer or food around, so much the better, but we'd be happy just to find a comfortable sitting room where we could lounge on the sofa monitoring daytime television.

Before long, the tour was over and we were back in Germany, swapping war stories. I actually found myself missing the buzz of Northern Ireland. Over there, I'd lived in a permanent state of alertness. I'd really felt I was living my life wide awake. I suppose I was also missing Elizabeth. She'd ring me regularly. In one of our phone conversations, we started discussing the possibility of my joining the Ulster Defence Regiment.

At first, I thought it was a mad idea. Apart from Elizabeth, there weren't too many UDR people I liked, and I knew my Irish-Catholic background discomforted the bigots. But I'd heard that quite a few English-born soldiers joined the regiment after serving in Northern Ireland. There was nothing else on the horizon for me, so I began to consider it seriously. After a few weeks mulling things over, I told Elizabeth to get me the application form. I was going back to Northern Ireland.

Before I left the army, I received my Certificate of Service. The range of Military Conduct Gradings is: 1) Exemplary, 2) Very Good, 3) Good, 4) Fair, 5) Unsatisfactory. I was given an 'exemplary' grading. Perhaps they'd hoped it'd guarantee me a job in Civvy Street and I'd never again don the uniform of the Crown.

CHAPTER 4

BRITS OUT

I ARRIVED IN FERMANAGH FOR CHRISTMAS. IT WAS GOOD TO SEE ELIZABETH AGAIN, but I felt strange walking around as an ordinary civilian. I moved into her flat in the centre of Enniskillen.

Until that time, her mother, father and brother had been an invisible presence, appearing occasionally in conversation, but never in the flesh. That was about to change. I'd been invited to spend Christmas Day with them.

I knew her father was a retired RUC officer and that her brother had followed him into the police. I also knew her mother was a devoted follower of the Reverend Ian Paisley. She'd even stood unsuccessfully in council elections as a candidate for his party. Elizabeth had also told me how in the '60s her mother had wrapped herself in the Union flag and lain in the road to block a civil rights march by Catholics. She'd been shocked when police had removed her from the Queen's highway.

Beyond those bare facts, I knew little else. I got an inkling of troubled times ahead when Elizabeth sat me down and told me she wanted to explain a few things before I met her family. She said her mother had quite extreme views on a number of issues and, however ridiculous I found them, she'd like me to respect them.

In essence, her mother was a fundamentalist Protestant who didn't like having anything to do with Catholics. Nor did she want her children having any such dealings. Elizabeth said she couldn't be honest with her mother about my background. In her mother's eyes, because I'd been born a Catholic, I'd always be a Catholic, at least until I'd been rebaptised as a born-again Protestant.

I'd never really liked the term 'born a Catholic'. I hadn't been born a Catholic. I'd been born naked and screaming. My religion had been imposed upon me. If I'd been born in India I'd likely have been a Sikh or a Hindu or a Muslim. The only God I'd ever worshipped was George Best – and he came from the Ulster Protestant tradition. Elizabeth knew my views and agreed with them to a large extent, but she asked me, for the sake of family harmony, to keep my Catholic background secret. In fact, she wanted me to lie.

She knew her mother would pick up on my Catholic name, so she suggested a cover story. If asked, I was to say my family came originally from Eire but had been Protestants for generations, the stain of Catholicism having been expunged long ago. Her other stricture was that I'd be sure not to swear or blaspheme in front of her mother. I said, 'Of course I'm not going to swear!' But she explained that, for her mother, swearing and blaspheming came together in the use of such words as 'Jesus', 'God' and 'bloody'. Nor could I expect to drink alcohol in her mother's house – or even give the impression I'd ever drunk alcohol anywhere in the world at any time. Apart from all that, she thought I'd get on fine. Elizabeth had yet to meet my family, so, out of pity for what the future might have in store, I agreed to her terms.

I felt deeply uncomfortable as I walked up the pathway to her parents' bungalow clutching a bottle of non-alcoholic drink. It wasn't the natural discomfort everyone feels before a first meeting with a partner's parents. It was more the uncomfortable feeling of knowing that, quite literally, I couldn't be myself.

The mother greeted us at the door, the personification of good manners. Very softly spoken, she was slim, about 5 ft 8 in., with silver-white hair. She led us politely into the sitting room.

I wish Elizabeth had prepared me for the appearance of it. I was faced with what I can only describe as a shrine to the Reverend Doctor Ian Paisley, scourge of Fenians and hater of popery. The face of Orange Number One beamed out from numerous photos in which he was often standing alongside Elizabeth's mother.

There was even a photo of the two of them together in that very room. Photos of the Queen and the Royal Family were also prominent, along with lots of little figurines and knick-knacks of historical figures such as King William of Orange.

Elizabeth's dad sat in one of the armchairs. He was about 60, short, thick-set with large gnarled hands. His white hair was balding. He got up to shake my hand and I noticed he had a bad limp. I found out later that this resulted from a wound received when the IRA blew up his Land-Rover with a culvert bomb.

Over Christmas dinner, his wife said he'd been taken to a hospital where, she claimed, he'd been refused treatment by the Fenians who worked there. He'd been airlifted to Belfast and had ended up being pensioned off. He was extremely quiet and hardly ever spoke. The conversation as a whole was polite and stilted. I was extremely edgy, worried I'd say something to identify me as a Fenian interloper. I sipped my ginger beer temperately, trying to anticipate the mother's questions in order to give myself time to prepare acceptable answers.

I was probably being over-sensitive, but I had the feeling she was analysing every word we said for signs of Catholicism or blasphemy. For instance, I might have said, 'My friend Patrick has got one of those cars.' And she'd have said, 'Patrick? That's a Catholic name. Is Patrick a Catholic?'

After dinner, we sat down again in the sitting room to watch the Queen's Speech. It was a first for me. Fortunately, they kept the television on after the speech, so at least I had a little respite from talking and the constant danger of betraying myself. But watching television held dangers too. Something happened on screen which made me say, 'Oh, God! I don't believe it.' Elizabeth's mother breathed in sharply, clutched her chest and walked out. Elizabeth whispered angrily, 'I told you not to swear!'

I tried to settle down into my new life with Elizabeth, but an uneasiness had crept into our relationship which hadn't been apparent before. Perhaps it was my fault. I'd expected something different from my new life. I suppose I'd almost expected to have my old army life back, but with more perks, such as the freedom to live outside camp with a woman I was fond of. But life as a civilian was very different. None of my friends was around and even from those very first days, I began to feel extremely isolated. I tried to enjoy myself, but deep down I knew I'd made a mistake in going back.

Shortly after my arrival, I went to the main RUC station in Enniskillen and enquired about obtaining a firearms licence. If the Provos did pay me a visit, I wanted at least to have the chance to defend myself. The policeman at the desk summoned a colleague who dealt with such applications. He asked me why I wanted one. I explained my background and what I was doing in Northern Ireland. He nodded sympathetically and said he didn't think that, as a former soldier, I'd have any problems. He asked me various questions from a prepared list. Was I on any medication? Had I ever received treatment for, or been diagnosed as having, a mental illness? I got through everything all right until he came to the question I'd been dreading. Had I ever been convicted of a criminal offence?

I suppose I could have lied, but I knew that, as a matter of course, he'd run my name through the police computer and find my record. Then I'd have committed another offence by lying to obtain a firearm. So I told the truth. I said I'd faced a few minor charges. He asked what they were. I said, 'Eh, assault, robbery, theft, threatening behaviour, possessing an offensive weapon and criminal damage.'

His manner became a little frosty. He told me I'd be wasting my time applying. There was no way someone with my record would be given a firearms licence. Not even if the Provos put up 'Wanted' posters of me. I was annoyed. I said I'd only recently spent four and a half months patrolling Fermanagh with a firearm. He shrugged his shoulders.

I had better luck with the UDR. After a short interview with an officer at St Angelo, and the lengthy processing of my application, I was told I'd been accepted into the ranks, although I'd have to wait six months to join the new intake.

I liked Elizabeth a lot. She was a lovely person, kind and gentle, and much of the time we got on fine. But we came from such different backgrounds that inevitably I began to feel how alien we were to each other. In the past at St Angelo, she'd laughed with me at the stupidity of some of the sectarian bigots at the base.

She'd often said, 'We're not all like that.' But living with her, and meeting her friends and family, I felt at times the evidence told me different. She certainly didn't hate Catholics, but the world she lived in had been formed by 'the Troubles'. Almost all her friends and family were involved with the Crown forces in one way or another. They saw themselves as frontierspeople barricading their homesteads against marauding natives. It was all hands to the pump-action shotgun.

Religion, or rather the religious denomination of others, dominated Elizabeth's thoughts and those of all her friends. Yet few of them seemed to practise their religion. Few went to church or Bible meetings or anything like that. The words 'Protestant' and 'Catholic' were used simply to identify friends from enemies, people whose company you could embrace from those whose company you had to shun. I felt a lot of her friends, especially those from St Angelo who knew about my background, didn't accept me. My blood tainted me – and even my prospective UDR uniform couldn't redeem me.

We used to go to a particular pub in the area popular with UDR and RUC people. I had a few good evenings there, but the pattern was always the same. I'd meet new people one evening, and we'd get on great, but the next time we met they'd be cold and distant, as if they'd been warned off me. Elizabeth would sometimes say I was imagining things, but I knew I wasn't.

I could see from Elizabeth's own behaviour how whispers about someone's untrustworthiness could start. Sometimes, we'd go round to the house of one of her friends. This friend used to share the house with her sister who, so far as I could tell, seemed to spend her days sewing. Before we went there for the first time, Elizabeth told me I wasn't to say anything to the sister. I asked her why. She said, 'She's not to be trusted. She mixes with the wrong people.' When I asked her to explain further, all she could say was that this woman occasionally drank in Catholic pubs and had Catholic friends.

I could understand the need for constant vigilance. I knew that careless cops and squaddies ended up dead, but at the same time I felt she was security-conscious to the point of obsession. Worse – she expected me to be the same. She started driving me mad with her list of things I could and couldn't do – you can't go here, you can't go there, you can't do this, you can't do that. I've never liked being told what to do – and nothing was more likely to make me do the opposite.

One day, I had a few drinks in a 'Provo' pub near the flat that she'd expressly ordered me to avoid. I told her what I'd done. It caused a major row. Our relationship, I realised, was not going to last.

This realisation made me less anxious about how her family viewed me and one peculiar development from that was that I started getting on really well with her mother. I suppose she'd never met anyone like me before. I used to make her laugh. She'd greet me with real warmth and affection. She genuinely liked me and I genuinely liked her, which began to sadden me.

I felt like a lying Judas. Yet I knew that if I told her I'd been born a Catholic, her attitude towards me would have done an about-turn. She'd have treated me like a nasty disease, despite the fact that in flesh, blood, mind and spirit I'd have been no different from the person she'd grown fond of. I'd grown up with anti-black racism, but to me, this was more poisonous – and less understandable. It was a seething hatred for others born on the same small island, if not in the same small street in the same small town – others who shared the same language, accent and skin colour. I felt like a phoney hiding behind an assumed identity. I couldn't tell anyone, Protestant or Catholic, who I really was. It began to get me down.

One evening when Elizabeth wasn't at home, I felt particularly down. I began feeling angry at being surrounded by the invisible enemy. As a joke, someone had given me a little blue-and-white shield-shaped badge on which was emblazoned the provocative symbol of militant Loyalism, the Red Hand of Ulster. I stuck it on my jacket and went for a drink in another so-called 'Provo' pub Elizabeth had warned me to avoid.

The pub was about a quarter full. I stood at the bar waiting to be served, my badge of defiance unnoticed by the elderly regulars. I couldn't see what Elizabeth was fussing about. None of the customers in this supposed IRA den looked violent or capable of violence. The barman, a stocky Lenin lookalike, came and said politely, 'And what can I get for you, Sir?' His eyes fell on my badge. It was like a crucifix to the Antichrist. I saw his eyes widening, then he shouted at me, 'Get out of here with that thing on.'

I told him I wasn't going anywhere: I wanted a drink. He continued shouting at me to get out, but I refused. The customers watched me with silent hostility, but no one intervened. The barman said he was calling the police, an unusual act for a republican, but I assumed the hated symbol of Loyalism on my jacket had unhinged him. Within a short while, two armed policemen came into the pub. I explained the situation, but they told me a landlord was under no obligation to serve anyone. They asked me to leave with them.

Outside, one of them said, 'You shouldn't go in there, especially not wearing that badge.'

I said, 'If I want to wear a badge, I'll wear a fucking badge and they won't stop me.'

He said again that I shouldn't return to that pub. I said I was sick of being told where I could and couldn't go: 'I'll go where I want.'

This time, I didn't tell Elizabeth what I'd done, but within a few days she knew anyway. Word had got back to her, even though I hadn't known those policemen. She couldn't believe I'd been so stupid. Elizabeth realised I wasn't happy. I could tell she was worried about the way I was drawing attention to myself. She'd try to remind me I wasn't in England where my loutish behaviour might only provoke a fist fight. She said, 'Over here, they'll learn who you are, what you are, wait for their moment and shoot you. You've got to take it easy. You've got to learn your boundaries.'

Elizabeth suggested we move out of Enniskillen into the countryside. An ex-UDR man rented us a house in a remote area near Maguiresbridge. We found ourselves about half a mile from the nearest neighbours, a mile from the main road and five miles from the nearest village. Worst of all, we were practically on the border, making us easy targets for the IRA.

There were still several months to go before I joined the UDR. I hadn't bothered looking for work, because I didn't want to be in a position where an employer would have to receive my P45 from the army. But boredom was really beginning to bite and I decided to see if the dole office offered any back-to-work retraining courses at the local college. I went to a dole office that Elizabeth had told me was 'safe' (that is, the one most likely to have Protestant staff and a Protestant clientele). They found me a place on an engineering course at a college in Enniskillen.

Memories of my schooldays filled me with dread, but I thought the course would at least get me out of the house. I'd arranged that my P45 from the army would be sent to the Department of Employment, which would effectively be my employer during my time on the course.

It turned out that most of my fellow students were Catholics, as was the instructor. On the first day, he went around the class asking people about themselves. Perhaps I was paranoid, but he seemed to pay special attention to me. I suppose I was an oddity, because there weren't to my knowledge any other people with English accents in the college. He asked me what I was doing in Northern Ireland. I said my parents were Irish. They'd moved back to Ireland and I'd decided to join them. I hoped that would be enough for him. But, no, he kept asking searching questions. Where were my parents from? What did my dad do? Where were they living?

Perhaps he was just being pally, but he made me feel uncomfortable. The other students weren't particularly friendly, although that could have been my fault as I wasn't overly friendly myself. I wasn't looking for a new group of mates. I felt that, even though they knew I had Irish blood, for them the most important fact about me was my English accent.

Later in the week, as we sat in the classroom before the start of the lesson, the instructor said clearly in front of the class, 'Bernard, could you come to the office later? Your P45 has arrived from the army.'

I thought, 'I'm fucked.'

I felt like punching the bastard in the face, but I just gave a little laugh and said, 'No problem.' I knew he'd done it on purpose. At the time, I thought he was trying to cause me problems – and I even considered giving him a bashing – but with hindsight, I think he might have been trying to do me a favour by letting me know that other people, apart from himself, could already have seen the P45.

From then on, the instructor remained friendly – more proof that I had more to fear from 'nice' people – but almost all the other students made a point of ignoring me. The only people who'd ever speak to me were Protestants – and there weren't many of them around. Within days, someone had scrawled 'Brits Out' on the back of my overalls. I'd come in to find my bits of practical work smashed to pieces or missing. I felt vulnerable, but angry. I used to make sure I carried a sharp tool around with me at all times. I was waiting for someone to say or do something overtly hostile, so I could justifiably smash his face in.

Then a few things happened which disturbed me and Elizabeth. Outside the college, I noticed two young men on a motorbike seemingly keeping an eye on me. Then our dog Jagger started barking a lot at night as if someone were outside. We wouldn't open the door to check, because even Elizabeth didn't have a personal firearm. It wouldn't have been worth her while applying for one so long as she was living with me.

One night, a car drove up to our front door. Someone got out and knocked loudly. We didn't answer. A few weeks later, we came home to find someone had painted the word 'SCUM' in large capital letters on the front door. All of this put a tremendous strain on us. The relationship began deteriorating rapidly.

Ironically, her mother, who thought I was still based at St Angelo – she'd have had a heart attack if she'd known we were living together 'in sin' – started dropping hints about our getting married. She'd say things like, 'Oh, you and Elizabeth are getting on well. I'll introduce you to the minister,' or, 'I hope you're not going to wear your army boots to the wedding. Ha! Ha! Ha!'

I thought, 'Wedding? What wedding?'

But everything came to a sudden end. I came out of college one day to find two green RUC Cortinas with bullet-proof windows parked outside. Elizabeth was standing in the road between them talking to two policemen. A UDR friend was with her. She was crying. I thought something drastic had happened. I ran to her and said, 'What's wrong?'

She said, 'You've got to go. You've just got to go.'

I asked her what she meant. One of the policemen said it was best that we didn't go back to the house. I asked him why. He said things had been happening and they were advising me to go. I said, 'Go where?' He said it had been arranged that I'd go back to England for a few weeks. Elizabeth would join me later. Everything would be fine.

I said, 'I'm not going anywhere.'

But he was firmly insistent: 'It's for your own good. We're going to drive you to the ferry now.'

I could hardly believe what was happening. I said, 'What about my gear?' He said they'd put all my possessions in the boot. I just caved in. I felt I had no choice in the matter. The fact was I didn't have any choice in the matter.

Elizabeth was still crying. I kissed her goodbye. She said she'd come over to England to see me soon. I got in one of the police cars and we drove off. They brought me to Larne and put me on the ferry to Stranraer in Scotland. I only discovered then that they hadn't brought all my possessions. They'd filled three cases, but most of the stuff I'd brought from England had been left behind: around 600 LPs and singles, all my photos and books, my army reserve kit, a lot of my clothes and other personal bits and pieces. I was too dazed to complain. I just got on the ferry. It set sail. For the whole journey, I stood on the deck watching the shores of Northern Ireland slowly disappear.

Elizabeth did come over to England a few times. I tried to get to the bottom of what had happened, but she'd say either she didn't know or she didn't want to talk about it. Her first and most detailed explanation was that she'd kept her policeman brother informed of everything – the men on the motorbike, the bang on the door, the graffiti on the house – and he'd told his superiors, who thought I needed to be moved back to England immediately for my own safety.

At first, I chose to believe that explanation, but over time it became more implausible. I came to feel that what had probably happened was that her parents had found out about my Catholic background and the fact we were living in sin – and they'd wanted me out of her life. The apparent danger I was putting her in with my occasional foolish behaviour, as well as the other incidents, would merely have added to their determination to have me physically removed from Fermanagh. I knew the family's RUC connections would easily have supplied the clout to have me put on a boat.

I couldn't help feeling Elizabeth had played a part. At the very least, she'd been complicit. The relationship, based as it was on a multitude of falsehoods, had become greatly strained. It wouldn't have lasted, but at the same time I hadn't wanted it to end the way it did. Elizabeth told me my possessions had been put at her parents' bungalow for safe-keeping. I was planning to pick them up myself eventually.

During one of her visits to England, I mentioned I'd have to get my stuff back urgently. I was missing my records and I needed my clothing and personal effects. She looked a bit embarrassed. Then she said her parents had destroyed everything. I was stunned. I asked her why. She said they didn't think I was coming back. I wanted to know why she, or they, hadn't contacted me before doing something so drastic. Again, she couldn't, or wouldn't, give a satisfactory explanation.

I felt angry and upset. I'd lost almost all my most personal possessions. Not just records and clothes, but photos and letters – the irreplaceable. There was no innocent explanation. It was a malicious and hostile act. It confirmed to me that her parents had discovered the horrifying truth that they'd allowed an Irish-Catholic (albeit with an English accent) into their front room. I imagined how shocked her poor mother must have been to discover she'd been trying to marry her daughter off to a Fenian. I thought of her falling to her knees and praying to God or the Reverend Ian Paisley, or both, in abject apology for her wickedness. I could imagine her, too, piling up my possessions in her garden, dousing them with petrol and, in an act of cathartic cleansing, flicking a lighted match onto the heap. The incinerated maharajah had finally had his revenge.

With my Irish blood, and my English upbringing, I should have felt at home in that truncated corner of Ulster. But I'd never felt, and would never feel, so alien. As I imagined my possessions going up in flames, my anger was tempered by a sense of relief. I'd never return there. They were welcome to their bonfires.

The only bit of my Wolverhampton past that had remained intact in Northern Ireland was my former MP, Enoch Powell. Sacked immediately from the Conservative Shadow Cabinet for his 'Rivers of Blood' speech, he later resigned from the Tories altogether – and joined the Ulster Unionists. He was elected MP for South Down, which he served from 1974 to 1987.

The army later awarded me a General Service Medal for my Northern Ireland tour of duty. For many years, my experiences there troubled me. Hated by republicans for being a soldier – and hated by some Unionists for being a Catholic. To me, my medal signified nothing but hatred and bigotry. On a drinking trip to Dublin some years later, I decided to give my British medal to the Irish. In an act of cathartic cleansing similar to that of Elizabeth's mother, I walked onto O'Connell Bridge and threw my piece of offical tin in the River Liffey. It plopped into the water and disappeared. No doubt it remains there to this day. The Irish people are welcome to it.

CHAPTER 5

MY MATE ADOLF

BACK IN ENGLAND, I DRIFTED INTO A JOB NORMALLY HELD BY THE SORT OF professional I used to hate. I became a bailiff, repossessing goods and evicting my fellow men and women from their homes and businesses. It wasn't an easy job and it didn't do much for my self-esteem. I felt like the rent man from whom my mother and I used to hide, someone trying to squeeze something out of people who had nothing.

I didn't mind descending on the affluent, but having to evict single mothers and other ordinary people made my task unpleasant and, at times, genuinely distressing. I soon became hopeless at the job. If I felt sorry for people – and quite often I did – I'd advise them about the best way to avoid payment. Then I began to lie to my employers. I'd say people hadn't been in or had moved. But when they sent another bailiff to the same address, and he 'succeeded' where I'd repeatedly failed, they realised I wasn't employee-of-the-month material. Eventually, they sacked me for incompetence. I didn't sue for wrongful dismissal.

My brother Paul invited me to live with him in Surrey. He'd moved into a house in Coulsdon with his new girlfriend, Linda. He told me not to mention our surname in front of her. He didn't say why, and I didn't ask why. In our family, it's always been the case that if one of us says something has to be, then the others accept it as such without question. In this case, he only told me the reason when he announced he was going to marry her.

Paul, forever suspicious of, and cautious about, 'new faces', had given Linda a false surname when he first met her. He hadn't envisaged a long-term romance. He'd given her a friend's surname instead of his own. Then, as the relationship developed and she'd got to know him under the other name, he hadn't had the heart to tell her who he really was. He feared the belated revelation of his true identity might undermine the bond of trust upon which a solid relationship is based.

Paul now planned to get married using his friend's surname. He asked me to be his best man. His only instruction was, 'Whatever's said during the service, keep your mouth shut.'

On the morning of the wedding, Paul took me for a drink with the friend whose surname he'd borrowed. He introduced him as 'Adolf'. And that's how I renewed my contact with Britain's Nazis.

They'd met after Paul's release from Borstal. The probation service had found my brother a job assisting nuns dishing out soup to the homeless in London's West End. Paul knocked the job on the head after a couple of weeks and started working on a building site. There he met Adolf, who was employed as a bricklayer's labourer – a job which he said boosted his fitness in readiness for the coming race war.

Adolf was a very angry young man, bursting with rage and resentment, ranting rather than conversing, but in a way I often found extremely funny. He viewed everything from what I then thought was merely an extreme right-wing perspective, but which I later discovered was in fact genuinely National Socialist.

He didn't tend to tell jokes or clown around; he just maintained a state of permanent rant, like a young Alf Garnett, talking about 'bloody women', 'bloody northerners' and, of course, 'bloody coons'. At that first meeting, as I've said, Adolf spent much of his time expressing disgust at my 'northern' roots and mocking my accent. I wasn't sure what to make of him. Was being rude his way of making friends? Or was he just a lunatic? My brother tended to associate only with lunatics, so I assumed the latter and didn't take his insults personally.

By the time we left for the registry office, we were all extremely drunk. Paul presented Adolf's birth certificate to the registrar and the ceremony got under way. About 30 guests had crammed into the room. I sniggered every time Paul's pseudonym was used. I couldn't stop myself. In the end, I was crying with laughter. The bride turned round and said, 'If he doesn't stop, I'm going home.' That made me even worse and I had to go outside. The formalities passed off without me.

Six months later, the marriage had ended. I don't know if Paul's wife ever found out about his false name. Even if she did, I suspect that, after six months living with him, she accepted it as one of his more minor shortcomings.

I returned to Codsall to spend the Christmas period with my mother. On New Year's Eve, I went drinking with a few of my old friends. Each year, the locals follow the same pattern: they walk from one pub to the next – there are only three – having a drink in each to see who's 'come home' and what's happening. I wasn't interested in doing the rounds, so my friends left me drinking alone in The Crown. The older members of a rival clique stood at the bar. They suffered from 'village mentality' – a delusional state of mind that causes the sufferer to believe he must be harder or somehow superior merely because he's older.

A girl called Diane walked past on her way to the loos. She looked upset. Her brother was my brother Jerry's best friend. I asked her what was wrong. She said she'd gone out for the evening with one of the rival clique. They'd fallen out over something and now he'd turned nasty. She went back to the group. Diane kept saying she wanted to go home, but he wouldn't let her. I thought he was taking the piss out of her. His friends were doing nothing about it.

I walked over and asked her 'boyfriend' what the fuck he thought he was doing. He grabbed me by the throat and tried to push me against a wall. I had a pint glass in my hand. I shoved it as hard as I could into his neck. The glass smashed. Blood poured down his shirt. He fell to the floor and started screaming. Other people joined the chorus of screams. I stood over him, called him a wanker and left the pub. I regretted the incident immediately, because the glass had cut one of my own fingers to the bone. I was now bleeding heavily.

Within five minutes, the police had turned up. Someone

grassed me and they arrested me nearby. Reluctantly, they took me to hospital, where a doctor sewed up my fingers while I stood handcuffed to a gloating policeman. The New Year dawned for me in the cells of Wombourne police station. I'd been in and out of these cells since I was a boy. I knew I'd broken the law, but I also knew I'd received little justice during my encounters with the justice system. I regarded most of the police who'd dealt with me as petty-minded, power-crazed bullies. The only thing we had in common was our mutual hatred.

As the bells chimed in the New Year, I could hear people cheering in the street outside. Alone in the cells, I felt my morale sag under the weight of other people's jubilation. Then I heard footsteps clicking on the cell-block's polished floor. A police officer was striding towards me. The thought of being in the company of another human being – albeit a policeman – at such a time of communal celebration lifted my deflated spirits. Glowing in the warmth of the moment, I found my ice-cold hatred of the police beginning to thaw. I told myself they weren't all bad. Indeed, some could pass for human. The footsteps stopped outside my door.

The uniformed bringer of festive cheer flung open the narrow steel hatch. A pair of eyes peered in at me. I found my lips forming themselves into a smile of friendship and gratitude. A voice said, 'O'Mahoney? Happy New Year, you fucking animal. Start the year as you mean to go on.' He then passed me a Jaffa Cake biscuit with a small candle stuck in it.

If the bastards thought I was an animal, then I'd behave like one. I pissed on the floor and in the morning, when they gave me some sort of slop for breakfast, I threw all my food at the walls. I've always avoided eating in police stations, because I believe the custodians almost certainly spit in your food. Later on, I spat in the face of my female probation officer after I heard her too describing me as 'an animal'.

The courts had closed for the festive season, so they convened a special magistrates' sitting just for me in the police-station foyer. The police led me out, still handcuffed. My right hand was three times its normal size, because the stitches had burst and the wounds had become inflamed. The swelling caused the cuffs to rub in a way which made my wrist bleed.

The prosecutor told the court that, because of the seriousness of the allegation, I shouldn't be granted bail. The magistrates agreed. They remanded me in custody to Winson Green Prison in Birmingham.

At 'The Green', as it's known, I was put in a cell with a middle-aged man who'd run over a traffic warden as she'd issued him a parking ticket. He'd never been in trouble before and was shocked to find himself in prison. He told everyone who'd listen, 'I'm not a criminal. I never saw her, honestly.' In the evenings, this man had the job of pushing the tea urn around. By the time he reached the end of the landing, the urn would be covered with made-up 'parking tickets'.

After three weeks of mind-numbing boredom in a filthy cell with this man and a credit-card fraudster, I applied for bail. This was granted, with several strict conditions, one of which was that I wasn't allowed to enter the county of Staffordshire, unless to attend court. I had to live at my brother Paul's address in Clapham, south London, where he'd moved after separating from his 'wife'.

As I awaited my trial, I began spending a lot of time with Paul, Adolf and a group of friends he'd grown up with. They came mostly from Brixton and Stockwell, from sprawling council estates with nicknames like 'Crack City', 'The Bronx' and 'Broadmoor 2'. Violence, or the threat of it, was a fact of everyday life. Every pub and estate had its own gang – and we managed to fall out with almost every one of them. One pub landlord nicknamed us 'the fire practice', because we caused alarm and forced everyone to leave in a hurry.

Apart from Adolf, there was 'Benny the Jew', Ray, Tony, Colin, Larry 'The Slash', Del Boy and Adrian 'Army Game'. Nearly all had been skinheads together in the '70s, staunch supporters of the National Front, British Movement and other far-right groups. Some had been brought up on estates in which as 'whites' they'd been in a minority. This fact hadn't helped them develop much understanding of, or tolerance for, the other ethnic minorities. Several said they'd always felt like foreigners in their own land. Every perceived 'slight' against them on their home turf was that little bit more painful and made them that little bit more resentful.

Our drinking base was The Royal Oak pub, opposite Stockwell tube station. A drink was always 'a full session', peppered with arguments, mischief or violence. Adolf, perhaps remembering the origins in the Munich beerhalls of Hitler's rise to power, took it upon himself to act as our political mentor. He saw his role as raising our fascist consciousness in preparation for the coming race war.

'Benny the Jew' (as Adolf, especially, liked to call him) had in fact been christened 'Maurice'. However, Adolf thought 'Maurice' sounded 'kikey' ('Maurice, shmorrish. Oy vay, oy vay.'). He was about 5 ft 9 in., had cropped hair and was fairly stocky, although Adolf insisted he was fat. He and Adolf were often at each other's throats. They'd end up brawling, rolling around at our feet while we continued drinking.

Ray and Tony were two brothers who lived in Railton Road, Brixton, known locally as 'the Front Line'. Ray, the elder of the two, was three years younger than me, 5 ft 9 in. and lean. His younger brother, Tony, was of similar height and build, but somewhat quieter than Ray, who tended to drink heavily and never shirk from violence.

Colin was short, about 5 ft 6 in., stocky with cropped ginger hair. He didn't have a violent manner. He could usually be found singing Frank Sinatra or Max Bygraves songs at the top of his voice while disorder raged around us. He was also in his early 20s. Despite his apparent unwillingness to cause trouble, he had no qualms about ending it quickly with a knife, bottle or whatever came close to hand.

Larry 'The Slash' was probably the meekest among us. He was about 5 ft 9 in. and thin almost to the point of frailty. He always wore a cream-coloured 'flasher'-type mac. His 'Slash' nickname came from a deep-red, angry scar which started at the bottom of his ear, ran along his jawline and tapered off under his chin. He picked it up one night down the Old Kent Road after Adolf got into a dispute with a black man. Unknown to Adolf and the others, the man was attending a party nearby. Around 20 of his armed friends then joined the dispute. A serious fight ensued and Larry was slashed with a craft knife. Nobody else was injured. The police arrived and both sides fled.

Del Boy was the oldest. He was well into his 20s. I don't know if he got his nickname from the small-time, south-London wheeler-dealer of the same name in the sitcom *Only Fools and Horses*, or whether that fictional character was based on him. He was an electrician by trade, but dabbled in everything from greyhound racing to drug smuggling, although he was never very successful at anything illegal. Everybody who saw him thought he was a policeman. He had an air of authority about him, perhaps because he always wore a suit. He also had short, black hair, neatly parted at the side, and a well-trimmed moustache.

One Saturday afternoon, I watched as he and Adolf bought a 'champion' greyhound in a Clapham pub. I say 'champion' because that's the word its owner used before selling it to the drunken duo for a few hundred pounds. Adolf and Del Boy used to train the dog in the local park for its debut race with them as owners. On the big night, we all made our way to the track in south London. Just before the race, Del Boy gave the dog a substance which he described as 'rocket fuel'.

The traps opened and the dogs sprinted out. Del Boy and Adolf's dog took the lead. We all jumped up and down, screaming encouragement. Adolf was shouting 'I told you so' at the non-believers and sceptics whose mockery he'd been shrugging off for weeks. The dog led the pack as the first bend approached. Our screams got louder with every second. The scent of victory filled the air, only to dissipate suddenly as the hound not only failed to turn, but failed even to acknowledge a turn might be necessary.

Without slowing down, it rocketed head first into an advertising hoarding. We could hear the crunch from where we stood. Badly injured, the dog never raced again. I next saw it being walked as a pet in the same park where it had trained. Adolf had given it away to a pensioner on his estate.

The other regular face in our circle was a teenager from Battersea called Adrian. He was broad, about 6 ft, with cropped fair hair. We called him 'Army Game' because of his obsession with all things military. The first night I met him he invited me and Colin back to what he said was 'his' flat in Battersea Bridge Road. We'd wanted to continue our drinking session after the pub. Adrian claimed his flat was full of beer.

We arrived by cab. As we climbed the steps to a three-storey townhouse, Adrian put his finger to his lips and slurred drunkenly, 'Wait here.' He went into the house and emerged a few minutes later with a set of keys. He said they belonged to his flat downstairs. I couldn't believe what we found when we walked in. One room contained cases and cases of Carlsberg lager. 'Help yourself, lads,' said Adrian, 'I'll put on some music.' He claimed the lager had been given to him by his father, who worked for Carlsberg.

He said we could drink as much as we wanted. He showed us a room full of new promotional Carlsberg clothing and electrical goods (such as a stereo and a TV). Some personal items were scattered around. Adrian said these had been left by the previous tenant. He said, 'Take what you want.' We raised our cans to his father and then spent the night drinking, trying on the promotional clothing and packing anything we liked into the previous tenant's suitcases. We got everything ready for carting off the next day.

In the early hours, someone banged on the door. I opened it to be faced by a West Indian man in his 50s wearing a dressing gown. He began screaming about the loud music. Before I had a chance to say anything, he said, 'Keep the noise down – or else.'

'Or else fucking what?' shouted Adrian over my shoulder. 'Or else fucking what?' I told the guy to fuck off and slammed the door. He shouted through the letterbox, 'I'll be back, you wankers, with my sons, and we'll see who'll fuck off then.'

We flung the door open and ran out, but he'd already disappeared. Around seven, we'd all lapsed into a drunken slumber. I heard someone putting a key in the lock. Then the letterbox clattered. I made my way on my hands and knees to the front room. I said, 'Colin! Colin! There's somebody at the front door. I think it's the black geezer and his sons.'

I picked up a knife, Colin a weightlifting bar. We walked to the front door and I shouted, 'Who is it? Who the fuck are you?'

A man's voice replied, 'Why can't I open the door? Who are you?'

Adrian had double-locked the door from the inside. I opened it. A well-dressed man, aged about 30, stood there.

I said, 'What do you want?'

'What do I want?' he said. 'What the hell do you want? This is my flat. And that shirt he's wearing is my bloody shirt.'

I looked at Colin, who still looked pitifully pissed. I said to the man, 'Give me five, mate.' I closed the door. The flat didn't look good. Cans, clothing and records were strewn everywhere. In the hallway, the stereo – speakers tied to it – had been put alongside the suitcases of clothes. Everything stood ready for transportation. In the bedroom, we found Adrian lying on his back, the nearby duvet covered in vomit. We tried rousing him, but he remained dead to the world. In the end, we decided to leave him. It was, after all, 'his' flat. We slipped out the back and hailed a cab.

Later that day, Adrian arrived at Colin's carrying a suitcase. His own suitcase. He'd left 'his' flat – and the house he shared with his dad. Apparently, the flat belonged to Carlsberg, for whom Adrian's father worked. A salesman currently occupied it. He'd gone away for the weekend, leaving the keys for safe-keeping with Adrian's father, who lived with his son in the company house above.

With the double-lock off, the salesman had been able to enter the flat after we'd left. He'd found the comatose Adrian, recognised him as the paralytic progeny of his work colleague upstairs and called dad down. The two managed to rouse Adrian. His furious father helped him upstairs.

About an hour later, the salesman knocked on Adrian's father's door. He was bleeding from the nose. He said someone had knocked on the flat's door. He'd opened it – and three well-built black youths had set upon him. They'd accused him of bad-mouthing their father and beat the shit out of him before leaving.

Alongside these drunken japes, Adolf made sure we never lost sight of the way 'our country' was being plundered by 'foreign invaders'. In fact, most members of our little group had at least one Irish parent. Some of us had two. So we probably weren't best qualified to represent British bulldog nationalism. That didn't stop Adolf enlisting us for 'the Movement'. For him, the most important facts were that we were white, working class and spoke with an English accent, albeit in my case with a regrettable regional variation.

None of us really bought into Adolf's fascist politics. But all of us bought into the widespread white, working-class sense of resentment of immigrants (especially non-white immigrants) and, in particular, of the perks we felt they enjoyed at the expense of 'the natives'. Adolf's sister had been born and bred in Lambeth. She was engaged to a man who'd also been born and bred in Lambeth. They'd applied for housing to the local authority, but were told they'd have to sit on a waiting list for at least five years. Yet they could see whole estates of council houses being filled with immigrants. It wasn't a figment of their racist imaginations. They used to say that every plane flying into England over Lambeth en route to Heathrow put them a few hundred places further down the housing list.

Foreigners could swiftly achieve higher priority over natives, because of what we regarded as the unjust way in which councils allocated public housing. Foreigners from alien cultures with no blood links to this country could arrive at Heathrow, be deemed 'homeless' (and therefore in greater and more urgent 'need' than natives) and shoot to the top of the queue. We felt strongly that these Third World shit-bins (as Adolf called them) should not have been immediately given the same rights to equal treatment as natives. Adolf's view, which we shared, was that if the government wanted to give them a home, and make them feel at home, it should have built a few tin-shacks or mud-huts for them on Hackney Marshes and let them shit in a big hole. Instead, as Adolf said, the Labour Government and all those lefty councils seemed to hand the best houses and flats to the wandering tribesmen of the Kalahari. It seemed so unjust. And that sense of perceived injustice bred resentment, frustration and, ultimately, hatred. Many white working-class people also felt they couldn't protest without being labelled 'racist'. Only extreme right-wing groups seemed willing to articulate their grievances and anger.

That spring, south London was simmering. You could feel the tension. It reminded me of Northern Ireland during the hunger strikes. I knew the simmering anger would soon boil over into violence. The police patrolling Brixton were just like the British Army patrolling Northern Ireland. It seemed like the men on the ground had their hands tied by politicians. The ordinary police seemed reluctant to enforce the law, particularly in the face of aggressive blacks, partly because doing so just wasn't worth the hassle and partly because their main aim was to survive their 'tour of duty' (which meant avoiding confrontation at all costs).

In the early part of 1983, officers on 'the Front Line' in Railton Road suffered several horrific attacks by mobs. These attacks received little or no publicity, presumably to avoid inciting copycat incidents. One day, I saw a policeman walking along one of the streets off Railton Road. A group of black youths hurled a milk bottle at him as he passed. The glass shattered at his feet. But he didn't even turn to look where it had come from. He just walked on and away. However much I despised the police, I still didn't like seeing them humiliated in this way.

The situation sickened me and my friends. Our resentment stewed. We talked about the 'repatriation' of immigrants and, if that failed, leaving England ourselves.

We used to drink with a couple of black blokes. They were friends of Ray's brother, Tony, and so were deemed 'OK'. We saw them as different from 'the others'. Of course, we didn't speak to any others.

In April 1983, I stood trial at Stafford Crown Court for the glassing incident on New Year's Eve. Charged with wounding with intent, I pleaded not guilty, knowing that 'intent' is very difficult to prove. I told the jury I'd gone to the aid of a woman in distress. I'd been alone and outnumbered by a gang with a reputation for violence. As a good citizen, I'd remonstrated with them regarding their obnoxious and anti-social behaviour. One of this gang of notorious hooligans had then grabbed me and, acting totally out of fear, I'd pushed him away, forgetting I held a glass in my hand.

The prosecution argued I couldn't 'forget' I was holding a glass. I said 'forget' probably wasn't the right word. I explained that I was wearing a pair of trousers, but I wasn't 'conscious' of that fact. I hadn't been conscious of holding the glass either.

The trial lasted three days. My victim put on an outstanding performance in the witness box. At one stage, the judge even let him sit down after he appeared to faint. I was genuinely impressed. Until then, I hadn't realised I'd assaulted such a gifted actor. However, the photographs of his injuries turned the stomach. He had a track of stitches along the length of his neck. His ear had nearly been severed and its remnants looked like they'd been in a dog's mouth. I could see looks of horror and disgust on the faces of the jury. I didn't fancy my chances.

On the morning of the third day, the jury retired to consider its verdict. Before leaving, the jurors had been given an alternative charge to consider: simple 'unlawful wounding', which is far less serious as there's no intent involved. They returned after six hours' deliberation. Not guilty to 'wounding with intent', but guilty to 'unlawful wounding'.

My barrister read out both the testimonial in my army Certificate of Service and a reference written by my former troop leader, attesting glowingly to my good character. I'd told my troop leader in a letter I needed it for a job. He hadn't been fooled. On a separate piece of paper, he'd written, 'Hope this is OK and you get off. Good luck.'

The judge told me that, because of my 'exemplary' military record, society owed me a debt. He said he'd considered sending me to prison for a considerably longer period, but, in the circumstances, nine months would suffice.

My mother was in court. Her look of anguish tore through me. It affected me more than the sentence, which I thought was pretty lenient, given the injuries I'd inflicted.

I served the first part in HMP Shrewsbury, known locally as 'The Dana'. Towards the end, I was moved to HMP Stafford, which had a bad reputation among prisoners, although to me it didn't seem any worse than 'The Dana'.

In both establishments, boredom reigned supreme. Life proceeded slowly and with great tedium. I was issued with prison-tailored jeans, a blue-and-white striped shirt, a grey jumper with a light-blue neck and a remarkably ugly pair of shoes. I felt the shoes in particular had been designed to deter escape attempts, because I couldn't imagine how anyone with a shred of dignity would consider wearing them on the street, whatever the circumstances. For one pound twenty per week, I worked on a sewing machine in the prison workshop making mailbags and jeans. Contrary to tabloid myth, there were no TVs in the cells.

The only TV I encountered was a long-haired effeminate Yorkshireman called Dan or Diane, depending on who was talking to him. I needed the patience of a saint to tolerate some of the fools around me. Occasionally, I'd meet an intelligent, interesting or amusing person, but by and large I found myself surrounded by idiots, fantasists, losers, bullies and the clinically insane, some of whom wore uniform and many of whom had very poor standards of personal hygiene. There was less violence than I'd imagined, but it happened now and again.

Just because I was in jail didn't mean I escaped the attention of the police. Detectives from my home town came to visit me at one stage. I guessed they hadn't come out of concern for the progress of my rehabilitation. They produced a list of around 20 petty crimes which they said I'd committed. I'd had nothing to do with any of them. My unwanted visitors had even prepared a statement they wanted me to sign. They said I wouldn't have to go to court. The crimes wouldn't even appear on my record of convictions. They'd simply be recorded as 'TICs' ('taken into consideration'). It was a popular police method of massaging the crime figures to boost the clear-up rate. I told them to fuck off. They said, 'Fair enough, Bernie. We'll arrest you at the gate and we can discuss it then.' That's something all prisoners fear. On the day you're released, the police are waiting for you outside. You walk your first steps of freedom into the back of a police car. I signed the statement. Such was the system that demanded my respect.

I fought back in little ways. At Stafford, I shared a cell with an Irish traveller called Finbar. He'd do anything for prison currency (biscuits, Mars bars, tobacco). We were on the third-floor landing. On the ground floor stood the Wing Office, outside which prison officers congregated every morning to drink tea and stroke each other's egos. I used to give Finbar a packet of biscuits or a Mars bar to fill a large plastic tea-mug with piss and throw the contents down onto the screws through the open metal grids underneath our feet. The screws would think they'd been accidentally splashed with tea or water by a careless prisoner. They'd shout up, 'Oi! Watch what you're bloody well doing.' Finbar would either apologise profusely or deny all knowledge. Little things like this helped me through.

I only had to serve six months of my nine-month sentence. Getting parole is easy, so long as you're prepared to toe the line and be dishonest.

'Do you regret your crime?'

'Deeply.'

'How do you feel about your victim?'

'Sorrow and remorse.'

'Will you offend again?'

'No, never.'

'Which lessons have you learnt for the future?'

'The importance of discipline and self-control.'

I just told them what they needed to hear. Lie, lie, lie. They didn't want me in their overcrowded hate-factory anyway. They were under-staffed, under pressure and underpaid. The truth was that the only regret I had was that I'd been caught and convicted. That's the only regret most prisoners have. But you can hardly be honest if you want to get out of jail. The system would find honesty 'unacceptable'. But perhaps if young offenders could be genuinely honest, then the roots of their behaviour could be explored in a constructive way. As it is, honesty only opens you up for additional punishment.

After prison, I returned to London to live with Lofty, the pacifist friend from my army days. He was renting a three-bedroom house in Perivale, west London, with his girlfriend Cathy. Lofty hadn't changed much since the army. He still spent his time puffing weed, reading Greenpeace leaflets and strumming his guitar. He didn't seem to be able to get his head together, probably because he couldn't find it.

Lofty's commitment to non-violence made him an unlikely pal for me. We were chalk and cheese, really, but I liked him. His semi-detached outlook on life and our cash-strapped situation always made me laugh. Each week was a struggle to meet the rent. On Friday nights, when the landlord called to collect his dues, Lofty would play the record 'Let's Lynch the Landlord' by The Dead Kennedys. I don't think the landlord ever got it.

One evening, my brother Paul came over from Clapham to see me. We were sitting in the front room watching TV when we heard a loud bang on the front door. Cathy had just gone to visit a neighbour and at first I thought it was her returning. Several more loud, urgent bangs followed. I became alarmed, because it sounded like someone was trying to kick the door down. I was concerned for Cathy. I thought something might be happening to her. I picked up a hammer and ran to the front door. Paul got there before me.

Whoever was outside was kicking the door and shouting, 'Open the door! Open the fucking door!'

Paul pulled it open and two men in their early 20s burst in and ran towards me. I swung the hammer and hit the first one on the side of the head. A jet of blood spattered the wall as he went down. His friend turned and ran back out. I stamped on the man at my feet until he stopped moving. Then I dragged him outside by his feet. It had been snowing. He lay there motionless with a bleeding head. His friend had disappeared. I didn't know the man, and neither did Paul nor Lofty, who'd joined us outside. Suddenly, the stranger sat up in the snow and began moaning, blood all down his head, chin and chest.

I said, 'What the fuck's going on, mate? Why were you trying to kick the fucking door in?' He saw the hammer still in my hand, so he lay back again in the snow, covering his face with his hands. He said, 'Please don't hit me again.'

With a little coaxing, he explained that he and his friend had been chased from a nearby fairground by a gang wielding weapons. He said they'd run for their lives to the nearest house. They'd banged on our door for help. I said, 'You should have said something, mate.'

He said, 'You didn't give us a chance.'

I felt bad about the poor bloke. But I believed that, in the circumstances, a forgivable misunderstanding had taken place. I gave him a towel to mop up the blood, called him a taxi and wished him a safe journey home. Lofty had been watching everything in disbelief.

Cathy came home and saw the blood in the snow, the damaged door and the arc of blood up the hallway wall. I couldn't pretend nothing had happened. Lofty filled her in and she went berserk. I was already feeling shitty, so I didn't need her on my case. Anyway, I thought her outrage stemmed from the minor damage to the interior decoration, rather than my inhospitable treatment of a fugitive seeking sanctuary. In the end, I told her it had fuck all to do with her. Lofty joined in on her side and, in a flash of temper, I ended up bashing him too, though not with the hammer. He was, after all, a friend.

The following day, I packed my possessions and moved to south London to live in a bedsit near Paul.

CHAPTER 6

AWAY DAYS

ONCE MY SELF–RIGHTEOUS ANGER HAD DIED DOWN, I FELT REALLY AWFUL ABOUT having beaten up a hippy. Lofty was a good bloke and I liked his company. Bashing him was hardly the best way to cement our friendship. I disliked myself for having lost my temper yet again. Sometimes, I just can't control it. I have this anger in me that never seems to go away. It can just well up and then explode, often for quite petty reasons.

I decided I needed to apologise to Cathy and Lofty. I thought I'd apologise first to Cathy at her workplace, then later I'd go round and take her and Lofty out for a drink. Cathy worked in a high-street shoe shop. I walked in and saw her at the other end, serving a customer at the counter. As I reached the shop's mid-point, her eyes met mine. The colour seemed to drain from her face and her mouth opened slightly, as if about to let out a scream.

In a few more steps, I was standing in front of her. I hadn't even opened my mouth when she shouted, 'Get out! Just get out! Or I'll call the police.' I tried to explain I wanted to apologise, but she didn't want to listen. To this day, I don't know quite how I did it, but I accidentally stepped back into some sort of glass display. It broke. The shop filled with the tinkling of glass. I was deeply embarrassed. Standing up to my ankles in plate glass, I said, 'Shit. I'm really sorry. Can I clear it up?'

Cathy just screamed at me, 'Get out now. I'm calling the police. Go!'

I found myself getting angry again, so I left. I never saw Cathy or Lofty again.

Moving back to south London brought me back into more regular contact with Adolf and the lads. They used to travel over to east London to sell National Front newspapers in Brick Lane, an area with a significant Asian population. I began joining them. There'd usually be no more than ten to fifteen of us selling the papers. At our side stood four police officers. Across the road, a group of Anti-Nazi League protesters would be screaming abuse. Another five policemen would keep them at bay.

There were no skinheads among the paper-sellers. Apart from me and my friends, the other regulars were three men in their 50s, sombrely dressed in dark suits, and two blokes in their early 30s who looked like City computer operators. Most of the people who ambled past the market stalls in 'the Lane' were Asians. Some would stop and buy a paper, which surprised me as they usually bore the brunt of the abuse inside. White customers would often shuffle up ashamedly, head down, as if buying a porn mag.

The paper, which I only rarely bothered to read, blathered on about 'war on the streets' and 'direct action', but when I once suggested to one of the suits that, instead of standing in silence, we ought to try now and again to bash the howling reds across the road, I was told to 'show restraint'. All in all, it was rather tedious.

Adolf invited me to a few meetings, usually held in the locked back-room of a pub. Behind closed doors, our 'leaders' bravely displayed bloodlust – before telling us to make sure we didn't leave any rubbish behind and to stack the chairs neatly. Equally tiresome.

I soon got to know a few of 'the Movement's' 'faces' and found myself being invited to go on 'away days'. These were coach trips to flashpoint areas like Liverpool, Leicester and Bradford. We'd go on marches and to meetings organised by groups like the National Front and the British Movement. We'd show support, swell the numbers and be on hand to defend the cause if these events provoked the violent reaction they were designed to.

The police always knew we were coming. Either they'd already be waiting or they'd turn up soon after our arrival. In Liverpool, they once met us at the motorway exit and turned us back. In

Bradford, they stopped us entering a community hall for a meeting. Around 250 reds had congregated for a howling session outside. A few bottles and stones flew towards us as we approached, and the police ushered us into a closed-off car park. Then they put us back on the coach and escorted us in two police cars to the city gates.

The coach, with about 50 on board, drove on, up into the hills. The meeting took place on a deserted and windswept slope far from civilisation. Having achieved what we'd come to do – that is, hold a meeting ('No Surrender') – we jumped back on the coach and headed triumphantly back to London.

It might sound naive, or slightly dull-witted, or an attempt to avoid taking full moral responsibility for my actions, but although I'd become more and more involved in these fascist activities, I didn't strongly identify myself or my mates with 'Nazism'. However, if you hang around with Nazis, go to Nazi events, support Nazi policies and express Nazi views, then you are, to all intents and purposes, a Nazi. I see that clearly now, but back then I didn't feel myself engaged primarily in a political struggle, an Aryan crusade. Mainly, I saw myself as just taking part, as I'd always done, in gang warfare.

I'd just found a new gang. White gang versus black gang, right-wing gang versus left-wing gang, working-class gang versus middle-class gang. Indeed, for me, the political dimension had a lot to do with 'class war': me and my mates, the white working class, fighting the red middle-class tossers. I saw these Anti-Nazi League, Socialist Worker, WRP, Red Army Faction 'students' merely as spoilt junior members of the bourgeoisie dabbling in left-wing activism before settling down to a comfy job in Channel Four News and a life sucking cappuccinos while reading *The Guardian*.

I felt that, apart from spending a short interlude slumming it in a free-love squat in a 'deprived' area, most of these middle-class red bastards would end up living in Kensington or Windsor, like mummy and daddy, and not in the sort of multicultural ghettos they wanted to foist on us. Those at least were the gut prejudices that filled my mind. As I never actually spoke to any of the reds, let alone had the chance to enquire about the circumstances of their upbringings, it was probably a bit ignorant of me to generalise in the way I did.

However, I can't say these ways of thinking helped me justify my actions, because for a long time I never thought I was doing anything particularly wrong. Self-righteousness came naturally to me. We returned several times to Bradford. Hostile crowds always greeted us. 'Winding up the Pakis', as Adolf called it, was a popular pastime. There was usually a bit of violence, but nothing serious. Sometimes, someone would get hit by a missile, or punched in the face by a 'dyke'.

We always went 'tooled up' with coshes, CS gas, knuckle-dusters and knives. On the coach, there'd be a lot of bravado, with people waving weapons about, boasting of their readiness to use them. On one trip to Bradford, someone produced a large, bone-handled Bowie knife and started bragging about its 'razor' sharpness. My mate 'Benny the Jew' disagreed. He said, 'That couldn't cut butter. It's blunt, mate.'

An argument developed. Benny suddenly snatched the knife and shouted, 'It's fucking blunt, see?' He jabbed his own chest with it only to discover he'd been wrong. The knife was sharp. Very, very sharp. The blade went straight in, right up to the hilt. He slumped back in his seat and went white.

I couldn't believe it. Everyone started shouting for the driver to pull over. I thought Benny was either dying before my eyes or already dead. Then he started making little moaning sounds. The coach driver took a few minutes to find an emergency phone on the motorway.

We came to a stop. I helped carry Benny from the coach. We laid him down on the hard shoulder. Someone phoned for an ambulance. The emergency operator was told it was 'a stab wound', so we knew the police would be sent too. We threw all our other weapons down the embankment.

The coach driver was panicking. He assumed one of us had stabbed Benny. Perhaps he feared he'd be next. He said, 'I don't need this, lads. Keep me out of it. I'm only here to drive the coach.' Everyone told him to shut up. He started walking nervously up and down the hard shoulder, chain-smoking and muttering to himself.

Benny had lost consciousness. I could see very little blood. A police car pulled up as we all stood around. The coach driver was now sitting on the grass, shaking his head and coming to the end of his cigarette packet. Two policemen got out of the car and walked briskly towards us. They looked down at Benny, who was moaning gently, with the knife still protruding from his chest. The first policeman said earnestly, 'Can anybody tell us what happened, lads?'

We told them the truth, but they didn't believe us. You could tell by their faces they thought a serious crime of violence had been committed, the perpetrator or perpetrators of which still skulked in their midst.

The second policeman said, 'He stabbed himself by mistake. Have I got that right?'

'Yes, officer. He stabbed himself by mistake.'

As Benny was being loaded into the ambulance, we were being loaded back onto the coach for a trip 'down to the station'. One of the policemen got on with us, presumably to prevent any 'evidence' being thrown out the window. The other led the way in his car.

At the station, they searched us before interrogating us individually. They remained steadfast in their conviction that someone had stabbed Benny. They fought hard to get at 'the truth'. The interrogators tried doggedly to break down my 'wall of lies'.

'You're lying, son. Tell the truth.'

'I'm not lying. He stabbed himself.'

'You think we're stupid up here, don't you?'

'No, but I'm telling the truth.'

'A bloke ends up with a big knife sticking out of his own chest, and almost dies, and it's just an accident, is it?'

'Yes.'

'He "accidentally" stabbed himself.'

'Yes.'

'You think we're stupid up here . . .'

In the early hours of the morning, they released us, reluctantly. They said Benny was recovering and was 'sticking to the same story' that he'd stabbed himself.

Benny stayed in hospital a few more days before returning to London. The knife had missed his important bits, so he recovered quickly. He said the police had visited him several times to implore him to tell 'the truth'. They'd said that only if he cooperated could they bring his 'attacker' to justice. They even sent along a 'Victim Support' officer skilled in counselling frightened witnesses.

On Saturday afternoons, we used to meet in a pub in Islington High Street, north London. One afternoon, we stayed later than usual and got very drunk. An argument about nothing developed between Adolf and Ray. They decided to settle their differences outside. Each first put a fifty-pound note on the table. The winner would not only prove his point, but collect a hundred pounds.

Once the two disappeared through the doors onto the street, Benny picked up Adolf's carrier bag and went into the toilet. A few minutes later, he emerged wearing a brand new pair of designer jeans Adolf had bought that morning. Benny had come to the pub directly from his job on a building site. His muck-and-paint-spattered jeans were now in Adolf's bag.

Adolf and Ray eventually returned, looking dishevelled, but uninjured. Each man picked up his own fifty-pound note. We continued drinking until afternoon closing time around three, when we headed back across the river to south London.

A few of us ended up at Adolf's flat in Stockwell. Adolf went to his bedroom. A few minutes later, we heard a scream of rage followed by a tirade of obscene language. 'Bastard, bastard, bastard,' Adolf shouted as he stormed back into the front room. He was holding Benny's dirty jeans in his hands. He said the Asian sales assistant must have knowingly swapped the new jeans for a disgusting pair of rags. 'He's had me over. The Paki bastard's had me over.' He couldn't believe it. 'I know when he did it,' he said. 'He bent down behind the counter to get a carrier bag and he must have done the switch then. Fucking sneaky Paki bastard.'

Adolf said he was going back to the shop. As soon as he slammed shut the front door, everybody collapsed into laughter.

Adolf returned a few hours later. He said justice had been done. He'd got a minicab to take him back to the Islington shop and told the driver to wait outside. He'd marched in and said he wanted to speak to the Asian sales assistant who'd served him earlier. This man turned out to be the manager. Adolf punched him in the face without saying a word. The manager had fallen to the floor. Before marching back out, Adolf had shouted, 'That's for the fucking jeans, you clever cunt.' Adolf wasn't told immediately about Benny's 'prank'. He wasn't amused when he found out. The jeans were returned. For the next few months, Adolf targeted Benny for abuse.

Larry 'The Slash' was looking for somewhere to stay, and I wanted to move out of my bedsit, so we decided to rent a flat together. Eventually, we moved into the ground floor of a terraced house in Evelyn Street, Deptford. The upper floor was occupied by a group of radical students who posted leaflets through our letterbox inviting us to attend anti-Nazi rallies and Rock Against Racism concerts. Most annoyingly, they played jazz all the time, really loud. Jazz is probably the only form of music I loathe and detest. The whole house would reverberate to the heart-sinking sound of Miles Davis.

We tried to be reasonable. At first, we asked them politely to turn down the music, which they did, only to turn it up again a few hours later. Gradually, we increased our threat level ('Turn the fucking music off or we'll turn you off.'). Finally, we decided we'd either bash them or burgle them.

We opted for the latter on a Friday night when we knew they'd be out rocking against racism. We broke in, stole their stereo and sent Miles Davis flying against the wall. 'The Jazz Cats', as we called them, never bothered us again. They even stopped leafletting us.

A barman called Buzz started working at our regular pub, The Royal Oak. He was either extremely brave or extremely fucking stupid, because he began giving evidence to the police when bad behaviour occurred on the premises. In the first incident, two of our friends, including Adrian 'Army Game', threw a few chairs over the bar after he asked them to leave. The chairs didn't even hit him, but he still made a statement. Both our friends ended up imprisoned for a few months. Buzz had placed himself in great danger. One evening, Ray knocked on our door in Deptford. He looked a bit shaken. He said he and Colin had launched a revenge attack on Buzz in the pub. In the fight, a barmaid's arm had been broken and Buzz had been repeatedly stabbed in the body. Buzz made another statement.

The police were now looking for Ray and Colin. Ray left home and came to live with us for eight months. Colin went to live with his dad in Stratford, east London. After a while, when he thought the police had lost interest, Ray started visiting his mother on Saturdays. One morning, the police swooped and arrested him. At his trial, he pleaded not guilty and refused to say who he'd been with on the night. Buzz went into the witness box and fingered him as one of his attackers. Ray was sent to prison.

Buzz's behaviour outraged us. He'd sent yet another of our friends to the hate-factory. That was a diabolical liberty that could not go unpunished. At least once a week, the pub's windows were smashed. Then a shot-put was thrown at Buzz from the second floor of a block of flats overlooking the pub. It didn't hit him, but it made him jump.

My old friend Hughie came down from Wolverhampton to visit. Everyone chipped in to pay him a hundred pounds to 'do' Buzz. Hughie agreed, but as he didn't know what Buzz looked like, he asked me to go with him to point him out. I didn't fancy it, because Buzz knew me and I knew he'd grass me too. But I wanted to avenge Ray. We'd become good friends in the eight months we'd lived together.

Del Boy had an idea. He said he had a disguise I could use – an actor's wig: 'He'll never recognise you, Bernie.' Del Boy's masterful disguise turned out to be a cheap ginger party wig. The only actor who might have worn it was the one playing Ronald McDonald, the burger chain's clown mascot. I tried it on. My friends began weeping with laughter. I kept saying, 'It looks fucking stupid.' But my friends assured me it looked good and no one would recognise me. We were all drinking at the time.

Del Boy and a man called Slippery Bill drove us to The Royal Oak. I put on the wig, then Hughie and I walked into the crowded bar. The regulars who saw me fell silent. A few who knew me began laughing, 'All right, Bernie. Love the wig, mate.' Someone started singing, 'There's a difference at McDonald's.'

I pointed Buzz out to Hughie. We walked to the bar. Buzz

came over to serve us personally. 'Can I help you?' he asked Hughie, who picked up a pint glass and lunged it at his face. Buzz saw it coming and leaned back. The glass broke across his forehead and he fell backwards. Hughie and I turned and ran from the pub. The regulars, many of whom liked and respected Buzz, gave chase. A hail of bottles and glasses fell around us as we ran to the car. My wig almost fell off in the excitement.

Del Boy was laughing so much he stalled the car. He finally got it going and we sped off, the angry mob shrinking in the rear-view mirror. We never heard anything from the police, so we assumed Buzz had got the message.

Ray's release from prison coincided with my birthday, so to celebrate we went up the West End to a bar called Sound and Vision. Banks of TV screens showing music videos covered the walls. A group of men from east London started behaving in a liberty-taking way, making snide comments about south London and jostling us as we walked past them to the toilets. They seemed to know the doormen, so must have assumed unwisely they could get away with their provocation. We played pool. One of the men walked past and deliberately knocked Del Boy into Benny. I didn't say anything. I just hit the man across the head with a pool cue, then proceeded to whack his mates too.

Both sides started throwing pool balls at one another. TV screens were getting smashed. The doormen came to the East Enders' aid, but we beat them back. We left the bar at our leisure and jumped on the nearest tube back to south London. The only place we could find open that would let us in was a tacky bar-cum-club in Vauxhall, frequented by gays and drug dealers.

As we stood at the bar waiting to be served, Adolf said to me, 'That bloke keeps smiling at me.' I looked across to see a man on his own at the other side of the bar. He was a bit older than us, and looked like he might have had one or two gay relationships in the past.

The handsome stranger smiled at me too. I told Adolf to ignore him. Adolf said if the man continued to smile at him, and therefore assume he too was gay, then he was going to bash him. I said, without wishing to appear too liberal, that, as it was a sort of gay venue, then it wasn't entirely unreasonable for a gay man to assume that perhaps other male customers might also be so inclined. A few minutes later, the man was on the floor, bleeding from the head, the remains of a light-ale bottle all around him.

For the second time that evening, a full-scale brawl erupted. Tables, chairs, glasses and customers flew around the room. The fight spilled out of the club and onto the street. Eventually, our opponents, in less than gay mood, just stood in the doorway, preventing our re-entry. We stood in the road, exchanged a few insults and started to walk off up the street. Only then did we realise that Larry wasn't with us. He had to be still inside the club. We turned and ran back down the road. As we reached the club, the doors opened and Larry was launched out onto the pavement. The doors slammed shut.

One of my friends arrived with a can of petrol. He'd bought it from the nearby garage in Nine Elms Lane. He started dousing the club's doors and windows with the fuel. Those inside could see what was happening. Through the windows, I watched panic breaking out. Screams and shouts accompanied the clambering to find a rear exit. Before the petrol could be ignited, a police car and van came hurtling round the corner. Everyone began to run. A policeman tackled me to the ground before I'd got very far. He said I was under arrest.

I could see Larry still lying immobile on the pavement where he'd landed. A victorious policeman stood over him, informing him of his rights. I was handcuffed, bundled into the van and told to sit on the floor.

Various revellers from the club were brought to the van to identify me. Only two of them implicated me as one of those who'd been fighting. Meanwhile, I watched Larry being hauled to his feet by two large police officers. Each time they got him upright, he collapsed again. Eventually, they gave up and carried him to the van, dumping him next to me on the floor. I tried speaking to him, but, between his mumbling and a policeman's telling me to shut up, I didn't get a decipherable response.

At the station, I was told I was being held on suspicion of attempted arson. Larry, still unable to stand or communicate (apart from the occasional slurred swear-word), was told he was being held for being drunk and disorderly. They tried walking him up and down the custody area to sober him up, but every time they let go of him he collapsed in a heap. They took me to an interview room for questioning. They took Larry to the cells to sleep it off.

I discovered later that, to be on the safe side, the police had called a doctor, who'd immediately summoned an ambulance for Larry. At the hospital, an X-ray revealed the reason why he couldn't stand up. He'd suffered two broken legs.

The police interrogated me for a few hours, but I knew I had nothing to fear, because neither my person nor my clothing had come into contact with any petrol. Then the two witnesses who'd been so sure about my identity outside the club failed to appear to make statements. I was released the next day. Larry later received a letter informing him that 'after careful consideration' no further action would be taken against him in respect of the drunk-and-disorderly allegation.

Effra Terrace in Railton Road, Brixton, had for several years been a source of irritation and anger for many locals, including my mates Ray and Tony, who lived almost opposite. The entire block of flats had been taken over by, according to Ray's description, a group of particularly smelly and offensive red squatters. We clashed occasionally outside Brixton tube station with the ones who sold Marxist propaganda sheets.

We were therefore delighted to watch the television news one night in March 1984. Police riot squads had moved in to evict the squatters. Later, Ray gave us his own eyewitness account. He said he'd been woken at four in the morning by the sound of shouts, screams and smashing bottles. At first, he'd thought we'd come to visit him.

It wasn't yet the rioting season – summer – so he got up to see hundreds of police outside. He realised gleefully that the squatters were finally being rehoused. Rampaging youths were hurling bricks and lumps of wood. Ray watched as they overturned a car, erected barricades and set a house on fire. He said if they hadn't been reds, he might have joined in on their side.

It was great news. However, their eviction would indirectly cause my brother Paul extreme grief a few weeks later.

I continued to travel home to Codsall now and again to visit my mother and see my old friends. When you've had constant problems with the police in a small community, you end up with a tag you can never shed. The police seem to work on the assumption that only certain people commit certain types of crime. Like at school, it becomes a case of, 'Who else could have done it?' So even on a short trip home to say hello to my mother I could find myself being pulled in for questioning about almost any crime of robbery and violence within a radius of 50 miles. On one occasion, when I myself became a victim of crime, I found the case being investigated as if I were the criminal.

I was drinking alone one day in a Wolverhampton pub. A well-built man came over to me. He was with a girl I knew from school. I greeted her and she introduced me to her friend. When he heard my surname, he said he knew my older brother Jerry. He added that Jerry was a wanker.

I haven't spent much time in my life with those of great charm and manners, so I don't expect much in the way of etiquette. However, I do feel, as a point of principle, that when one is meeting strangers for the first time one should – at least in the intial exchange of greetings – try to avoid expressing insultingly derogatory comments about one of that stranger's close family members.

I said to the cheeky bastard, 'What did you say?'

He repeated that my brother Jerry was a wanker. He based his contention on the fact that Jerry had left the Hell's Angels. No one wants to upset the Wolverhampton Hell's Angels – especially not Asian potato-pickers – but Jerry had been involved with them, got locked up, come out of prison and moved on.

I punched my new acquaintance in the face and a fight started. When we were pulled apart, the landlord, who'd seen and heard everything, told the other man to leave. At closing time, I walked out of the pub to get a taxi at the rank directly opposite. As I stepped onto the pavement, I was hit over the head from behind with some sort of heavy weapon, possibly an iron bar. I fell to the floor and covered my face as I was now being kicked about the head.

The attack stopped and my opponent from earlier walked away.

I could hear him laughing with his girlfriend. I got to my feet slowly. I was dazed and could feel blood pouring down my neck and back, but I was shaking with temper for having been so easily caught out.

A rubbish bin stood nearby. I pulled out its metal insert and ran up behind the man. I belted him over the head with it as hard as I could, then I began to kick and punch him. He fell to the ground. I made the mistake of standing directly over him. He forced himself up into my body and I fell backwards, losing my balance. I twisted in an attempt to regain my footing, but ended up falling face-first into the plate-glass window of a clothes shop. The glass shattered and I fell through into the shop itself. The impact knocked me out. Luckily, two nurses on their way to work stopped to give me first aid. They called an ambulance.

At the hospital, I had 56 stitches put in a wound that went from the top right-hand side of my forehead, across the corner of my eye and onto my cheek. I received a further seven stitches in the wound at the back of my head. As soon as I could focus, I got up and discharged myself. I went home, gave my mother a fright and retired to bed.

The next day, the police arrived. They hadn't come to bring me grapes and wish me a speedy recovery. They wanted to question me about my 'attempt to burgle' the clothes shop. Fortunately, the two nurses, and a woman who'd been on a passing bus, contacted them. I wasn't troubled further. Apparently, according to the woman on the bus, after I'd fallen through the plate-glass window, my attacker had climbed into the shop after me and kicked me in the head several times as I lay unconscious among the mannequins.

I went to great lengths to find my attacker. I was hoping, obviously, to make a citizen's arrest, but he left the area before I could bring him to justice.

I put in a claim to the Criminal Injuries Compensation Board. I walked into a hearing, which I thought would debate how much cash I was going to get. Instead, I was told I wouldn't get a penny. My 'character and way of life' made me 'unsuitable for compensation'.

I returned to London and moved out of Deptford. The flat there was beginning to fill up with fugitives from justice. I moved into a tiny flat in Earls Court. It was pretty awful – cramped, noisy and with a neighbour who was insane. Officially, that is, with the certificate to prove it. If somebody knocked on my door, my neighbour would knock on his own for the next ten minutes. Occasionally, he'd knock on my door, too. I'd answer it and he'd just stand there laughing. Day and night he'd march around his flat, or hang out of his window, shouting, 'West five! West five!' I moved to a larger flat in the Putney Bridge end of Fulham.

My old friend Stan from Codsall came to visit me for a week. Adolf invited us to a BNP meeting on the Euston Road in north London. He said there'd be trouble later with the reds. Members of a group called the 'Red Army Faction' (RAF) would be passing through nearby King's Cross station after a march in south London. The plan was to ambush them.

The BNP meeting took place in a building called 'The Friends' Meeting House'. I thought at first I'd come to the wrong place, because the noticeboard overflowed with posters for Third World charities and other compassionate causes. I was told the building was actually owned by the pacifist Quakers, who let it be used cheaply by worthy groups. I assumed someone in the BNP hadn't been entirely honest when making the booking.

At the meeting, Adolf introduced me to Tony Wells, who later became national organiser in the 'reformed' BNP. Adolf said Wells's real surname was Lecomber, but he'd dropped it because he thought it sounded Jewish. Almost a year later, in 1985, Lecomber would become known as 'The Mad Bomber' after an incident involving Adolf.

After the usual rabble-rousing speeches, about 20 of us waited around for the encounter with the reds. A BNP 'spotter' who was following them from south London rang on a mobile phone to say they'd just got on a train heading for King's Cross.

Our group headed over to the station. A skinhead with us produced a flare gun and promised to shoot a leading RAF member with it. Flares are designed for use as distress signals or to illuminate targets. If they hit someone, the end result is horrific.

A flare, unlike a bullet, doesn't smash its way through flesh and bone – it burns its way through.

There was a real air of menace that day, perhaps generated in part by the bloodlust speeches. Everyone felt something 'big' would happen. Instead of the usual fisticuffs, we thought at least one of the reds would be seriously injured or even killed. There'd been a dramatic fall in the number of people supporting extreme right-wing parties. The feeling was that a 'spectacular' was needed to thrust 'the Movement' under the spotlight again and re-awaken the public's interest. A red being maimed or murdered in such a horrific fashion would fit the bill.

The spotter phoned to say they'd be at King's Cross in 15 minutes. We went down into the tube station to meet them. The owner of the flare gun loaded it for us all to see, before putting it back in his pocket with a now-we-shall-see look. There must have been about 20 of us down near the ticket barrier as the first reds came up the stairs. As soon as the reds saw us, they tried to turn and go back down the stairs. We advanced towards the barrier, screaming and shouting, 'Fucking red scum! Come on! Come on!' Suddenly, from further down the stairs came a great roar of manly voices. The reds who'd been retreating were pushed back up towards us by the ones following. About 50 reds were now advancing towards us.

Everyone in our group was shouting 'Stand! Stand!' but most were retreating as they said it. Adolf began shouting at the man with the flare gun, 'Shoot the cunts! Shoot the cunts!'

But the man just turned and ran. Tony Lecomber was shouting, 'Stand! Stand!', too, but before long he was legging it as well. Only Adolf, Stan, myself and two others remained as the reds began clambering over the barriers to get at us. We looked around, looked at each other and said, 'Fuck this.' We legged it. On the stairs to the street, Adolf stopped and said, 'We'll hold them here.'

As the first reds reached us, we began kicking and punching them, but realised the space was too confined. As more reds arrived, we'd be pushed back or, worse, over. We ran up the stairs and into the street.

Adolf, Stan and I ran into the overground station. The other two men ran down the road. The leading reds took off in pursuit of the other two. The other reds followed them. No one came after us.

We sat on a platform bench to get our breath back. Adolf then began shouting abuse: 'We should have fucking done the bastards. What happened to that prick with the flare gun?'

Stan looked at me, and we both started laughing. Adolf didn't find it amusing. He stood up and stormed off, vowing to 'do some red bastard'.

That evening in the pub, we learned that the two men who'd been chased up the street had been captured in a car park off the Caledonian Road. The reds had kicked and punched them to the ground, then whipped them with a car aerial. As a final act of humiliation, they'd pissed on them.

We heard a new landlord had taken over at The Royal Oak in Stockwell. Buzz the barman was no longer around. We went there one Saturday morning after spending the first part of the day at an illegal drinking den called Freddie Head's in Railton Road. We were already well pissed when we staggered in to meet the new landlord. He turned out to be a scruffy man, who looked more like a care-in-the-community patient than a landlord. I suppose, with us as customers, The Royal Oak could never expect to attract the cream of the brewery trade.

The landlord didn't want to serve drunks at eleven in the morning. He told us to leave. Del Boy told him to shut up. He said he was calling the police. His threat was met with jeering, wolf-whistles and laughter. The landlord went to the lounge to phone the police and await their arrival.

Around ten minutes later, two policemen walked into the bar. Del Boy, as always, smartly dressed in a suit and tie, was up on his feet explaining the situation before anybody else could say anything. He claimed he was the manager and that 'the troublemaker' was a scruffy man skulking in the lounge, refusing to leave. Del Boy told the officers confidentially, 'He keeps saying he's the landlord. He's not the full shilling, if you ask me. This isn't the first trouble I've had with him. Could you please just put him out? Be careful.'

The two policemen marched into the lounge, grabbed the

landlord and frog-marched him to their van. The prisoner protested loudly the whole while, but his protests only made Del Boy's story seem more convincing. The police just threw him into the van, like rubbish. As soon as the van pulled off, we fled the pub. We learned later that the landlord had been taken to Brixton police station. He was only released after his wife turned up to identify him.

Around this time in 1984, the ceiling of my brother Paul's council flat in Clapham collapsed. The man upstairs had forgotten to turn off his bath taps, causing a flood. Paul was given temporary accommodation nearby.

On the Sunday morning before he was due to move back in, he went round to check everything. He discovered the locks had been changed. He knocked next door. His neighbour told him that, in his brief absence, a group of squatters had moved in. Apparently, there'd been a large influx of them into the borough following the mass eviction at Effra Terrace in neighbouring Brixton.

Paul banged on his door, shouted through the letterbox and knocked on the windows, but no one answered. He decided he'd wait until the squatters returned, rather than damage his windows and doors trying to get in. He intended removing the squatters promptly and permanently, without recourse to the law.

Paul came round to the pub where we always met on Sunday mornings and told us about the squatters. I said when the pub closed we'd go round and evict them for him. Everyone was egging each other on, ranting about 'scum' taking over our towns and now our very homes. No fucking reds were going to take the roofs from over our heads. 'Kill, kill, kill' expressed the general mood. At closing time, Paul went back to his temporary accommodation to pack his bags. Meanwhile, five of us went round to his flat to evict the red scum. When we arrived, the back door was open, so we walked straight in. Nobody was home.

We picked up the squatters' belongings and threw them onto the pavement. We deliberately smashed things like the stereo, the television and the chairs. We ripped up all their clothes. Then, after carrying out the beds, we slashed the mattresses and pillows. As soon as we'd completed our squatter-cleansing mission, Colin and I went round to Paul's to tell him he could now move his stuff back in. Paul looked puzzled. He said, 'What do you mean, "move all my stuff back in"? Has it all gone then?'

Most of the property we'd trashed was his.

He never did see the funny side of it.

CHAPTER 7

STEAMING THE RED RABBLE

THE ANNUAL 'TROOPS OUT' MARCH IN LONDON WAS A MUCH-LOVED AND EAGERLY awaited event in the Nazi social calendar. Supporters of a withdrawal of British troops from Northern Ireland would march from south London to somewhere in the centre. And the Nazis would traditionally attack them.

I had mixed feelings about this. My time as a soldier in the six counties had actually strengthened my sympathies for the Troops Out cause. My Irish blood and my encounters with Catholic-hating Loyalists, as well as the fact that my dearest possessions now existed as a pile of ashes in an Orangewoman's garden, made me support the idea of a united Ireland, although I didn't want IRA violence to achieve that goal. Adolf, too, with his Irish father, wasn't entirely opposed to the key aspects of the republican cause.

However, both of us looked forward to taking part in the planned attack on the Troops Out march for the simple reason that we wanted to bash some reds. We felt sure the marchers would be the same 'red rabble' we saw marching against Nazis, apartheid, Margaret Thatcher, the destruction of the rain forests and the clubbing of baby seals, not 'real' Irish republicans locked in a war with the Brits. In our eyes, members of this red rabble deserved a bashing whenever and wherever we could find them.

It was around Easter 1984. The night before the march, Adolf and I helped leaflet squaddies' pubs in the Victoria area. The leaflets described 'IRA scum' marching through our streets while waging a dirty war 'against our people'. That night, we also attended a Nazi meeting at a pub in the West End. Upstairs in a small, wood-panelled room stood a long table on a small stage. A Union flag covered the table. A flag of Ulster decorated the wall behind. The speakers included two men from the Loyalist paramilitary Ulster Volunteer Force. Dressed in jeans and combat jackets, and with strong Belfast accents, they ranted for ten minutes about the 'Marxist' IRA before urging the congregation of around 50 fascists to give generously to the cause.

I gave nothing. I had no intention of ever giving a penny to the Orange bastards. Not even if they gave me my stuff back.

The meeting ended with a full-throated version of God Save the Queen. It could have brought a tear trickling down the cheek of Elizabeth's mother, if not the Reverend Ian Paisley himself.

Adolf got talking to one of the Loyalists. He said to him, 'You're not a Nazi, are you? You only dislike the Provos. What are your views on blacks, Asians and other immigrants?'

The Loyalist wasn't entirely sure what to say. A black in Northern Ireland at that time was about as common as a four-leafed clover. Most blacks encountered by Loyalists would have been wearing a British Army uniform. The Orangeman struggled for words before saying he couldn't understand why blacks had it in for Unionists. His response puzzled us.

During the meeting, we'd been told that the two most likely opportunities we'd get to steam the reds would be when the march passed either Lambeth North tube station or The Bear pub in Kennington Road. If the police presence was too strong at these locations, then we were to head to a 'redirection' point at Waterloo Station, from where we'd be sent elsewhere. Very few meetings or 'actions' took place without our being herded around first from one non-location to another, the final destination being kept secret until the last moment in an effort to thwart the reds. If the latter knew of a venue before a meeting then they'd sometimes try to launch an attack. The men who stood at the redirection points had a dangerous job. The reds beat them up regularly.

On the morning of the march, we met up in a local pub when it opened at eleven. By the time we had to head for Lambeth North tube station, we were all drunk. As we made our way to meet the red hordes, other people from pubs along our route joined us. Around 70 of us prepared to do battle – Nazis, squaddies, ex-squaddies and ordinary members of the public who'd seen their city bombed by those the marchers seemed to represent.

Soon, we could hear the pipe-and-drum band accompanying the marchers. Before long, the republican flags and banners came into view. The enemy column remained a few hundred yards away when somebody began shouting, 'The fucking scum! Kill the fucking scum!' Screaming like primitives, we all began running towards the marchers, who probably numbered about 500.

I felt like a footsoldier in a medieval battle as we charged across the road towards our foe. I was half-expecting a hail of arrows to meet us. We crashed into the front of the march, a clash of mutual hatred. I hit several people, but I don't know who. I just lashed out in a frenzy. The leading marchers had difficulty fighting because many carried large banners. Some tried retreating, but found themselves pushed forward again by those at the back.

In a few seconds, it was over. Everybody, including the marchers, began shouting, 'Police! Police!' I turned and started to run. I looked over my shoulder to see a line of police officers running towards us. I kept running until I was several streets away. Then I made my way back to the pub where we'd agreed to meet.

Adolf and my south London mates had got there first. The assault on the reds left everyone excited and laughing. It had been such good fun that everyone wanted another crack at the bastards. We decided to attack the march at another point. We walked to a pub half a mile away where we knew the march would have to pass. We planned to run out at the marchers as soon as they arrived. But the police put officers on the doors of both exits and told us to stay inside until the march had passed.

A few people got angry with the police. They asked how they could protect people who supported groups that murdered police officers. 'Why don't you just go round the corner and let us at the bastards?' The police ignored them. A fight with the police began to seem the most likely scenario.

The march soon reached the pub. We tried to run at the marchers through the police line. The marchers saw us – and tried to run at us too. The police pushed us back into the pub. Adolf lunged forward and two officers wrestled him to the ground. They told him he was under arrest before bundling him and others into a van. Adolf was charged with a public order offence and bailed to appear at Horseferry Road Magistrates' Court in Victoria. We all agreed to go with him on the day of his court appearance, because we guessed the Anti-Nazi League would congregate outside. We were right. Around 20 reds and the same number of police stood there. The reds shouted abuse, took our photos – something they always did – and hissed at us, but no scuffles occurred.

Members of the BNP and the NF stood inside the lobby, trying to recruit those who'd been arrested. Both groups offered to pay the fines of their members: 'Join us. We look after our members. Unlike the others.'

In his defence, Adolf claimed not to have been part of any group that day. He always met with his friends in that pub after work on a Saturday. On this occasion, when he'd gone to leave he'd been prevented from doing so by the police. A fight had then broken out among other people with whom he wasn't associated. Fearing he might be about to get caught up in an unpleasant altercation, he'd tried to flee, but the police had pounced on him, mistaking him for a troublemaker.

My wealth of experience in the dock qualified me to become Adolf's star witness. The prosecutor began cross-examining me. He asked if I'd drunk much alcohol in the pub that day. 'No, I don't drink, actually.'

'You regularly go to this public house and yet you abstain from alcohol. A bit odd, don't you think, Mr O'Mahoney?'

'Not really,' I replied. 'You see, I can't drink because I've got a problem.'

'A problem, Mr O'Mahoney. And what might that be?'

Before I could answer, Del Boy shouted from the back of the court, 'He's run out of money.'

Even the magistrate laughed. This witticism didn't help Adolf. He was found guilty. Before fining him, the magistrate said that in a democracy people had a right to demonstrate, however distasteful others might find their cause. He added, 'I fought in the Second World War, young man. But that doesn't give me the right to walk around the West End assaulting German tourists.'

He warned Adolf not to come before him again – or he could expect a trip to prison. We left the court laughing. Not surprisingly, neither the NF nor the BNP paid Adolf's fine. We began meeting regularly in The Falcon pub in Battersea. Nazi football hooligans from the Chelsea 'Headhunters' also congregated there. A lot of them came from Kent and Croydon and places like that. I had a fight with one idiot who said they had the 'hardest firm' in south London. I gave him a good bashing for his insolence and, as a result, my reputation rose in Nazi circles. It was after that incident that Tony Lecomber, the future BNP national organiser, began turning up to try to recruit us. Far-right groups viewed the simmering racial tension across south London as an opportunity to swell their diminishing ranks. They also needed thugs like us to protect their meetings from attacks by the reds. There's a long and well-documented history of far-right groups trying to recruit football hooligans. As one Nazi magazine put it: '99 per cent of football thugs are white and 99 per cent of those are nationalistic and patriotic and displaying the warrior instincts that made Britain and our race great.'

I grew to like Lecomber. He was intelligent and well spoken, full of energy and ideas. You wouldn't have thought him violent, but he firmly supported 'direct action'. He wanted trouble. He wanted to cause the reds grief. So we got on well with him. Adolf, in particular, seemed to have found a soulmate.

Lecomber was always handing out leaflets and papers for us to distribute at football matches and pubs. One time, drunk, I agreed to take 200 newspapers off him. He wanted me to distribute them to football fans at a Brentford v. Wolves game. I threw them over a hedge on the way to the match. Lecomber also encouraged us to attend more fascist meetings. The major political drama taking place in the background at this time was the Miners' Strike. It had started in March 1984 and lasted just over a year. We didn't sympathise with the miners. They might have been white working class, but they struck us as whinging northerners led by a loathsome red bastard called Arthur Scargill, who wanted to hold the country to ransom in the name of Marxism.

All of us lived with job insecurity, so we didn't see why the miners should be the only people guaranteed a job for life. We found especially laughable the idea that the mining industry should be preserved so that the workers' children could themselves later descend into the pit. Adolf ranted regularly on this theme, describing the miners as 'typical backward northern bastards'. He'd often say, 'What sort of sick fucks want to send their kids down a mine, anyway?'

On visits from London to my mother in Codsall, I'd met and started going out with a girl called Sarah Milner (known to me as 'Millie'). It was a case of opposites attracting, because she was quiet, caring and extremely well mannered. We got on very well, and when I was with her I found myself beginning to feel like a 'normal' human being. In Millie, I'd found a real soulmate. We did all the normal things that normal people do. Indeed, it was the 'normality' I really enjoyed. We just did everyday stuff together and she never mentioned my 'reputation'. She even used to laugh at me for getting excited about doing the most mundane things.

However, in a place like Codsall, you can never escape your past. The village gossips soon started 'warning' her parents about me. Naturally, her parents became concerned. I met them a few times. They were good, decent people and I liked them. At first, they accepted me and tried to ignore the gossips, but then the rumours became more venomous and bizarre.

People claimed Millie had had two abortions. The innocent truth was that, although we'd been together more than a year, we'd never even slept together. But, as the old saying goes, a lie is halfway round the world before the truth has got its boots on.

Despite my assurances that I'd treat their daughter with the utmost respect, Millie's parents made it obvious they wanted her to stop seeing me. Both of us felt deeply hurt by the desire of some locals to destroy any chance we had of a future together, but we both knew the gossip-mongers had won.

Millie's parents had no reason to fear for their daughter's well-being on account of me. Indeed, by that stage, the evidence showed that my mother should have feared for my well-being on account of Millie. In the mid-point of our relationship, I'd visited her at her parents' house. We'd been fooling around by the kitchen sink as she did the washing up. At the same time as I stepped towards her, she turned towards me with a steak knife in her hand. The blade penetrated my left chest, pushing through my ribs and puncturing my lung. I pulled the knife out and, without waiting for an ambulance, got a lift to hospital.

Millie stood over me as I lay gasping for breath on a trolley. I said, 'Fucking hell, Millie. I might die here.' Her demeanour became agitated with what I thought might be anguish caused by my plight. Then she slapped me hard across the face. 'Don't you dare swear in front of me,' she said. I don't think she ever did grasp the gravity of the situation.

On Christmas Eve 1984, Millie's father arrived at my mother's house and gave me back the present I'd bought for his daughter. He told me not to contact her again. It really hurt me. I felt devastated. More than anything else, Millie and I were good friends who understood one another. The girlfriend–boyfriend thing was secondary. I wouldn't have dreamt of asking her to fall out with her parents over me, so our demise as a couple just had to be.

I went out that night with a heart full of hate for my fellow man. Given my mood, I decided to avoid The Crown after the last violent incident during the season of goodwill two years earlier. I went instead with my friends to The Wheel Inn. There, I bumped into a female 'friend' of Millie. This person's mother had been one of the gossips passing on vile rumours to Millie's parents. When this 'friend' tried talking to me, I told her to fuck off. Her boyfriend objected. At that moment, all the resentment I felt for the good people of Codsall erupted. I picked up a bottle from a nearby table and smashed it over his forehead. It wasn't personal. It was just a release for my anger and frustration.

As before, I was arrested, charged with wounding with intent, put in front of a special court and remanded in custody to Birmingham's Winson Green Prison. This time, I didn't even get a Jaffa Cake.

I spent two weeks in prison before being bailed. In the mean time, someone confronted one of the witnesses with a hammer. Then the injured party began to wonder if he'd actually imagined the incident. He said at my committal hearing he didn't have a clue who'd hit him. The prosecution didn't appreciate this divergence from his original written statement. They deemed him a 'hostile witness', which meant his verbal evidence could effectively be disregarded in favour of his written statement. I was committed to stand trial at Stoke Crown Court.

I returned to London to await my trial. I knew I'd be sent to prison again, but this thought didn't have much effect in turning me into a better citizen. I'd had enough of 'decent citizens'. I felt I was damned if I did right and damned if I did wrong. I decided to stop giving a damn altogether.

Larry 'The Slash' had been a Millwall fan all his life. He'd often told me about the violence he'd witnessed at their games. Millwall's hooligans were the hooligans' hooligans. Organised and determined, they feared no one. As far back as 1920, Millwall's ground had been closed for two weeks after hooligans beat up the opposing goalkeeper. The future England manager and Knight of the Realm, Bobby Robson, had once said flame-throwers ought to be turned on them. The BBC publicised, and inadvertently glorified, their violent reputation with a *Panorama* documentary in 1977.

As a teenager, I could remember Millwall's visit to Wolverhampton when the local paper had described the streets after the game as 'running with blood'. I fancied joining them. My birthday was coming up and Millwall had drawn Luton Town in an FA Cup quarter-final tie at Luton. The ground stood just down the road from where I'd been born.

All the talk in hooligan circles around Deptford and New Cross was of the Luton match. People who hadn't been to a Millwall game for years said they were 'coming out of retirement' to attend. Everyone knew there'd be trouble.

Larry, Benny, Tony, Ray, myself and a few others hired a Transit van, filled it with beer and headed off to Luton. We arrived around lunch-time in a town that had already been occupied by invading Millwall troops. We went into the first pub we found. Inside, Millwall fans sang loudly and chanted '*Sieg Heil!*' at any Asians foolish enough to pass by on the street. As the pub filled, fans became more boisterous. They knocked over tables and hurled chairs and glasses across the room. The landlord phoned the police, who moved us on to the next pub, where fans wreaked similar havoc, until the police moved them on again. While making our way from pub to pub, I watched shop windows being smashed and Asian drivers at a taxi rank being attacked and beaten up.

Everyone seemed pretty drunk by the time we reached the ground. Then we found ourselves being crammed like cattle into a small enclosure. Just before the game started, the Millwall fans surged forward. Fans at the front feared a crush, so they spilled onto the pitch, delaying the kick-off for 25 minutes.

Throughout the game, I watched fights breaking out in different parts of the ground. With 10 minutes to go, Luton led 1–0. Hundreds of Millwall fans poured onto the touchline to try to get the game abandoned. The police struggled to hold them back. The match ended. Millwall had lost. Everyone surged forward and most found themselves on the pitch. Nobody knew quite what to do. I couldn't see Ray and the others, so I just followed the mob.

We ran towards the seating enclosure. Everyone started ripping out the plastic seats and hurling them at the police, who scattered, but then regrouped and baton-charged us. Total chaos reigned. I looked up into the night sky and could see only plastic seats flying through the air, their trajectory captured in the powerful floodlights.

Outside the ground, the rampaging mob damaged houses, shops and cars before wrecking a train in the station. The day's events had left 47 people injured, 31 of them police. It was front-page news.

The next day, UEFA awarded the Euro '88 competition to Germany. The British Football Association attributed their decision to the rioting at Luton. Even Prime Minister Mrs Thatcher, fresh from winning the Miners' Strike, condemned the Millwall hooligans. Her words became a source of great pride and encouragement to us all.

A few weeks later, I was summoned to appear at Stoke Crown Court for trial over the bottling incident. I didn't go. I knew I'd be sent to prison and that thought didn't fill me with joy. In order to avoid arrest, I moved out of the house in Deptford and into a squat near Clapham Common. Normally, I disapproved of squatters. Indeed, until the point at which I myself became a squatter, I hadn't considered the possibility that squatters could be anything other than bash-worthy red scum. Del Boy, an electrician by trade, employed me as his labourer for a few weeks, although he didn't really need me. He then invited me to go with him to Holland for a job wiring-up oil-rig platforms. The money was good, so I said yes. I also thought I'd have a better chance abroad of avoiding arrest.

The only problem was my lack of electrical qualifications. I'd learnt a few things from Del Boy, and I'd changed a few light bulbs and plugs in my life, but I didn't feel qualified to take on a responsible job. Three hours after our arrival in Rotterdam, they sent us to work on a huge oil rig in a dry dock. The foreman handed me a very complicated wiring diagram and told me to get on with it.

I'd hoped to stick by Del Boy's side, but we'd been split up. A Scottish man called William was my partner. I had no choice but to explain my problem. He did the decent thing and said he'd help me. We worked twelve-hour shifts, from seven to seven, six days a week. Everything I did was guesswork. I suffered more electric shocks and burns in a twelve-hour shift than most electricians suffer in a lifetime.

A few years later, the Piper Alpha oil rig went up with a bang, killing scores of people. I often wonder if some of the electrics on that platform had been done by someone with similar professional skills to mine.

The job came to an end. I didn't want to risk returning to England, so I told Del Boy I'd head for Amsterdam. He said he'd go back to England for a month, then join me. Drug addicts, con-men and sleazeballs preyed on the thousands of young tourists in Amsterdam. I saw several street robberies, including one particularly bad stabbing when a German tourist refused to let go of his wallet.

I slept in the train station until the police moved me on. Then I slept in the park, but I didn't like my roommates. I booked into a hostel run by American Christians. Cheap and clean, its only drawback was the staff, who spent their time trying to lead me to

God. I couldn't sit anywhere without one of them sidling up to say, 'Bernard, are you seeking inner peace?'

I met someone called Billy. He came from Leicestershire and was also on the run from the law, though he never told me why. He'd moved to Holland with his girlfriend Angie, who was about 17, attractive, streetwise and a prostitute. She'd almost been murdered a few weeks after her arrival. A man had taken her for sex to one of the floating hotel boats at the dock behind the central station. In the room, he'd turned nasty, taken out a carving knife and stabbed her seven times. It took her five months to recover. But, as soon as she could, she went back on the game. She'd started taking heroin.

At first, I got on fairly well with Billy. He invited me to stay at the flat he shared with Angie. She worked nights and slept during the day, so I didn't see that much of her, though every time I did see her I thought she'd slipped another few yards downhill.

Billy introduced me to two scumbags from Surinam called 'Orlando' and 'Johnny'. They made their living selling drugs and stolen passports. They also pimped, preying on teenage girls, the younger the better, most of them drug addicts. I think Billy hoped to open up some business opportunities for us, but I wanted nothing to do with his mates. I started hanging around with a Dutch giant with a very English name – Henry. He worked as a nightclub doorman. I asked him to try to fix me up with some work. The next day, he invited me to meet a club manager, a little pumpkin of a man, with a bald head and a sleazy manner.

I expected an offer of work on the door or in the bar. In fact, the pumpkin wanted me for sex. That is, as a performer in a live-sex show. The job entailed going on stage dressed as a gorilla and performing a full repertoire of sex acts with two women and various types of fruit. He showed me my would-be co-performers' photos. Both looked gorgeous, but – on a stage, in front of an audience, brandishing bananas and wearing a gorilla suit – I had to decline. Henry and the pumpkin seemed genuinely surprised by my refusal.

I rang Del Boy. For one reason or another, he kept postponing his return. I concluded he wouldn't be coming back. I decided I wanted to leave Amsterdam. I'd only been there a few months, but the sleaze had begun to get me down. My money was getting low and I didn't think much of the work opportunities. Billy had also been talking about leaving – without Angie. By now, she was a total wreck, her mind and body ravaged by heroin. I wanted to hitch-hike, to follow the road wherever it might take me.

I'd done that once before in England. Aged 17, I'd made pregnant my girlfriend of three years. She gave birth to a boy, Adrian, but then dumped me. With hindsight, I know she made a wise decision, but at the time I felt heartbroken. I decided to leave the area. I packed a holdall and said goodbye to my mother, not knowing where I was going or what I was going to do when I got there. Saying goodbye to my mother devastated me. I walked the five miles to the M6 motorway in tears. I decided to leave my final destination to fate: I'd stick my thumb out and go wherever the first car to stop was going. That night, I found myself trudging in a blizzard through a run-down area of Glasgow. I slept in a tin workman's hut near the Celtic football ground and in the morning I explored the city. I'd heard unemployment was high in Glasgow, but I didn't think things could be that bad. Then I found a jobcentre that appeared not to have any jobs on its boards. When I enquired at the desk, the clerk started laughing. He called over his colleagues to show them the Englishman who'd come to Glasgow to find work. As he sent me away, he said, 'You're at the wrong end of the motorway, Dick Whittington.' I lived rough in Glasgow for a few days before moving on and doing the same in Edinburgh and then Dundee. After six months, I ended up back in Codsall.

Billy said he wanted to leave Amsterdam and move on with me. I agreed to let him travel with me, though I felt I'd probably made a mistake. I'd been growing gradually to dislike him. His callous treatment of Angie had accelerated the plunge in his personal ratings. I asked him to tell her about our plans, but he wouldn't, and he forbade me to say anything. He didn't care about her. Her prostitution had kept him fed, clothed and boozed for several months, but now he couldn't even be bothered to say goodbye.

We packed our stuff and left in the early morning before she returned. I felt guilty, so I left her a note. I kept thinking she'd go completely under when she discovered Billy had left her. He didn't give a toss. He said, 'She's only a whore.' God only knows what happened to the poor girl.

On the road, our 'friendship' deteriorated further. We couldn't get many lifts and we ran out of money. Billy kept moaning and moaning and moaning, like a whining child. Outside Maastricht, I finally had enough. I told him to stop moaning or fuck off on his own. We had a brief but intense exchange of views, then he pulled a knife on me. He kept jabbing it at me, calling me a wanker and saying, 'Come on, then! Come on, then!'

I didn't fancy bleeding to death on a deserted road, so I ran away. But Billy shouldn't have jeered as he did, because I wasn't running far. I'd merely spotted something I wanted. I jogged 30 yards to an embankment where out of the ground I pulled up a long, thin, metal rod (which workmen use when taping off trenches). Then I jogged back to my dear, dear friend, whose recent pride in victory was now evacuating rapidly into his underpants.

Billy seemed transfixed as I bore down upon him. I swung the rod and clubbed him across the head. He fell to the ground. I kicked him in the head and body before taking the knife off him. I was tempted to stab him, if only for Angie, but I thought better of it. I punched him a few more times in the head and just left him there, moaning again, though this time with good reason.

Blood had spattered over my face, hands and clothes, so I knew I'd now have even greater difficulty hitching a ride. I cleaned myself up in a petrol station before setting off on my own.

It soon dawned on me that I was never going to establish myself anywhere without money, so I returned reluctantly to London by jumping trains and conning my way onto the ferry.

It was late summer 1985. Nothing much had changed. My friends were going about their unruly business much the same as before. I was told that the police had called at my old address a few times looking for me. But they hadn't bothered searching it. They hadn't even asked too many questions, so I felt they weren't in hot pursuit. Then again, I'd hardly committed the crime of the century. A bottle over the head in Codsall wouldn't be competing with the Great Train Robbery for a place in the annals of crime.

I got back in time for the Live Aid concert at Wembley Stadium. This event, televised live and watched by hundreds of millions throughout the world, aimed to raise money for famine victims in Ethiopia. Many of the entertainers taking part had sung on the so-called 'Band Aid' single 'Do They Know It's Christmas?' at the end of 1984. That record sold 3.5 million copies in the UK. I went along with a closet fascist to hear a few bands and to laugh at the outpouring of what I saw as bogus compassion for the Third World.

For some years, I'd loathed the event's organiser, Bob Geldof, and his band, the Boomtown Prats. My friends and I had seen them as perfumed maggots on the joyfully stinking corpse of punk. Now that the public had tired of buying his crap records – I ranted to myself – Geldof had dreamt up this 'Feed the World' bollocks to boost his diminished status. The idea of all these hugely wealthy, if not multimillionaire, pop stars getting on stage to browbeat poor people into handing over money to 'feed' even poorer people really brought out the Adolf in me. I couldn't believe the gall of these 'musicians', many of whom led lives of extravagant and wasteful luxury, publicly weeping crocodile tears for the poor little black kids going to bed hungry. I felt sure a single restaurant bill from one of these fucks would keep a Bangladeshi village in rice for a decade. Chief phoney Bob Geldof was the sort of person I wished I'd been at school with. I'd have sentenced him to hang long ago.

Another pop star showing signs of becoming a similar 'Messiah of Compassion' was U2's Bono. In 1985, Bono, unlike fellow Irishman Geldof, could at least say he'd once led a decent band. Sadly, too much time spent with Geldof looked like infecting Bono with the same drooling Jesus complex. My closet fascist friend felt the same way. When the band U2 took to the stage, a man near us began waving an Irish tricolour. My friend told him to take it down. 'Wembley,' said my friend, 'ain't the place for IRA scum to wave their colours.'

An argument developed between us and the man. My friend grabbed the flag. Inevitably, a fight broke out. The crowd parted to avoid the flying fists. My friend started rolling about on the famous turf, punching 'the red scum', until the security staff intervened. They threw us out, pushing us into the street still clutching the snatched flag.

Within a few weeks, events occurred which made me and most of my friends wonder again if we should bother staying in England. An incident in the Handsworth district of Birmingham in which young blacks accused the police of racism led to two days of rioting, arson and looting, costing millions of pounds and the lives of two Asian men who died trapped in a burning post office. Around 120 people were injured, two-thirds of them police officers. A total of 437 people were arrested.

A few days later, so-called 'copycat' riots took place in Dudley, West Bromwich, Wolverhampton, Coventry, Moseley in Birmingham and St Paul's in Bristol. It seemed, from our extremist viewpoint, as if our familiar, British way of life might collapse for ever under the weight of all these immigrants trying to take over our country, with no regard for our laws. As we saw it, they would go shopping when the shops were shut and, if the police intervened, they'd petrol-bomb them and accuse them of being 'racist'. We'd have been happy for the government to send in the Paras to carry out another 'Bloody Sunday' on British soil, though this time with black victims. Some of us began to dream of emigrating to a country where the authorities knew how to deal firmly with uppity darkies. South Africa was mentioned for the first time as more than a possible holiday destination.

I guessed it wouldn't be long before south London joined the list of riot zones. I think the police agreed. There seemed to be a lot more of them on the streets. And the local papers reported more police raids on illegal drinking and drug dens and the like. I wasn't entirely unhappy with this part of the situation. I felt if the police were concentrating on the possibility of major civil disorder, they were hardly likely to devote any resources to hunting me down.

On 28 September 1985, the police raided a house in Brixton searching for a black man called Michael Groce. They wanted to question him about the illegal possession of a shotgun. During the raid, his mother ended up being shot by a policeman. A few hours later, around 300 youths, most of them black, attacked the local police station with petrol bombs. The shooting of Mrs

Groce had finally kicked off the riots we'd felt had been waiting to happen.

We all rang each other with the news. Later on that afternoon, seven of us, including Adolf, Colin, Adrian 'Army Game' and 'Benny the Jew' met up for a drink in Stockwell. Benny lived just around the corner from Ray and Tony's house on the front line. We decided to head over there to see what was happening. Police had cordoned off the area and were stopping non-residents from entering. Resident Benny convinced them to let us all through to go home. As we made our way down the road, we passed some white teenagers who warned us about blacks attacking whites. We relished the thought of a row. Nothing prepared us for the scale of the trouble. Hundreds of people filled the streets – most of them engaged in law-breaking of one kind or another.

Screams and missiles hurtled towards police cowering behind riot shields that were being tested to the limits of their brick-resisting endurance. Petrol bombs added colour and warmth to the occasion. And, in an early pre-Christmas non-sales rush, mask-wearing bargain-hunters emptied shops of their goods.

We passed people we felt sure were trying to organise this chaos. I saw white individuals with whistles which they seemed to be using to send signals to other people with whistles. I didn't ask them to show their party cards, but they looked like members of the red rabble we'd encountered countless times before.

One man stood on a small pair of stepladders. Perhaps he just wanted a better view, but he seemed to me to be watching the police's movements. Then he'd make hand signals – and I don't think he was waving to his mum. I'd seen this before in Northern Ireland, where riots were rarely as 'spontaneous' as they appeared and, once they'd kicked off, were often led and directed by people with a politically motivated agenda. We felt a confrontation in this situation would be unwise. We left the main theatre of riot and headed towards Benny's house.

At a junction, we heard the sound of hammering. It was coming from the back of a jeweller's shop. We lifted ourselves up onto a wall to have a look. A group of black youths ran off. We climbed down to see what they'd been up to. Instead of using their sledgehammer to tackle the shop's heavily armoured back door, they'd opted for trying to smash a hole through the brickwork.

Our conversation until that point had been filled with outrage at the 'black criminals' running riot and looting in our cities. Now the thought of getting our hands on a few trays of gold necklaces prompted us to join in. We took turns trying to knock through the wall. Every few minutes, a police siren would wail nearby. We feared they were coming for us. After a while, having made little progress through the reinforced wall, we gave up.

We spent the rest of the night at Benny's, watching the riot on the news. By midnight, the police had shed their defensive tactics and charged the crowd. The disorder had subsided by 2.30 a.m.

Next day, a few sporadic clashes occurred, but they dissolved quickly. In all, 43 civilians and 10 police officers had been injured. The police arrested 230 people, half of whom were white, and recorded 724 crimes, including more than 90 burglaries. A photographer later died from injuries sustained during the riot. A few days later, other smaller riots occurred in nearby Peckham and in Toxteth in Liverpool.

In the days after the riots, some of the local pubs resembled electrical superstores. Cut-price TVs, microwaves and stereos were in abundance. The people who'd looted them didn't give a fuck about politics. We could have bought everything off them wearing Ku Klux Klan robes, and they wouldn't have cared, so long as we paid cash.

A week or so later, the police organised a public meeting at Brixton Town Hall aimed at trying to heal the damage caused by their shooting of Mrs Cherry Groce. A group of six of us went along. Adolf hoped to contribute to the debate by making a speech about the 'foreigners' burning our cities. He abandoned his plans when we arrived at the town hall.

It seemed like every red from miles around had descended to chant abuse at the 'fascist' police. Some of the reds were dressed in black, paramilitary-style uniforms with dark glasses. We stood around at the back near the door.

The audience in the packed hall was being whipped up with a series of chants: 'Murdering fascists', 'No more butchery' and 'Violence is the only solution'. Adolf agreed. He slapped one of the chanting reds hard across the ear with the flat of his hand. The man staggered and swayed as he clutched his head with both hands before falling to his knees.

Other reds saw the slap. They alerted their comrades and gathered together to launch themselves at us. Fortunately, the fascist police saved us. A phalanx of police moved towards us, effectively forming a line between us and the reds, who surged at us. The police then shoved us out the door. They kept shoving until they'd pushed us outside onto the street. We walked swiftly away as soon as we reached the pavement.

I read in the papers that the meeting had later collapsed into chaos. The police blamed agitators from eight different left-wing and anarchist groups. They announced they were looking in particular for a woman called 'Liverpool Pat' as one of the chief ringleaders.

Looking back, I can see how Nazi leaders exploited our hostility to blacks (and 'middle-class reds') and our hooligan willingness to fight all-comers for whatever cause. They used the Brixton riots to fuel our hatred. They knew if they stoked us up we'd react in the only way we knew how – with violence.

In the months following the riots, I attended a lot of Nazi meetings. Some of the speeches had a powerful rabble-rousing effect. The speakers would rage about 'the immigrants' looting and burning shops on 'our manor', beating up 'white men' on 'our streets' and terrorising 'white women' into staying indoors.

Down the pub afterwards, we took it all very personally. No 'unemployed coons' and their middle-class red supporters were going to take the piss on our doorstep. On Friday nights, especially, as the alcohol flowed, we'd sit around in the bar having a communal rant. By closing time, everyone would be seething, desperate to seek revenge.

We'd all pile into Del Boy's old blue Transit van. Armed with bats, bars, hammers and chains, we'd cruise up and down the road that runs between Stockwell and Clapham Common underground stations, looking for groups of blacks to attack. Our victims rarely fought back. They could usually flee as we jumped out the back of the van and ran at them. But twice we managed to capture someone. On both occasions, we bundled the young black man into the back of the van, gave him a good beating, then dumped him near The Windmill pub on Clapham Common.

One evening, an excited BNP member we knew came running into The Royal Oak. He said Gerry Gable – a man hated and feared by Nazis as the force behind the anti-fascist *Searchlight* magazine – had been spotted drinking with a few friends in The Bull pub in Clapham old town. A group of BNP members had already gathered near The Bull to attack him. We all jumped into Del Boy's van and sped off to join them. Gable, who had lost relatives in the Holocaust, was often targeted for abuse and threats. People like Adolf regarded him as the incarnation of ZOG. In later years, a group of British Nazis on holiday in Prague sent Gable a parcel containing an old-fashioned suit, a pair of shattered pebble glasses, some chicken bones and a sprinkling of mud. The accompanying note said they'd just visited a former concentration camp and had managed to locate Gable's grandfather.

When we arrived, the BNP members were already running from the pub, having carried out their 'attack'. They jumped in our van and we drove back to The Royal Oak. They were laughing excitedly, almost screeching with delight. I thought their attack must have been a real success. But when we all sat down to hear their war stories, I was disappointed. They said that, because of the 'panic in the pub', they hadn't been able 'to do him properly'. From their description, I felt they'd probably done the most panicking. I guessed they'd probably lost their bottle, thrown a couple of wet punches and legged it. Later, I discovered that the target hadn't even been Gerry Gable. It had been the then chairperson of the WRP. It wasn't the first time, and it wouldn't be the last, that I'd experienced an incident in which Nazi loudmouths talked war, then ran a mile at the first sign of trouble.

One afternoon, Del Boy was driving me and Adrian 'Army Game' through the back streets of Brixton in his newly purchased car. Adrian was in the front seat; I was in the back. We spotted a black man working under the bonnet of a mini-van. Del Boy slowed down next to him and Adrian shouted, 'Oi, you fucking nigger!'

The black guy stood up and said, 'Fuck you, boy.' Del Boy slammed on the brakes and we all moved to get out. As it was a two-door car, I had to wait for Adrian to go before I could push forward the front seat and get out myself. Adrian was only half out when the black man ran over and started punching him.

As the two struggled, the black man started shouting, 'Help me! Help me!' In seconds, around ten other blacks had surrounded the car. I still hadn't had time to get out. I pulled Adrian back in and he slammed the door shut. Del Boy also got back in, but before he could slam shut his door someone hit him on the head with a spanner. He rammed the car into gear and we sped off down the road, chased for a few yards by a group of angry blacks.

Blood ran down the back of Del Boy's head and his hands shook as he clutched the steering wheel. I kept laughing at the stupidity of it, and probably out of shock. My companions didn't see the funny side. They kept telling me to 'fucking shut up'. I felt that if they lacked the bollocks to fight these people, then they should have kept their mouths firmly shut. Simple as that.

We began talking more often of emigrating. Many of us felt England had already lost the race war. It seemed like the blacks and the Asians and every other toerag called Abdul living in every other Third World shithole would soon be making a home in our green and pleasant land. The alien culture had already swamped us.

I can't remember who first started talking about South Africa, but the country of apartheid began to shine out to us as a beacon of hope and a focus for our escape fantasies. It was hot there, English was spoken, more whites were needed and the blacks knew their place. Colin, in particular, often brought up the subject of this white paradise. He seemed genuinely to want to emigrate there. South Africa represented a new beginning, away from those bloody invaders and their appeasing hosts.

At first, I thought it was just 'pub talk', but one day I asked him if he was serious. He convinced me he was. On the spur of the moment, I said, 'Why don't we go together?' He agreed. The night before we left, I stayed with him at his father's house in Stratford, east London. I didn't fancy flying out of Heathrow because of my outstanding warrant. Passport checks were less vigorous on the ferries, so we agreed to take a boat from Harwich to Holland, then to fly out to Africa from there with our tourist visas.

I still laugh now when I think back to the day we left England. We both wore our Sunday-best suits and behaved like robot model-citizens. Very sober and correct. Indeed, as the train pulled out of Liverpool Street Station, we vowed never to drink alcohol again. Alcohol only brought trouble. And we were determined to avoid trouble in our new life. Even Millie's parents would have been proud of me.

We were on our way to white man's heaven.

CHAPTER 8

WHITE MAN'S HEAVEN

OUR IRON-WILLED COMMITMENT TO A NEW LIFE WITHOUT ALCOHOL REMAINED intact throughout the journey to Amsterdam. On the train, we drank only tea. On the ferry, we ordered only soft drinks. In the duty-free shop, we bought only postcards. As we set foot in Holland, still wearing our suits, we felt pride in our self-mastery. Our abstinence had set us firmly on the road to a new beginning.

In Amsterdam, we booked into one of the floating hotels where Angie had nearly met her death. After a shower and a change of clothes, we decided to watch a football match on the telly. Holland were playing Belgium. We had to go down to the bar to see the match. Again, we ordered soft drinks. We sat sipping them for ten, perhaps eleven, minutes. Then the football chants combined with the holiday atmosphere to weaken our teetotal resolve.

After a short discussion, we agreed it might be possible to relax our puritan restraint without compromising our good intentions. We'd proved to ourselves we could go without alcohol. Now we needed to prove we could drink in moderation. With that goal in mind, and nothing else, we decided to allow ourselves a few beers. Just a few. Nothing to excess. There'd certainly be no relapse into drunkenness.

After a few hours' heavy drinking, we felt the agreement needed alteration. It was now all right to get drunk so long as we avoided trouble.

We were having a good time drinking with a group of Dutch

football supporters. 'Boisterous, but relaxed' is how the police might have described the scene. A fat but otherwise nondescript young woman waddled over and, with an English accent, told me and Colin to keep the noise down. I said I didn't think we were being too noisy. No one else was complaining. She disagreed and added that her boyfriend, who'd be down in half an hour, would also take exception to the volume, especially as he was a staunch Welsh nationalist who didn't like English people. This confused me. I asked what he was doing with her if he disliked the English. She said, 'My mum's Welsh.'

We both laughed at her. Looking riled, she said, 'I'm advising you, for your own sake, not to be so loud when Dai comes.' I told her to fuck off. She said, 'You won't say that when Dai gets here.'

She waddled back to her friends at the bar. Together, they kept glancing at us and the door. They seemed to be counting the seconds till Dai's arrival, eager to witness the English loudmouths' comeuppance at the hands of the destroyer from the valleys.

Over the next half hour, various characters came into the bar. I'd say to Colin, 'D'you think that's Dai?'

Colin would say, 'Naaa'. Then he'd make some derogatory comment about the potential gladiator.

A slightly built creature with permed, peroxide-blond, shoulder-length hair arrived. He looked like the female flatmate in an unfunny 1970s sitcom. I said, 'That can't be Dai.'

Colin said, 'Naaa, that's Princess Di.'

We both laughed. Then the fat woman waved at the new arrival and shouted, 'Dai!' We laughed even more.

Dai spoke briefly to his Bacon, turned and walked towards us. The look on his girlfriend's face said, 'Now we'll see.' Dai was a pace and a half away from me. As he opened his mouth to say something, I punched him hard into the side of the head. He fell back onto a table and crashed to the floor. As his girlfriend started screaming at me to stop hitting him, I stamped on him a few times. Dai stayed where he was. I don't think the Welsh warrior had encountered the direct approach before.

Next morning at breakfast, Colin and I sat at one end of the room. All the other guests sat at the other. Only the sound of toast being chewed broke the perfect silence. Colin and I agreed that the new life, the new beginning, would start when we reached Africa. We flew first to Cairo in Egypt, then on to Nairobi in Kenya before landing in Johannesburg at midday after 16 hours in the air. As we shuffled through passport control, I vowed never to sit in a plane again. If necessary, I'd walk back to Europe.

We found ourselves an apartment suite in the rather lavish Mariston Hotel and paid a month in advance. We wanted to ensure that, come what may, we'd have a roof over our heads. Only a month earlier, I'd been stranded in Europe without food, money or shelter. Now I was relaxing in opulence with black servants to cater for any wishes that occurred to me as I lazed in our spacious quarters or occupied myself in the sauna, swimming pool, bar and restaurant.

It was all very pleasant. You could almost forget the civil war on the horizon. A real civil war, that is, not a few bricks being thrown in Brixton. It seemed to come a little closer with every day spent downing beers by the pool. You only had to watch the censored television news to see what was coming. The South African Army's supposed 'victories' against 'terrorists' on the borders filled those parts of the bulletins not taken up with reports of rebellion in the black townships or violent crime in the once 'safe' white suburbs.

We treated the first fortnight as a holiday, sunbathing by day, clubbing by night. Then we started looking for work. Given the shortage of whites in a country that sought to preserve their dominant status – they represented about 18 per cent of the population, while around 68 per cent were classified as black, 11 per cent as coloured and 3 per cent as Asian – we thought it wouldn't be too difficult to find a slot somewhere. But as we'd entered the country on tourist visas, we found the search for work more challenging than expected. Everyone asked for work permits, which we didn't have.

The South African authorities strictly enforced the permits, largely as a way to control the movement of blacks. Employers who chose to ignore the law could find themselves in a lot of trouble.

Someone told us that foreigners could enlist in a branch of the South African Army to fight on the Namibian border. Given the seeming absence of other employment possibilities, we decided to offer our military services to the cause of white rule, although we didn't see our actions quite like that at the time. We just wanted adventure, although, to be honest, the adventure was the thought of a war where the enemy wasn't very good.

I'm not saying my actions had nothing to do with politics, but for me the political dimension lay in the enjoyment I felt at doing something I knew would piss off those right-on, middle-class leftists I'd left behind in England. At that time in the mid-'80s, to do anything in support of 'white South Africa' and 'the apartheid system' was to break a widely enforced taboo. You weren't supposed to bank at Barclays or eat Rowntree's sweeties or drink South African sherry or chomp Cape apples. It was as if everything bad in the world was only taking place in South Africa. The millions of people enslaved by the various sects of communism and socialism didn't seem to count.

This obsession with the evils of apartheid just struck me as the most awful bollocks – and encouraged me to support the Boers. On a good day by the pool, with a few beers inside me, I could even agree with the white South Africans' view of themselves as a victimised minority fighting for the Free World against the communist forces of darkness.

We had to travel by train to the capital Pretoria to see if the South African Army would let us strap on the jackboots. We asked a taxi-driver to take us to the main barracks. We told the duty officer at the heavily fortified main gate that we wanted to join up. He ordered a soldier to take us to the relevant person, who turned out to be a middle-aged major sitting in a wood-panelled office, shuffling papers.

We told him we wanted to enlist and fight on the border. He seemed surprised – and impressed. He asked us a few questions about our backgrounds. I told him I'd been in the British Army. He asked us why we wanted to join the beleaguered Boers. We said we felt South Africa was a country worth fighting for – and we didn't want the reds to take over.

He looked at us with eyes almost moist with respect and approval. He said he'd sign us up on the spot if he could. Unfortunately, he couldn't. First, we weren't South African nationals. Second, we only had tourist visas. The information we'd been given about an official South African 'Foreign Legion' was false.

He regretted having to reject us. He felt the army needed more young men with our backbone and moral fibre. He said many young whites had been infected with defeatism and cowardice. Hardly anyone wanted to join the army, especially since the increase in fighting on the border. Young people were moving abroad, waking up as – spit – conscientious objectors, or even – horror of horrors – deserting. He regarded the country's youth as riddled with commies and conchies, pooftahs and pansies, whackos and weirdies. He sounded just like Adolf.

He told us not to be dispirited. He said many Afrikaner farmers would employ an ex-British Army soldier as an armed security guard. He also mentioned a new 'private' police force that was being set up. He plucked a newspaper cutting from the papers on his desk and handed it to me. It read:

> Low-profile patrol squads plus community participation and suburban security equal a three-cornered crime crackdown unit.
>
> This equation is the brainchild of an ex-Rhodesian who heads the Johannesburg Community Crime Counteraction Squad with thousands of members.
>
> The scheme, the first of its kind in South Africa, is based on similar operations in strife-torn areas of America.
>
> For 15 Rand per month, anyone may join the Community Policing Services scheme which guarantees 24-hour patrols in marked and unmarked vehicles, as well as regular house checks.
>
> Members display a triangular board depicting a skull and crossbones to enable the crack unit and other community participants to identify their homes.
>
> Clients are also given two 24-hour emergency telephone numbers. 'If we receive an emergency call we send out the nearest vehicle as quickly as possible to sort out the problem,' said the company director. The car is usually there in five minutes. 'We are not Nazi pigs, thugs or bully

boys. We don't do this for fun,' he stressed. 'Our squad members are highly trained. All have police or military experience and are armed. Our job is not to investigate, but to protect.

'We try to use minimal force, but if my men are in a dangerous situation, they are fully entitled to protect themselves.'

About a week later, we found ourselves sitting in a classroom with around ten other recruits to the Community Policing Services. At the interview, we'd been told by the company director – a Londoner by birth – that he could only offer us a position in the sales team. Later, when they'd (or we'd) recruited more customers, we could go over to the security side. He said our lack of work permits could be overlooked for the time being.

The job didn't represent for me the fulfilment of a dream, but it was a start. We spent the first week learning sales techniques. The strategy hinged on terrifying people. Instructors taught us various techniques for playing on white people's fears of violent black criminals.

Every word of the spiel that we had to learn by heart contributed towards making potential customers see their homes as little more than neon-lit invitations to every passing black burglar, rapist and murderer. By the end of our training, we could have turned up at Fort Knox and made its commander feel insecure.

When they finally sent us out to meet the South African public, we didn't have to work too hard to sign up customers. Apart from our newly acquired sales skills, the escalating unrest (and the resulting climate of threat and insecurity) helped us reach our sales targets quite easily. We hadn't planned on ending up as door-to-door salesmen, but in the beginning, at least, the job amused us. We had a lot of fun striking fear into people.

We'd stand on doorsteps hitting them with crime statistics (most of which we'd fabricated). Then we'd point out that 80 per cent of the state's police were engaged in fighting township violence, leaving only a pitiful remnant to protect the suburbs. Then we'd invent some awful crimes that had supposedly happened in the neighbourhood only recently, but which the authorities had hushed up to avoid scaring people.

We'd bring the horror show to a climax with a 'free' security survey of their homes. Many of these homes already bristled with the sort of defences normally found at high-security military complexes. But, regardless of the fortifications, we'd always reach the regrettable conclusion that a gruesome fate beckoned for those who chose to live unprotected in such potential death traps.

'High walls don't keep burglars out, Madam. They merely hide them once they've scaled the wall.'

'Husband at work, Madam? So you're alone in your home with the children, are you? Very brave, if I may say so.'

For that rare housewife who still seemed undecided, we'd glance accusingly at her children and say, 'Surely your children's safety is worth fifteen rand a month [around five English pounds at that time]?' Hardly anyone turned us down.

However, after a month or so Colin and I felt bored. We asked the boss if we could start providing the physical protection our terrified customers now needed.

He asked if we fancied working in nightclubs. He'd been approached by a few club managers after a dramatic increase in trouble at city-centre nightspots. Knife, and sometimes gun, fights had become commonplace. Bar takings had sunk.

In Wolverhampton some years earlier, I'd served a sort of apprenticeship in the distinguished profession of the door. I'd worked both for a friend's band and in a town-centre pub. Since then, I'd done the job now and again, but, as with the salesman's post, it wasn't part of the dream that sustained me.

However, I suspected the job would be more of a challenge in South Africa. Knives, handguns and even automatic rifles were held quite legally and openly by people. So they tended to be produced more readily in disputes. After only a few weeks in paradise, we knew that someone being shot or stabbed on the street, night or day, wasn't uncommon.

The boss sent us to a nightclub in the centre of Johannesburg owned by a Greek family. Before letting us set off for our first shift, he issued us each with a pair of handcuffs, a heavy rubber baton, a 9 mm pistol and – presumably for the more difficult customers – a single-barrelled, Russian-made shotgun with 12 cartridges. He must have detected a slight flicker of disquiet on our faces. He tapped the shotgun and said, 'You probably won't have to use this, boys. But just in case. It'll scare the bastards.'

Everything, apart from the shotgun, was attached to a gun-belt worn on the waist, so as not to restrict our mobility. Colin and I had already spent quite a lot of time as paying customers in Johannesburg nightclubs. We'd never encountered such heavily armed doormen. I mentioned this. Our boss confirmed that such weaponry might be considered unusual, but he'd promised the club manager that we'd stamp out the gang fights that were harming business. He thought the sight of us on the door would scare off troublemakers, reassure decent customers and generally encourage better manners on and off the dance floor. It was a new approach to customer service.

But it worked. Gang fights ceased, and the club became very easy to manage. There were still the occasional scuffles caused by excess alcohol and wronged boyfriends (or girlfriends), but the manager and bar staff assured us that the general level of politeness and consideration to others had risen appreciably since our arrival. We moved out of the hotel into a flat in a high-rise block in Hillbrow, an area of the city centre which most considered 'rough'. Our neighbours were mostly Portuguese who'd been booted out of countries like Angola following the collapse of Portugal's colonial empire.

Technically, I suppose, the Portuguese were 'whites', but in this land of obsessive racial classification I didn't meet any whites (that is, Afrikaners, Anglo-Saxons and others with passably pale skins, preferably of European origin) who regarded the Portuguese as being on an equal footing with them. The whites I spoke to seemed to regard them as on a par with (or even slightly below) the Asians, who themselves were on a par with (or even slightly above) the mixed-race coloureds, who, like everyone else, were above the blacks, who themselves were just above the dogs. But only just. The Portuguese had a reputation – unjustified, no doubt – for being small-time criminals with a penchant for stabbing.

During the day, Colin and I would be 'stacking Zs' – a popular local term to describe sleeping – or drinking gallons of the local brew, Lion Beer, in a bar called The Moulin Rouge, which lay within staggering distance of our flat and was popular with British expatriates. Despite the French name, like most things in Johannesburg it was done out in 'American' style, with 1950s jukebox, pool table and high stools around a bar offering an array of vomit-provoking cocktails. We were popular there, at least in the sense that many customers went out of their way to make conversation with us. This may have had something to do with the fact that we were sometimes armed with the guns we were carrying to, or from, work.

The barmaid was an absolutely stunning blonde South African who looked as if butter wouldn't melt in her mouth. She had her own little staff of 'pot-men' – blacks who'd collect and wash the glasses, clean the ashtrays and top up the peanuts: the sort of tasks a barmaid in England would perform herself.

I used to watch in amazement as she slapped and shouted at the pot-men for making the slightest mistake. One minute, she'd be screaming at and slapping a cowering man, the next she'd be politely serving a customer as if nothing had happened. I watched horrified one day as, for no apparent reason, she gave a pot-man a particularly vicious slap. I asked her why. She said, 'I have to. If you don't let them know who's in charge, they'll turn on you one day.'

She told me not to feel sorry for them, but rather to regard them as dogs. She added, 'Dogs know who their masters are. And dogs don't often bite their masters, do they?' Her views were quite common among many of the whites I met.

A lot of the younger people in there were English. They'd moved to Jo'burg with their parents several years earlier. The young men now whinged about the most unpleasant consequence of the move – having to do national service in the South African Army. Most of them planned dodging it somehow, either by fleeing the country or taking up a non-military alternative, like working in a hospital. As our own attempt to join the army had been rebuffed, we used to taunt them for wanting to forgo such a 'great opportunity'.

We became friends with a group of people from Essex. These

included a brother and sister, Shane and Claire, who lived with their parents in Hillbrow, and their two cousins, sisters Susan and Karen. All came originally from Romford. They also had a friend called Tim, who used to tag along. He came from Yorkshire and regarded himself as a real ladies' man. In fact, he was a fool. I assumed his life had been changed by watching John Travolta in the film *Saturday Night Fever*. He appeared to model himself on Travolta's 'Disco King' character, while lacking the original's looks, talent and charm. He became the target for some of our more unpleasant practical jokes.

I became attracted to one of Karen's friends, Debra, who came from Basildon. She'd come over for a holiday, but had kept extending her stay. She'd been there around nine months when we first met. She'd had a few jobs in that time. During the day, she worked as a hairdresser in a downtown salon. She told me that to earn a bit more money she'd taken on a part-time job behind the bar in a nightclub.

One evening, she'd refused to serve two drunken Afrikaners. An argument had blown up. One of the Afrikaners had pulled out a handgun, pointed it at her and shouted, 'I'll kill you, you bitch.' Others in the bar had wrestled the gun from him before ejecting him. Debra said she'd been speechless with shock and fear. She'd left the job immediately. She was still a bit nervous when we first met.

These new friends were different from our old friends. They were all reasonably balanced people with no interest in, or understanding of, the violent world in which we roamed. At first, we tried to give the impression that we were nice people just like them (although, obviously, the weaponry we sometimes carried slightly gave us away), but gradually the mask slipped.

One evening, we found ourselves drinking with an American who claimed to be a 'Vietnam veteran'. He even wore a baseball cap inscribed with the name of 'his' elite unit, the 509th Arizona Penis Pullers, or something like that. At the beginning of the third hour of his storytelling about his incredible one-man war against the Vietcong, I told him to fuck off. He sat back in his high stool and said, 'No, you fuck off.' I punched him somewhere in the head. All I remember is his vet's cap flying off, Claire screaming hysterically and Colin jumping on me piggyback-style, shouting, 'Bernie. Calm down, you crazy bastard.' I was asked to leave.

The next day, I bumped into Debra and Claire on the street. I mumbled a sort of apology and gave the excuse that I'd been mixing my drinks. They seemed to forgive me. But things were never really the same again. My true self had been exposed in the harsh and unforgiving light of the South African sun. Or, rather, in the dim rays from the 100-watt bulbs of The Moulin Rouge, to which we soon returned without anyone mentioning 'the incident'. Colin and I, despite our fitful attempts to hold on to our fresh-start ideals, soon reverted to our south London ways. That is, boozing, then abusing and sometimes beating people, such as our 'mate' Tim, the wannabe John Travolta.

The problem with Tim was Tim. There was just something deeply irritating about him. One day, we invited him to our tenth-floor flat. Being a fool, he came. We handcuffed him gently to the balcony railings, sprayed him lightly with CS gas, then clubbed him playfully with our riot batons until his whimpering became pitiful and decency impelled us to desist. He stopped spending so much time with us.

We still met up with the others, although usually in the club's alcohol-free areas, like the swimming pool. They seemed to avoid drinking with us. Claire, especially, seemed a little nervous around us. However, I was getting on very well with Debra. I wanted to ask her out, but kept putting it off, because I didn't think she'd be interested in anything more than friendship.

Colin and I used to ring home once a week to keep in touch. When we rang in early October 1985, we heard there'd been more rioting in London, this time on the Broadwater Farm Estate in Tottenham. More than 200 police officers had been injured and one of them, PC Keith Blakelock, had been hacked to death.

Our South African friends goaded us 'Brits' for letting 'the kaffirs' get away with it. 'Your government should break out the rifles,' they'd say.

About a month later, we got a call from 'Benny the Jew'. He said Adolf had been injured by a car bomb in Clapham High Street. Benny didn't have any more details. My first thought was that Adolf had been caught up in an IRA attack. But then I couldn't think of anything in Clapham that the Provos might have regarded as worth blowing up.

Benny rang back a few days later with more information. That's when I first found out that Adolf had been travelling as a passenger in a car with the future BNP 'national organiser' Tony Wells/Lecomber but had got out just before it had exploded. Both Adolf and Lecomber had been injured. Adolf had minor burns to his face and hands; Lecomber was quite badly chewed up. Both had made their own way to hospital, where they'd been arrested.

The fact they'd been arrested suggested the police didn't think of them as victims. Press reports mentioned that the headquarters of the far-left WRP stood 200 yards away from the site of the explosion.

I wouldn't hear the full story until I'd got back to England. In the mean time, we sent Adolf a 'Get Well Soon' card.

The success of our heavily armed approach to club security meant our job had become extremely tedious. Trouble had almost disappeared. Colin and I would sit at a table in the restaurant from early evening until the early hours of the morning, totally bored. We'd been planning to stay in South Africa and then apply for citizenship so we could join the army. But that remained a long way off.

Colin suggested moving to Cape Town: 'It's full of English and we'd be near the sea.' I said we could think about it. Colin said he'd only stay in Jo'burg if the company gave him a more exciting job. The next day, he told the boss he was bored and wanted to leave. He was asked to 'hang on', because something was coming up that might interest him.

I didn't want to be left out, so I told the boss the same thing. He told me the same thing, 'Hang on. Something's coming up.' The something coming up turned out to be another club, also in the city centre, but in the basement of a hotel. It was the haunt of various biker and Portuguese gangs. It had a reputation for trouble. This wasn't quite the new position Colin had hoped for, so he left the company.

I decided to rise to the challenge, although without Colin I had no back-up. I was expected to handle any situation that arose, alone. In fact, most of the customers turned out to be all right.

The manager represented the problem. A half-witted, aggressive little shit, he caused more trouble than anyone else. His decisions, always arbitrary and irrational, seemed designed to provoke.

He'd point at individuals he wanted me to eject from the club. Then he'd make a big show of the fact that he'd ordered their ejection. Most of these customers, so far as I could tell, hadn't actually done anything wrong. More than once, I saw him, blind drunk, threatening customers with a handgun. He'd never explain their supposed offences.

One evening, he decided – again for no apparent reason – that jeans were no longer an acceptable form of dress. Given that bikers formed the largest segment of the clientele, his request struck me as even more markedly unreasonable than usual. Not only did he order me to turn away at the door any people wearing jeans, he also demanded that I eject every jeans-wearing customer already in the club.

But I did as I was told, although I expected trouble. Fortunately for me and the manager, almost everyone left without much fuss. Only one group of Portuguese men took exception. They felt they were being singled out. As they left, they threatened to return to smash up the club – and me. The barman told me they had a reputation and that I ought to keep my wits about me for a while.

I finished work about 3.30 in the morning and walked the half mile or so home. There was no one about. I got in the lift and stepped out at my floor. A group of six or so men were standing around outside the first flat while being shouted at by a Portuguese woman. I'd never seen her before, although she only lived a few doors down from me. As soon as she saw me, she ran over. She started saying, 'Arrest him! Go on, arrest him!' She'd assumed I was a policeman. Our uniform was similar to theirs and, as I was also carrying a baton, handcuffs and firearms, I could understand her mistake.

I tried telling her I wasn't a policeman, but she wasn't interested. She just kept gibbering on. 'I had a party in my flat. It ended. But these people want to come back in.' Her manner was agitated and she smelt of alcohol.

I told her I didn't want anything to do with her guests: 'I'm not a policeman, I live here.' I walked a few steps with her. As I got to the men, I realised they were the same men who'd threatened me earlier at the club. 'Small world,' I thought. And it was almost my last thought ever, because the men recognised me too. One of them stepped forward, called me a bastard and lunged at my chest with a knife. The blade cut me, but I managed to turn away, so preventing it going right in. Holding the shotgun in both hands, I swung round and belted the knifeman across the head with it. The wooden butt crashing into his skull made a wincingly loud noise. He fell to the floor, unconscious and injured.

I raised the shotgun and pointed it at the others. I made as if to shoot. They tore off down the corridor. The woman was standing there, muttering in Portuguese. I wasn't sure what to do with the man on the floor. His head was bleeding quite badly; one of his eyes had closed completely. I grabbed his feet and dragged him to the lift. I ferried him down to the ground floor, then dragged him out into the street, where I left him alongside the rubbish. I took the lift back up. The woman was still standing near her flat, alone. She started shouting in Portuguese. She seemed angry with me. I couldn't understand why. After all, I'd got rid of her unwanted guests.

I told her to calm down. I walked with her to the door of her flat. Her evening's alcohol consumption had really started kicking in. She became abusive in English. I'd had enough. I was bleeding too, my stab wound was starting to hurt and I wanted to go to bed. She was lucky I wasn't a policeman: I'd have arrested her.

I grabbed her by the arm, pushed her into her flat and told her to fuck off. I walked off down the corridor. She followed a few paces behind me, screaming abuse. Colin was awake when I got in. He said he'd heard a row, but hadn't realised I was involved. I warned him that if the Portuguese man ended up in hospital, we'd probably get a visit from the police. And, whether or not he made it to hospital, we'd probably get a visit at some point from him and his mates.

I washed and cleaned the wound in my chest, then put the knife I'd picked up from the floor, and my torn shirt, into a bag and went to bed.

I slept uneasily with the guns by my side. I was expecting either the police or the Portuguese to burst through the door, but no one came. Early next morning, the company telephoned to say they needed every available body to attend an incident near the black township of Soweto.

An hour or so later, I was picked up in a company van which drove at speed out of the city to Soweto. I hadn't realised we had customers out there. I couldn't imagine how we'd recruited them. Perhaps we'd scared them with stories about the white police ('Flimsy shack, Madam? That's not going to stop a determined Boer in uniform, is it?').

In fact, I discovered our customers were the South African police. They called occasionally on freelance help for 'non-political' incidents when they were overstretched. I was told in the van, which contained around ten other heavily armed colleagues, that two black factions had been fighting over ownership of a 'shebeen', that is, an illegal drinking den, often a venue for gambling and prostitution. (When I first heard the word 'shebeen', I thought it was native South African. Only years later did I discover it comes from an Irish Gaelic word for 'bad ale'.)

By the time we got there, a gang fight had already taken place. One young man of about 20 had been trapped by rivals, put against a wall and stoned. He lay there motionless, blood spattered all over his broken body. I thought he was dead. Another man had been stabbed in the head. He was reeling around the street, clutching his head and screaming in pain. After a while, he collapsed.

A police pick-up truck arrived. A few policemen got out, grabbed hold of the two men and dumped them both into the back of the truck, like sacks of rubbish. They drove off, leaving us standing in a cloud of dust.

When I got back to the flat, I found an anxious-looking Colin waiting for me. He said that armed police had raided the flat. Apparently, the Portuguese woman had alleged I'd assaulted her. Colin said the police had made plain they planned to arrest me. I decided to seek legal advice. As I left the building, two policemen suddenly stood up, guns drawn, from behind a car near the entrance. Pointing their guns at me, they shouted, 'Raise your hands and turn around.' I wasn't going to argue. They came over, searched me, handcuffed me, then asked me where my guns were. I said, 'In the flat.'

They told me to get into their car. As we drove off, one of them said they were taking me to John Foster Square police station. It had a worse reputation than my bikers' club. Numerous prisoners had died after supposedly 'jumping' from windows on the upper floors during interrogations.

They brought me into a detention room. Sweating – and not just from the heat – I waited on my own for a few minutes before a detective entered the room. He asked me about the events of the night before. I told him the truth and added that I still had the knife and torn clothing at home. He produced a statement made by the Portuguese woman. She claimed that, for no reason, I'd grabbed her by the arm, pushed her about, threatened her with a gun and even sexually assaulted her (although she'd given no explanation of how).

I was furious. I said, 'Why the fuck would I attack someone who lives on the same fucking landing as me, without reason? I'm not fucking stupid, mate.'

I needn't have worried. The detective said he didn't believe the woman and he wasn't going to look into the matter any further. He said she was known to the police and added, 'Be careful of these people. They're trouble.' He wrote out a statement for me, asked me to sign it, then told me to go home and forget about it. Less than 30 minutes after being arrested, I was released. I thought that was the end of the matter. In fact, it was only the beginning.

The company heard about my arrest. The boss didn't like having any bother with the police. He decided I needed a break from the nightclub. He thought that, between us, me and the manager were causing more trouble than we were preventing. He said he wanted to transfer me temporarily to 'patrol work', that is, patrolling the suburbs of Johannesburg in a pick-up truck.

I was owed a few days, which I took before starting my new duties. During this time, I spoke a lot with Colin about moving on to Cape Town. At that time, a luxury train called 'The Blue Train' connected the two cities. We agreed we'd travel on it if and when we left Jo'burg, although it was becoming a case of 'when' rather than 'if'. It was now December. Debra missed her family, as she'd been away now for almost a year. They'd thought she'd only be gone for a month or two. She said she'd travel with us on The Blue Train, but first she wanted to spend Christmas in England.

We booked three tickets for The Blue Train, due to depart Jo'burg on 14 January 1986. I don't know why, but something told me I wouldn't be on it. I just couldn't look forward to the journey (and the new 'new start'), because I knew it wasn't going to happen.

Debra planned to leave for England in the second week of December. I told myself I'd ask her out for a meal the night before she left, but I bottled out of it. I thought she'd make some excuse and hand me the basket. She planned a final drink with her friends. They did invite me and Colin, but I said I had to work. I hoped to pop in to the club at some stage, but I never did. I don't know why.

The following morning, Debra came round to say goodbye. I was surprised at how sorry I felt to see her go, even though she'd only be gone for a month. But thoughts of romance soon receded when I started my new duties patrolling the suburbs. Until then, I'd foolishly regarded myself as unshockable.

CHAPTER 9

BLACK MAN'S HELL

'LET'S GET THIS STRAIGHT, BERNIE. KAFFIRS ARE FUCKING VERMIN. THEY'RE NOT human, OK?'

Dougie, my senior colleague in the pick-up truck, was explaining the cornerstone of his world view as we drove around the tidy and well-tended suburbs of white Johannesburg and the less tidy and less well-tended suburbs of coloured Johannesburg.

Most of the blacks we encountered were either domestic servants or – at least in Dougie's eyes – potential criminals. Our job was to answer emergency calls from Community Policing Services customers. We had white and coloured householders on our books, but calls from whites tended to be treated with the greatest urgency. These white callers were usually reporting suspicious people near, on, or in their properties.

Dougie was in his mid-30s. Slightly built and not very tall, he bolstered his otherwise unimposing presence with an arsenal of weapons strapped to his body. I don't know if he was an Afrikaner or an Anglo, because we didn't have the sort of conversations in which I could have asked a question like that. Any details about his background emerged incidentally through anecdotes he'd tell about his past.

These tended to describe his beating, shooting and humiliating 'kaffirs'. He said he'd shot his 'first kaffir' as a teenager. He'd been cleaning a handgun in his house when he'd heard his sister screaming in the garden. He'd run out with the gun, seen a black man standing over her and fired twice. The first bullet hit the man in the shoulder; the second slammed into his head, killing him instantly. He'd told the police the man had been attacking his sister. That was the end of the matter. No charges, no inquest, no nothing. I didn't really believe him. Naively, I thought he had to be lying or, at the very least, exaggerating. After a few shifts with him, I changed my mind.

On one shift, I discovered in the truck's glove compartment a photo of a black man with his face covered in blood. Dougie said he'd taken it as a souvenir after attacking the man during a raid on a shebeen. He told me to keep it as a 'memento'. I didn't really want to, but he urged me to take it, so I put it in my jacket pocket to shut him up.

On one of my first shifts, we were called out to a coloured person's house in the west of the city. The householder had reported five black youths trying to smash their way in. Apparently, they'd smashed his windows with sticks and were now trying to break down the front door.

We pulled up leisurely at the address. The youths were still there, throwing rocks against the door and trying to shoulder it open. Dougie didn't say anything. He just jumped out of the truck and started shooting. The youths skedaddled. Dougie ran up the path towards the house, firing his pistol wildly at the fleeing figures. He wasn't just shooting in the air for effect: he seemed to be aiming his shots. Luckily for his targets, he couldn't shoot well on the move and, anyway, the juveniles were probably running faster than his bullets. I'd jumped out of the truck and was running behind him. His behaviour left me speechless. Everything was happening too quickly for me to say or do anything. We started chasing the only youth still visible. He was streaking down the road with the velocity of an Olympic sprinter.

Dougie fired again. As he did so, a police car came round the corner. The terrified youth ran straight up to it. Without even stopping to talk to the policemen inside, he opened the rear door and jumped in. It must have seemed a better option than summary execution. For the second time in a week, I found myself back in John Foster Square police station. The fact that shots had been fired meant a bit of paperwork needed completion.

I expected a hard time from police keen to discover why a

security guard had been shooting at a member of the public in a residential area. But, apart from a few unprobing questions from a bored sergeant, no one seemed too concerned. We could have been reporting a stolen bike. I told the police I'd been talking on the radio when the shooting started. I'd only just got out of the vehicle as the police arrived, so I couldn't throw much light on the events. However, Dougie not only told the full truth, he also exaggerated the more illegal aspects.

I knew security guards could get away with a lot, but I'd also been told the law was crystal clear about self-defence. You could shoot if you considered your life in danger, but not if that danger had passed. Someone whizzing gazelle-like down the road away from you could not be regarded as a threat.

They released me. Dougie stayed to make a statement. I thought he'd be charged with something, and perhaps suspended, but next day he was waiting for me as usual at work. He said the police considered the matter closed.

I now guessed they wouldn't have done anything even if he'd shot someone dead – so long as that someone was black. Dougie had obviously learnt early what he could get away with. What I'd thought were his tall tales had probably been faithful depictions of reality.

One day, Colin and I found the lamp-posts outside our block of flats posted with flyers decorated with swastika-type symbols. They advertised a meeting for the far-right Afrikaner Resistance Movement (AWB). Its leader, Eugène Terre'Blanche, would be present. I didn't know that much about him, but I'd seen him described in the British media as a would-be South African Hitler.

Colin and I decided to go along. Outside the venue, khaki-clad paramilitary types sat on horseback or stood holding flags decorated with the swastika-type symbols we'd seen on the flyers. Inside the packed hall, I spoke to Colin. A few people nearby moved away from us, muttering in Afrikaans. A few minutes later, a group of six guards stormed over and ordered us to leave immediately.

Taken aback by their hostility, we asked why. An aggressive paramilitary with a beard said the British weren't welcome there – or anywhere in South Africa. He and his mates all carried firearms, so we decided not to protest at their racism. We made our way to the door, followed by the guards, who looked like they wanted to bash us. I think they were still bitter about the Boer War.

I began to feel very uncomfortable working with Dougie. He had a spitting aggressiveness fuelled by paranoia, suspicion and hatred. I knew a lot of violent people, and I wasn't particularly gentle myself, but Dougie was different. I could never feel at ease with him. Not only would he start waving a gun about for little or no reason, he'd also threaten and beat blacks just for fun. His brutality would astonish me. I'd often tell him to ease off, but he'd just look at me as if I were mad. I think he regarded me as some sort of humanitarian goody-goody.

Over the next few weeks, I came to realise the law didn't exist as something blacks could call on for help. I witnessed officialdom's contempt for black lives every hour of every day. I saw a policeman kung-fu kick a black man in the chest on a crowded street for no reason; I attended an incident where a white man who'd knocked down a black man in his car was asked by the policeman if the victim had caused the vehicle any damage. It was an odd, brutal world that seemed on the brink of boiling over into a bloodbath. For the first time since my arrival, I started thinking about leaving Africa altogether. I just couldn't stomach the misery and injustice I was witnessing. I saw a black family living in an abandoned car surrounded by corrugated iron. I watched black women and children sharing a meal of thin gruel from the paint tin they'd cooked it in. Yet only a few miles away, white families lived in bloated luxury. I was beginning to think like a *Guardian* reader. I thought I was cracking up.

One night, Dougie and I were on duty, but had been whiling away our shift drinking outside The Moulin Rouge. We should have been patrolling the streets in our truck. We had pagers, with which the company contacted us in emergencies. Claire was sitting with us. Normally, she tended to avoid me when I was drinking. But she'd arranged to meet someone, had arrived early and didn't want to wait on her own. My pager started bleeping. We were being called to a reported burglary. The address was just round the corner. We got up to leave. I told Claire we wouldn't be long. She asked if she could come along, because she didn't fancy sitting on her own. Foolishly, I let her jump in with us.

We arrived quickly at the address. A young white woman told us the offender had only just run out of the house. She gave a brief description of a black man wearing jeans and a T-shirt. Dougie ran one way; I the other. I bolted down the street and round the block, but couldn't see anyone. After a few minutes, I made my way back to the house. A few hundred yards away, I could see Dougie frogmarching someone towards me. Before long, the two of them reached me. On Dougie's face was a smirk; on his black prisoner's, was blood. Then Dougie suddenly belted the man across the back of the head with his pistol. He crumpled to his knees. Dougie started pistol-whipping him. I said, 'Leave it out, Dougie. Leave it out, man.' But he was in a real frenzy.

'Dirty kaffir, dirty fucking kaffir,' he spat as he booted the man, who by now had curled up into a defensive ball. I heard the sound of pounding on a window. I looked up. It was Claire. She'd been watching everything from the truck. She looked distraught. Banging on the window with both hands, she was crying her eyes out, shouting at Dougie to stop.

Dougie eventually tired, and stopped. He pulled his blood-smeared victim to his feet and forced him up the path to the house he'd allegedly burgled. Dougie rang the bell. The young woman opened the door – and let out a scream. She didn't scream because she recognised the quivering man. She screamed because his face was a mask of blood. Dougie told her to call the police.

In a few minutes, they arrived in a van. Dougie said, 'I've got a burglar for you.' The police didn't ask how the alleged burglar had ended up in such a state. Trivial points like that didn't interest them. Dougie said he'd attend the station to make a statement. The police pushed the man into the van and drove off.

We drove Claire back to The Moulin Rouge. She was still upset, but had stopped crying. She asked Dougie why he'd had to hit the man like that. He said, 'He was a burglar.' We dropped her off and drove on.

I didn't feel well. It struck me that the man hadn't been wearing jeans and a T-shirt. He didn't fit the householder's original description. I asked Dougie if he could be sure he'd got the right man. I said, 'Do you really think he's the burglar?'

Dougie laughed, 'Don't be stupid. Of course he isn't.'

He said he'd seen the man walking up the road with his girlfriend. He'd asked him where he'd been and he'd 'got lippy'. Dougie had then pistol-whipped him on the spot. He added, 'Fucking kaffir. His black bitch got a kicking too.' He claimed that as he was kicking her, she'd wet herself. Her urine had gone all over his boots and trousers. 'That's why he got what he got.'

I felt sick, just sick, and dirty. I asked myself what I was doing with such an animal. I was holding the shotgun in my hands. I felt like smashing the butt into the side of his head. I really wanted to damage him, but I didn't. He was white. The law would have punished me severely for harming even a hair on his head.

I felt like going to the police and telling them the man was innocent. But I guessed my intervention wouldn't have made any difference. The man was black: he was already guilty. It seemed to me that so long as some black man was in custody for an offence, it didn't matter to the police if he was the wrong one. Dougie would make his statement and 'the burglar' would probably receive a lengthy prison sentence. The next day, I went into the office and told them I didn't want to work on patrols any more.

Some people might think I'm exaggerating the way things were for blacks. I'm not. The more independent papers were full of stories of astonishing official cruelty. One story in particular has stuck in my mind. It involves the so-called 'Pabello 26'.

Pabello is a black township. A policeman had been murdered outside his home by demonstrators who'd just been dispersed from a nearby football pitch with tear gas. He'd been struck on the head with his own rifle after he'd shot indiscriminately, paralysing an 11-year-old boy. The courts convicted 26 blacks of having played a part in the murder. Six received community service, six were sent to prison and fourteen were sentenced to death. The controversial law of common purpose had been used to convict all of them, but the trials never established who'd actually struck the policeman.

It subsequently emerged that five of the blacks sentenced to death had only been arrested by chance. They'd been stopped at random in the street seven months after the murder and asked to make up the numbers in an identity parade. The police witness had picked out all five of the innocent men. Despite the public outcry, all were hanged.

I knew too that the state didn't reserve injustice for non-whites alone. I heard enough stories to know that anyone who displeased the authorities could be locked up without charge, fitted up and even, in extreme cases, murdered.

The boss found me another nightclub. Neither as big nor as busy as the last one, it shared a similar biker clientele. The bikers, mostly older men in their mid-30s to early 40s, involved themselves in most things criminal. Mercifully, however, my new manager didn't indulge in provocative and irrational behaviour, so life became easier.

On my second weekend at the club, Colin visited me for a drink. We shared more than a few beers together over the next couple of hours, until the manager came over. He said a group of men had started bothering customers outside the club. Even though Colin wasn't working, he went with me to the door. Rather foolishly, I left the shotgun behind at the reception desk upstairs.

To my undelight, I recognised the troublemakers – four of the Portuguese men I'd last seen on the landing near my flat. This time, I didn't have my shotgun to hand. Their number didn't include the knifeman I'd battered with the butt. I hoped he was still in hospital. I explained politely that they should return forthwith to their slums.

One of them stepped forward and kicked in the glass door. The others ran at us. We backed off into the foyer. They ran in after us and picked up chairs and tables. Furniture was soon flying through the air towards us. I grabbed one of the chairs and began to smash it over anyone within striking distance. Unfortunately, in the confusion I smashed Colin over the head too. The blow knocked him out – and down a flight of stairs. Now alone, I knew I could lose. Only my shotgun could save me. I ran back up the stairs to reception, grabbed the gun from behind the counter and spun round to level it at the Portuguese charging up after me.

The police arrived before the situation could deteriorate any further. They'd drawn their guns. I felt pleased to see them, but I sensed the feeling wasn't mutual. I think they'd had enough of me, the English holidaymaker. They ignored the Portuguese men and arrested me. I saw Colin still lying comatose downstairs as the police marched me out to the van.

Once again, I found myself standing in front of the desk sergeant in John Foster Square police station. I felt I'd been treated unjustly. I was also worried about Colin. These feelings combined to make me less polite and respectful than usual.

I kept interrupting the desk sergeant, who then said something insulting about my mother. I lunged at him but, before I could grab him, his colleagues brought me down to the ground with a crash. Several of them dragged me along the floor to the cells, punctuating my journey with kicks. They opened a heavy metal door and shoved me into what seemed more like a cage than a cell. The door slammed shut and for a moment I lay still on cold concrete. Looking up, I could see the stars in the night sky. The architect had forgotten to sketch in a ceiling. Only the security bars offered protection from the weather.

The cell was about six paces wide and twelve long. At one end sat a broken, stinking toilet. At the other, a small round hole in what appeared to be a coal bunker. In fact, the hole formed the entrance to the sleeping area, which contained no beds, only a few manky blankets. Crawling through the hole made me feel like a dog entering its kennel.

I managed to fall into an uneasy sleep, but the unbearable heat from the rising sun soon made that impossible. In the morning light, I could see that around the wall of my cell ran a cast-iron gutter containing water for drinking and washing. You had to pull a chain to set the liquid flowing. I didn't fancy catching amoebic dysentry, so I avoided the water.

The accommodation had one other drawback – I had to share it with five others. I introduced myself to my cellmates. All had been arrested for drink-driving. Breakfast was served at sunrise. It consisted of one scoop of cold porridge on a piece of dry bread. I asked the policeman on breakfast duty if I could use the phone. He said, 'Yeah, sure. I'll bring it to you. I'll just fetch it out of my arse.' He slammed the door shut with a sneer.

I didn't have the stomach for breakfast. I gave my meagre portion to one of the others. I sat there in my torn leather jacket and pondered my options. I hoped Colin was all right, because I knew he represented my best hope of finding a way out. He was probably the only person in the entire country who'd be concerned about my well-being.

I needed to contact him to tell him to get me a lawyer. One of the other prisoners, a Welshman (no relation to Dai, I prayed), was to be released that morning. I scratched Colin's telephone number on the back of his belt buckle. He assured me he'd ring him to let him know where I was.

During the afternoon, the police came and moved me to another cell-block. It was marked 'Category A: Serious Crimes'. This worried me, to say the least, because I didn't think a brawl in a club represented a serious crime. The policeman opened the door to my new cell. It looked much the same as the other one. It just smelt a bit more. I relaxed a bit when I met my new cellmates. None had committed any serious crimes.

Johnny had been arrested for using a stolen cheque book. He'd been in custody for seven months and was still waiting for other matters to be investigated before his case could be heard. Mario was in for drink-driving and driving while disqualified. Two teenagers were in for burglary and theft. The fifth man, Andrew, didn't know what he was in for, because he'd lost his memory. He said the police had told him he'd be staying put until he started remembering things. My colleagues told me to abandon any great hope of getting out swiftly. I could expect to be held for a long time while 'investigations' continued. They told me the police kept some people in custody indefinitely for no reason other than some officer taking a dislike to them. I wished fervently I hadn't tried to grab the desk sergeant. I hoped he wasn't the type to bear a grudge. I wondered if it was too late for an apology.

Some hours later, as the others dozed, Johnny whispered that I should be wary of Andrew, the supposed amnesia sufferer. He said, 'He's a cop.' Apparently, the police moved him from cell to cell to gather information. Normally, I'd have considered such a suggestion ridiculous. But now nothing done by these upholders of the law could surprise me.

Around two in the morning, a policeman called me from the cell. He led me to a room which was empty apart from a single chair in the middle. He told me to sit on it. I assumed I was about to be interviewed. I sat there for around 45 minutes before the policeman returned. He ordered me to follow him. He took me straight back to the cell, slammed shut the door, and walked away. I felt a bit unnerved. I asked Johnny if this procedure was normal. He laughed and said, 'Anything is normal in this place.'

During the day, the heat in the cell was unbearable. It didn't matter where you moved, you couldn't escape it. In the early evening, the rain fell heavily for about an hour, flooding the floor. The clouds cleared and the sun beamed down again, turning the cell into a Turkish bath. It stank to white man's heaven.

The one other meal of the day, delivered late afternoon, wasn't any more appetising than breakfast. It looked like a bowl of hot water with some sort of plant life floating on top. And more dry bread. Again, I let one of my cellmates have it. The police came for me around seven that evening. Once again, I was led to the room with the single chair. After half an hour, a detective came in and told me to follow him. He was in his mid-40s and looked mean, very mean. I was thankful I wasn't black.

He brought me into an office, sat me down and stared at me. He said, 'You English bastards. You're worse than the bloody blecks.' That was all I needed: an anti-English racist. His face seemed familiar. I had a feeling I might have met him at that meeting for the Brit-hating Afrikaner Resistance Movement. I could imagine him, khaki-clad on horseback, hunting blacks and Anglos across the veld.

He began questioning me about the guns that had been in my flat when I'd been arrested. I explained they'd been issued to me by my company. I admitted I didn't have a work permit.

'What?' he said. 'No fucking permit? You're a tourist, and you think you can stroll round our city, armed to the teeth, assaulting and threatening our citizens? You've come to the wrong place, sonny.' He said that, come what may, he'd make sure I was deported. He seemed to take my presence in his country very personally. I'd really upset him. I prayed the desk sergeant wasn't his mate.

He questioned me about the assault on my friend Colin and about my threats to kill the Portuguese which he said I'd shouted at them during the disturbance. He seemed to be fishing around to see what charges he could bring. I tried explaining that everything stemmed from the incident some weeks earlier when I'd been cut by one of their mates outside my flat.

This seemed to turn on a light in his head. He left the room and returned a moment later with a file. He sat there reading it for a few minutes. Then he held up the statement I'd signed regarding this earlier incident. He said, 'Is this yours?' I said it was. He tore it up into about eight pieces, threw the remains in the bin and said, 'Well, we won't be needing that then.'

He led me out of the room to the reception area where I was charged with assaulting the Portuguese woman two weeks earlier. I felt gobsmacked, but for the moment there wasn't much I could do. The detectives told me they'd be seeking my deportation and therefore needed my last address outside the Republic. I didn't want to give them my English address in case they contacted the English police, who'd no doubt inform them of my wanted status. I gave them the address of Angie's flat in Amsterdam. I was told that, when the time came, I'd be deported to Holland.

They photographed me, fingerprinted me and noted all distinguishing marks on my body before returning me to my cell. The other prisoners told me that, now I'd been charged, I'd be taken to court the following morning.

At night, the cell turned into a fridge – the frozen-food compartment. My mind filled with ifs and maybes, and I couldn't sleep. The cells never fell silent. The slamming of doors and the despairing cries of prisoners didn't stop. Around midnight, I heard shouting outside. A woman started screaming. I heard the door of our adjacent cell being slammed shut. As the jailer's footsteps faded, I could hear a woman sobbing uncontrollably. I called out to her and asked if she was all right. Her voice conveyed a sense of absolute terror. She said, 'Please help me! Please help me! The guards have threatened to rape me!'

I told her they were just trying to scare her. I said nothing would happen to her. She shouldn't show she was scared, because they'd just play on it. In truth, I couldn't be sure nothing would happen to her. As Johnny had said, and as I'd already found out myself, in this place anything was possible and everything was normal.

She said she'd been arrested for 'stealing' a car which she'd bought legitimately from a showroom two weeks earlier. 'They want me to say I stole it. I've never broken the law in my life. I'm married with children. Please help me.'

I spoke to her on and off throughout the night. She became a lot calmer.

I never found out what happened to her, because in the early morning I was loaded with several other prisoners into a truck with a wire-mesh back door. About 15 minutes later, the truck drove into a courtyard. We all got out. Police led us into what seemed like a long tunnel under the courts.

For the first time since my arrest, I found myself sitting with black prisoners. One black youth sat there sobbing. He had a gaping wound in his side. It had been dressed, but badly. I was told he'd been shot by police as he ran from a car that had been broken into. Another man stood there completely naked. His clothes had been taken away, supposedly for forensic examination, and hadn't been replaced.

I kept thinking about my ex-colleague Dougie and the events I'd witnessed; the events I'd allowed to happen. No doubt, our black victims had ended up down here, bewildered, humiliated and terrified, yet usually guilty of nothing. I felt like scum. I wanted to fly a thousand miles away from this demented country. I could hardly believe that only a few weeks earlier, I'd wanted to defend this system and way of life.

After a few hours' waiting, I heard my name being called out. A jailer escorted me uptairs to the courtroom. I looked up into the public gallery and saw Colin. For the first time since my arrest, I felt a surge of relief. He indicated with hand gestures that he'd got me a solicitor. South Africa had no legal-aid system. Either you paid for justice or you didn't get it. That was another reason so many black people ended up being railroaded to jail – or the gallows.

I couldn't understand what was being said, because my solicitor and the court officials spoke in Afrikaans. But after a few minutes of, to me, incomprehensible jabber, my lawyer leaned over and said, 'You can get bail if you're willing to surrender your passport and pay 1,000 rand in cash.' I said, 'Tell them it's done.' I told him to sort out the cash with Colin.

Moments later, I was being led back down the stairs into the tunnel. It's hard to describe the awful atmosphere below. The air stank of sweat and fear. Everybody sat staring at the floor. Everyone looked troubled. Some looked desperate and defeated. I could barely imagine the suffering this miserable place had witnessed over the years. You could sense it in the heavy air.

I'd relaxed considerably, because I thought I'd soon be walking out. But, to my alarm, the police loaded me back into the truck and said I was being taken to the notorious Deepcliffe Prison. I kept saying I'd been granted bail, but no one wanted to listen. My heart sank to my toes.

In the truck, I sat near the exit, looking through the wire mesh as the driver pulled out of the courtyard. Then a little morale-booster brought my heart back up: Colin was following in a car. I had one of those strange, dreamy moments when everything seems peculiar. Here I was being driven through the streets of Johannesburg in the back of a prison truck on a beautifully sunny day with my friend in desperate pursuit. This was hardly the new life of which we'd dreamed.

We reached Deepcliffe in an hour or so. They unloaded us and led us into a reception area. One by one, we were called forward. When my turn came, I had to stand on a wooden box and answer a series of mundane questions from a screw standing behind a counter. Name, age, address, religion, birthmarks, mother's maiden name. I told him I shouldn't be there. I said, 'I got bail, mate. Check with the courts.'

He gave a look of mock concern and said, 'Oh, really! Don't tell me – we're swapping you for Barabbas. Put this name-badge on, hold these papers, stand over there and shut up.'

I had to stand there for another half-hour as they documented everyone. Then they led us through the prison. I'd just about resigned myself to another spell in custody when I heard my name being called. I was taken back out to the reception area and into the office of a man I assumed was the prison governor.

He said, 'Your bail's been paid, O'Mahoney, and your passport's been lodged with us. Do you understand that if you don't appear in court, your friend who paid your bail will lose his money?' I said I did. I wasn't concerned about the money. I'd told Colin to take it from my own account. I signed a form and in two minutes I was walking back out the main gate as a free man. Colin was waiting for me.

It was 30 December 1985 and I had only one thought in my mind: how to flee the country before New Year. Trying to travel without a passport presented a significant hurdle. But I had an idea. I drove with Colin to the capital, Pretoria, where a few months earlier we'd tried to enlist in the army. I already had an open return ticket. I went to a travel agent's, showed them my ticket and said that, because of a bereavement, I had to get back to England as soon as possible.

The earliest available flight, leaving on New Year's Day and taking me as far as Brussels, involved flying via Nairobi, Cairo, Madrid and Geneva. I said, 'No problem. I'll take it.'

Ticket in hand, I then went to a nearby police station. I told them I'd been visiting my sister to help her pack. She was moving back to England to get married. Unfortunately, I couldn't find my passport. I had a horrible feeling I'd accidentally packed it away in my sister's belongings, which were now on their way to England.

I had to fly out the day after tomorrow. What could I do? I showed him my plane ticket. He walked off, returning moments later with a lost-property form. He filled it out, stamped it and told me to take it to the British Embassy down the road. At the embassy, they checked I held a valid passport before issuing me with an emergency 'one-way' passport. This 'passport' was in fact just an A4 piece of paper declaring my right to travel on one journey only from Johannesburg to England.

I now had all I needed, apart from the certainty that I'd get out of the country. I knew if they carried out proper checks at the airport they'd suss me out. I'd be arrested and wouldn't get bail until my case had been dealt with. I imagined the next year stuck on remand in a South African prison cell.

I'd let a few people in on my plan. Not everyone thought it was a good idea. Someone suggested it might be better to cross a river on the northern border. But I discovered the river was crocodile-infested – and the far shore a haven for anti-apartheid guerrillas. Someone else suggested travelling to Durban or Cape Town and stowing away on a ship. I felt on balance that my own plan was the best, so long as I kept my head and didn't appear suspicious at the airport.

The next day, New Year's Eve, the day before my planned departure, Colin, a few of our friends and I went to a huge street party in the centre of Johannesburg. The city was celebrating its centenary and the streets were packed with people: white people. In the evening, the city centre became a black-free zone. Black people lived under a curfew. Apart from those with special work permits, all blacks had to be back in their townships by ten at the latest.

Cheers went up as the New Year swept in. A few glass bottles fell to the ground. The police must have thought they had a potential riot on their hands. Using loudhailers, they ordered the crowd to disperse. Nobody paid attention. Everybody kept partying. The occasional bottle could still be heard crashing to the ground. I watched as a line of riot police formed up across the street. Again, the police used loudhailers to order the crowd's dispersal. Again, everyone ignored the order.

Suddenly, the police started firing tear gas into the crowd. Then the riot police began advancing, batons in hand. I suppose it was a fitting end to a century of oppression.

I didn't enjoy my last night in South Africa. I walked the streets alone until five in the morning. I went into a couple of bars, but felt so sick with worry that I couldn't even drink. I knew if I was caught, I'd have no legal rights. They could pretty much do with me what they wanted, for as long as they wanted. There'd be no civil rights lawyer to read the police the Riot Act on my behalf. I wouldn't just be dealing with a few bent Old Bill trying to give me a hard time. The whole fucking system was in on this one. I knew I'd done wrong. Perhaps I deserved punishment. But surely I was entitled to my rights? I found myself sneering at myself. In my head I'd started sounding like a bleating-heart liberal blubbering about bully-boy Nazis. I remembered an old joke. Q: What do you call a liberal? A: A conservative who's been arrested.

Or, in my case, a Nazi who's been arrested and imprisoned in South Africa.

The next day, I packed my bags and went to the airport with Colin and a few other friends. Another piece of bad news was that Claire's brother had been repeatedly stabbed in an unprovoked attack by Portuguese. He remained quite seriously ill for some time. Hillbrow, where we all lived, was getting more and more violent. When he'd made a full recovery, the family moved back to Essex.

I checked in for my flight, handed over my luggage and went for a drink in the bar in the hope of steadying my nerves. I kept looking at my emergency passport, that pathetic piece of paper. I thought any official with a spare brain cell was bound to check it out. My 'passport' seemed to grow more laughably, transparently bogus with every second that ticked by.

My time came. Colin was flying home to England in a fortnight. I told him I'd see him either in half an hour – being led back to the cells – or in two weeks' time. We said our goodbyes and I walked off towards passport control.

I asked myself if I was walking too fast or too slow. Being normal is easy. Trying to act normal is a nightmare. I didn't know where to look or where to put my hands. I stood in the queue, trying vainly to control my sweat glands. Then it was my turn to show my passport. The man at the gate gave it a quick glance – and waved me through. I'd done it. I'd fucking done it. I felt elated.

Then, more doubts. I wouldn't be safe until the plane had taken off. Surely some Nazi bully-boy could still jump on and do a spot check? I sat shaking in my seat on the plane. I just wanted the 747 to move, to fly off, but it just sat there. I really began to believe they'd checked all the names on the boarding cards and had identified me as a fugitive from justice.

The stewardesses shut the doors. Relief. The plane began to ease itself backwards away from the terminal. More relief. It taxied onto the runway and came to a halt. Then the engines began to roar. Finally, my metal bird of freedom accelerated up the runway and zoomed off into the clouds.

I knew I was safe. I was going home. Even the thought that I might be heading for arrest and imprisonment didn't worry me.

CHAPTER 10

FUNERAL FOR A FRIEND

'PASSPORT, PLEASE.'

I'd just stepped off the ferry at Dover. Earlier that day, I'd arrived in Brussels. I'd hoped to have a better chance of sneaking unnoticed into England on the ferry. A vain hope.

A very vain hope, because I couldn't have made myself more conspicuous if I'd had rabies. Unlike my fellow foot-passengers, each of whom carried at most a rucksack and a few plastic bags of duty-free, I was laden with three large suitcases and a bulky sports bag. And, unlike their pale skins, mine had been burnt so brown the Afrikaners could have classified me 'black' and allowed Dougie to shoot or hack me to death.

So the official's request to see my passport came as a disappointment, but no surprise. My disappointment intensified when I saw Debra at the other side of the barrier. I'd rung her in Brussels and explained my situation. She'd agreed to pick me up in her car. We'd exchanged a few letters and phone calls since we'd last seen each other some weeks earlier. She'd been disappointed I hadn't asked her out in Johannesburg. Now she'd have to wait even longer for our first date.

The official looked at my A4 piece of paper. He said, 'One moment, Sir.' He walked into a nearby office. A few minutes later, he came back out, accompanied by two men in suits.

'Bernard O'Mahoney?' said one of the detectives.

'That's me,' I said.

'Are you aware there's a warrant out for your arrest?'

'No, there must be some mistake.'

'Make it easy for us, Bernard. You're not going anywhere till we've checked it all out. So do everyone a favour.'

In a cell at Dover police station, Debra and I shared our first kiss. The police had allowed us a few minutes alone together when they discovered she'd driven down from Basildon in Essex. They'd also given her permission to take my luggage. And they'd even allowed me to phone my mother. If this decent treatment had continued, I could well have turned into one of those pub bores parroting, 'British justice? Best in the world, mate.'

Within 12 hours, I found myself sitting in a cell beneath Stafford Crown Court agreeing to a prosecution deal that involved my pleading guilty to 'unlawful wounding' in return for their dropping the 'wounding with intent' and other charges relating to my failure to appear.

Later in court, the judge told me a custodial sentence was unavoidable. He said, 'You cannot go around Staffordshire beating people up at your leisure, Mr O'Mahoney. You will go to prison for 12 months.'

It could have been worse. In six months, I'd be eligible for parole.

Over the next four weeks, they shifted me around various establishments until I ended up at HMP Ranby in Nottinghamshire. While there, Adolf came to visit me with Debra. They'd travelled up together on the train after meeting at London's Liverpool Street Station.

Debra told me later that, at the start of the journey, Adolf had given her a package wrapped in brown paper. It was about four inches wide and twelve inches long. He said, 'It's for you. Don't open it till you're on your way home.'

When they arrived at the station nearest the prison, Adolf put Debra in a taxi and said he'd follow later. He thought she should spend the first part of the visit alone with me. He announced he was going for a drink.

Halfway through the visit, a commotion of raised voices indicated Adolf had arrived. He stormed into the visiting room, looking dishevelled and phlegm-spattered, then strutted urgently towards our table. He sat down without saying hello and started ranting. 'Fucking Third World northerners,' he said. 'Fucking cunts. Unwashed, redundant scum.'

I pieced together that he'd started playing pool in a pub with some locals. A dispute about the rules had resulted in his chinning one or more of his fellow players before being bundled out the door.

'Cunts, fucking cunts,' he said. 'I never saw one of them drink a pint. Four of them huddled over two halves of lager and a packet of peanuts. Tried telling me "their" pool rules.'

On and on he went. He even started ranting at some of the screws. I didn't usually relish the end of a visit, but I was happy when this one reached the goodbyes.

Debra told me afterwards she'd sat opposite Adolf on the journey down. He hadn't eased up for one moment. She wasn't given the chance to speak a word. When he left her at Liverpool Street, he told her not to forget to open her 'present'. He said, 'This town's full of mugging scum. Don't be worried about using it.' Alone on the train home, she unwrapped his gift. It was a small machete.

I hadn't been at Ranby long when they put me in solitary confinement for allegedly trying to escape. I hadn't been trying to escape. I'd merely gone for a stroll in an out-of-bounds area. But the screws wouldn't listen. They refused to let me shatter their fantasy. They'd foiled an escape attempt. And nothing could be allowed to detract from their achievement. Not even the truth.

It was my first experience of solitary. My new apartment suite had been fitted out to minimalist standards. A slab of concrete represented the bedroom, a plastic bucket the bathroom. My permitted possessions comprised – although not all at the same time – the prison clothes I stood in (minus shoes) and the bedding (pillow, sheet and cover). At night, I had to hand over my clothes in order to get the bedding. I had nothing to write with or read, not even the Bible, and certainly no telly or radio. You'd have provided more home comforts for a dog.

A small, high window made of thick, frosted glass ensured I could barely distinguish night from day. The cell had obviously been designed to destroy any traits of humanity remaining in its occupant. The only human contact – and I'm probably stretching the definition here – came from twisted screws. Mercifully, this contact never lasted more than a few minutes each day. I came to understand how silence can sometimes be described as deafening. The dirty beige walls seemed to close in on me.

Hearing the jangle of keys would make my heart jump. I'd hope the screws were coming to let me out. And they knew it. One screw used to put his keys in my door, take them out again and laugh. Another told me that long-term prisoners could apply for ownership of their cells under the Conservative government's 'Right to Buy' scheme.

I didn't want them to think they could get to me. When I heard them coming, I'd sit cross-legged on the floor with my back to the door. I wouldn't even turn round at mealtimes, when they'd slide a tray of slop across the floor towards me.

It really used to annoy a few of them. One used to say, 'You think you're fucking clever, don't you?' After a fortnight, they let me return to the normal prison.

A man from Stafford called Mac left the solitary block at the same time. They put us both in a prefabricated hut which housed about ten prisoners. Our hut-mates were out at work when we arrived. We noticed a pigeon on top of one of the lockers. Mac tried shooing it outside, but it kept flying about. I told him to forget about it. He wouldn't listen. 'Pigeons are bloody vermin,' he said.

The bird reached the seeming safety of a rafter. Mac picked up a small but heavy block of wood being used to keep the door open. He threw it and, amazingly, scored a direct hit. The pigeon dropped dead to the floor.

Mac said, 'Fucking bingo! Did you see that? Incredible!' He threw the corpse outside.

Around four in the afternoon, the other prisoners started returning. Several of them were miners who'd fallen foul of the law during the year-long strike that had ended the previous year. When you asked them what they were in for – usually the first question one inmate asks another – they'd say, 'Political prisoner' or 'I'm not a fucking criminal'.

I didn't have much sympathy for them. I regarded them as red rabble who'd justifiably had their Marxist-led arses kicked by Mrs Thatcher.

Just as I was getting acquainted with some of my new Scargillite comrades, I heard shouting outside. The door burst open. A bald-headed man wearing thick-rimmed NHS glasses stood there holding the dead pigeon. He said in a loud voice trembling with emotion, 'I want to know . . . I want to know . . . I want to know who did this?'

I looked over at Mac. He rolled over as if to go to sleep. I said, 'I saw it on the ground when we came.'

We learnt that on the outside this man kept racing pigeons. During his stay in prison, he'd adopted the recently deceased bird. It used to sit on his bedside locker, patiently awaiting its master's return. The bereaved pigeon-fancier sat down tearfully on his bed. For half an hour, he stroked the still-warm feathers of his dear departed. Then he gave it a send-off not seen since Churchill's funeral.

Next day, without warning, Mac and I were moved 'for security reasons' to Lincoln Prison. The move left us both puzzled. We hadn't realised they took suspected pigeon murder so seriously.

Adolf sent several neo-Nazi publications to me at Lincoln. I didn't get a chance to read them, though, because the censors seized them. I was informed that 'racist' reading material was banned in the prison. Debra then paid me a visit. After her five-hour train journey, they allowed us just 55 minutes together. I told her not to bother again. They could fuck me about, but not her. I applied to move to HMP Stafford near my home, but they turned me down. The same thing happened to Mac.

I had an idea for getting us transferred. Prisoners had to post their letters unsealed in a special mailbox, so the censors could check their contents. Some prisoners also used this box to post notes informing on other inmates. Mac and I wrote a note informing on ourselves. We accused us of supplying 'gear' (that is, heroin) and hiring out 'a works' (that is, a syringe). Stafford is the prison system's dustbin, where the screws send violent and unruly prisoners, so we felt sure we'd end up there if the governor wanted to rid his model establishment of two suspected drug dealers.

1	2
3	4

1. My father Patrick in Birmingham in the 1950s.
2. My mother is holding me as my brothers Paul (left) and Jerry stand on either side.
3. My brother Paul wearing his American cop's uniform, with pistol, in the back garden in Codsall in the late '60s.
4. Me holding my brother Michael in a field outside Wolverhampton in 1968. Out of shot, my mother is picking potatoes with the Asian workers terrorised by Hell's Angels.

THE FOOLS THE FOOLS
THEY HAVE LEFT US OUR FENIAN
DEAD AND WHILE IRELAND HOLDS
THESE GRAVES IRELAND UNFREE
SHALL NEVER BE AT PEACE

5. Me wearing my parade uniform at Catterick Barracks in Yorkshire just before passing out in 1979.
6. Me (right) blacked up with fellow soldier Phil Evans at St Angelo's in Northern Ireland in 1981.
7. Me alongside a republican wall mural on Belfast's Falls Road.

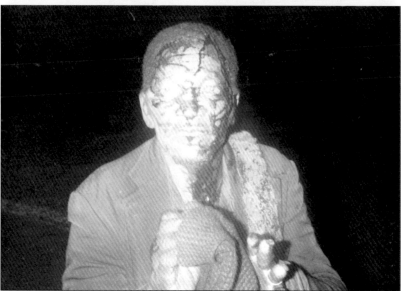

8. Colin and I fully equipped to start our nightclub shift in Johannesburg, South Africa, in 1985.

9. Dougie's photo, given to me as a 'memento' of South Africa. A homeless black man beaten during a raid on an illegal drinking den in Soweto.

10. Our 'good friend' Tim is manacled to the balcony of our Johannesburg flat, still smiling, unaware he's about to be sprayed with CS gas and beaten with truncheons.

11. 1987. The last time I was together with my elder brothers: Jerry left, Paul right.

12. Adrian 'Army Game' Boreham pictured some months before his death in a car accident in September 1987.

13. Me wearing a National Front T-shirt behind the right shoulder of a television presenter at the Vauxhall by-election count in Brixton Town Hall in June 1989. Screaming Lord Sutch of the Monster Raving Loony Party can be seen on the presenter's left.

14. From left: Ray, Del Boy, Adolf and me on an away day in 1990.

15. My 'business associates' Tony Tucker (left) and Pat Tate (middle) with me (right) on a night out at the Epping Country Club in Essex in late 1995, a few weeks before they were murdered in a Range Rover with Craig Rolfe.

16. Me with my mate from Raquels, fellow doorman Gavin.

*7 IKON/SQR
00:28:1 18.MAY99

TAXI

THE ORDER
ISSUE 16
BM BOX 5608
LONDON
WC1N3XX
ENGLAND

NOT SO CLEVER NOW, ARE YOU!

11:02

17. CCTV footage captures Gaffer, 'the most dangerous man in Britain', fleeing from me outside a Basildon nightclub.
18. Picture secretly taken inside the Ku Klux Klan meeting in Birmingham in 1996. I'm turning away from the table.
19. My photo is splashed across the front page of Combat 18's magazine, *The Order*, threatening me as 'red hack scum' for having exposed their 'kith and kin', the Klan.

20. Prior to his bombing campaign, David Copeland (wearing a baseball cap) stands behind BNP leader John Tyndall, whose face is bloodied after a brush with political opponents in east London.

21. Patsy Scanlon's would-be lover, nail-bomber David Copeland.

22. Me (left) with brothers Paul (centre) and Michael at Ray's funeral in October 2002.

23. Larry 'The Slash' smoking at my wedding reception in July 2004.

24. Some of my south London gang hidden among other friends and relatives at Ray's funeral. From left: 'Benny the Jew', my brother Paul, Mark, Sean, me, Colin, Alan, Ray's brother Tony, Steve, Del Boy, my brother Michael.

25. My wedding in July 2004 with family and friends, old and new. Back row, from left: Rashed, brother Michael, son Adrian, Natasha (my wife's cousin), my wife Emma, me, daughter Karis, my mother, Hughie, Adolf, Gavin, son Vinney. At the front, my brother Michael's son Finn is wearing the top hat. The bridesmaids are, from left: Sophia (Natasha's daughter), Lauren and Ebony (the daughters of Emma's sister Siobhan), and Lilly (Michael's daughter).

That evening, a team of grim-faced screws burst into our cell. These were rubber-gloved men on a mission. They ordered us to strip, then dug determinedly into our arse-furrows for hidden treasure. They combed our clothes and possessions meticulously. They could have been panning for gold, so intense and concentrated were their faces. I kept saying, 'What's all this about?'

The chief screw would only say, 'You know, O'Mahoney. You know.'

The following morning, they came for us at work. They searched the workroom with painful meticulousness. Again, they left frustrated. The chief screw assured me, 'We'll find it in the end, O'Mahoney. Don't worry.' I told him I resented his insinuation I might be involved in something illegal.

We put another note in the mailbox. It said the gear being sold by those two evil slags O'Mahoney and Mac was so bad there was going to be trouble.

The next day, they wouldn't let us go to work. We asked why. They said, 'You're being transferred to Stafford.' These sorts of little victories helped make prison life bearable.

I stayed at Stafford until the end of my sentence. I was finally released in July 1986, having endured several months of industrial action by the Prison Officers' Association. Lock-up for 23 hours a day, no work, no visits and delayed mail provoked a major riot during my time there. A large minority of prisoners destroyed everything destroyable in their cells, burnt down the canteen, took to the roof and hurled tiles onto the street. But not me: I stayed out of it. I didn't fancy jeopardising my impending freedom.

On the day of my release, the screws took me to the reception area. I had to strip off my prison clothing and put it in a laundry bag. Then they ordered me to shower. As I stood there naked, a screw handed me a cardboard box containing the clothes I'd arrived in.

Naturally, they hadn't been washed, aired or folded. However, I still felt good putting on my own clothes, even if they stank of prison and made me look like a vagrant. A screw called out my name. I began my walk to freedom. I stood in front of the inner gate. The screw opened it and I stepped out onto the pavement, a free man determined to make a new start.

I went to live with Debra in Basildon. Both of us wanted to settle down and live a normal life. I felt I'd endured enough trouble to last a lifetime.

But within a few days I'd arranged to meet my old friends in south London. Adolf, Del Boy, Larry 'The Slash', 'Benny the Jew', Ray and his brother Tony were there to greet me. I asked where Adrian 'Army Game' and Colin were. I was told they'd tried joining the French Foreign Legion. 'That lasted about three weeks,' said Adolf. 'Now they've gone to live in Canada.'

Everyone wanted to know about South Africa. They treated me like a white knight returning from the crusades. I felt uncomfortable. Adolf, in particular, seemed to think I'd struck some sort of blow for the Aryan race. He chose to regard my forced departure as being the result of my being too right-wing. He doubted whether the Boers could maintain white rule for much longer if they continued to expel decent Nazis like myself.

Adolf also told me the story behind the bomb in Clapham High Street that had injured him while we were in South Africa. He said the police believed that Tony Lecomber's plan had been to bomb the headquarters of the far-left WRP as a response to the Tottenham riots and the hacking to death of PC Keith Blakelock. Lecomber had packed explosives and nails into a biscuit-tin. The device was being transported on his car's back seat when it exploded 200 yards from its destination. The police thought a radio signal from a nearby West-Indian-owned cab office had detonated it.

Adolf escaped prosecution. The police accepted his claim that he'd known nothing about the bomb. They believed him when he said he'd just accepted a lift from a friend.

A few months later, in November 1986, future BNP 'national organiser' Lecomber stood trial at the Old Bailey charged with making an explosive device intending to endanger life. However, the jury believed his defence that he'd only been 'experimenting' with bomb-making as a hobby and had not built the bomb for any political use.

The judge could only sentence him on the lesser charges. He

got three years' imprisonment for possessing the contents of the biscuit-tin (and ten home-made grenades, seven detonators and two petrol bombs).

By the end of the evening, I was so drunk I had to be helped to Liverpool Street Station by my friends. They put me on a train. I don't think it was the right one, because I woke up in Clacton early next morning. Debra, though unamused, seemed pleased I hadn't got into any trouble.

I did my best to settle down into a 'normal' life. I couldn't find work locally, so I ended up driving tipper lorries for a south London firm. I had to leave the house at 4.30 a.m. to catch the train. I never got home before seven in the evening.

We lived in a block of flats in the roughest part of Basildon, on a housing estate known as 'Alcatraz'. It got its nickname from the maze of alleyways connecting the cramped, Legoland-type flats and houses. One of our female neighbours would hold a party whenever she found a new boyfriend. So I could rely on my sleep being disturbed at least three times a week. The barking of her dog would accompany the pounding music. Revellers would urinate, fornicate, vomit and argue on the stairs outside my front door.

One night, I reached the end of my short tether. Around two in the morning, the sound of a screaming row tore me out of my sleep. I put on a pair of boxer shorts and opened the front door. My neighbour and her latest boyfriend stood in the stairwell exchanging unpleasantries. I walked the few paces over to them and said to the boyfriend, 'I'm not having a debate about it, mate. I get up in two hours. Fuck off or I'll kill you.'

He just grinned at me moronically. The alcohol fumes from both of them could have put me over the drink-driving limit. I'd had enough. Bang. I chinned him. He flew backwards down the stairs. His girlfriend started screaming. I told her to shut up, closed my door and went back to bed.

A short time later, someone started banging loudly on my front door. I got up again. I thought, 'If it's the boyfriend, he's going over the balcony.' I opened the door to be faced by a policeman. Several other officers stood in the background with dogs. Alsatian dogs, that is, not my noisy neighbour and her female friends.

I could see my neighbour and her boyfriend, the latter bleeding from facial wounds. As soon as he saw me, he shouted, 'That's the cunt! Arrest him!' The officer said he wanted to question me about an alleged assault and threats to kill.

I said, 'For fuck's sake, mate. Unlike most of the fuckers round here, I work for a living. I'm up in less than two hours. How can I not react when these people are pissing, puking, fucking and fighting on my doorstep all night?'

The policeman looked at me in my boxers, then looked at the drunken boyfriend – who'd now begun screaming obscenities – and told me to go to bed.

My neighbour found herself a new boyfriend. The partying continued. In the end, I broke into her flat one day when she was out. I smashed her stereo to bits, stamped on all her tapes and tried to hurl her snarling dog over the balcony. However, the hound sensed my hostile intentions. It scampered round the flat, bared its teeth whenever I got near and stayed just out of my grasp. I was making too much noise. To avoid being caught, I abandoned my mission. The dog lived to bark another day, but my neighbour became quieter.

During the week, I had no time for anything other than working, eating and sleeping. On Saturdays, I'd start work at the same time, but finish at lunch-time. Then I'd allow myself a few beers with my friends in south London.

Within a few months, Adrian and Colin had returned from Canada. They declared the country to be 'full of Jews' and therefore, in their opinion, unfit to live in. With everyone back home, the 'few beers' on Saturday afternoons soon turned into full sessions, complete with inevitable bar-room brawls.

One day, my eldest brother, Jerry, rang to tell me his mother-in-law had shot her husband. I suppose I should have been surprised, but years of drama connected to our family had deadened my shock-sensors. Jerry said it had 'come out' that his wife had been abused by her father. The mother had picked up a shotgun and chased her husband through the house. He'd locked himself in the downstairs bathroom, but she'd fired through the door, then run outside, pushed the barrel through the small, open window and fired again. Pellets had hit the man in his foot and head, but Jerry said his injuries weren't life-threatening.

'They will be when we catch him,' I said. I told Jerry I'd bring up a few lads to sort out the 'child abuser' while his wife sat in custody. I don't know why I took everything so personally. I shouldn't have wanted to stick my nose in, because I didn't even know the family. I'd met Jerry's wife briefly, but not her parents. I suppose stories of abused children always trigger extreme reactions in me. I rang my friends. Only Ray, Benny, Adrian and Colin were available at such short notice. After a drinking session, we decided to steal a car and drive up to the Midlands.

Adrian spotted an old Morris Traveller parked in a Clapham street. He opened the door and soon got the engine turning, but the car wouldn't start. It needed petrol. We walked to the nearest garage and bought a can. We delegated Benny to put it in the tank, while we stayed at the garage. We didn't want nosy neighbours alerted by a group of dodgy-looking men standing around a car late at night.

When Benny returned, Adrian said he'd start the car, then pick us up. He arrived back on foot a short while later. He swore at Benny, 'You fucking dickhead. You've filled up the wrong car.' We bought another can of petrol. Eventually, we got going.

It was almost daylight when we drove into Wolverhampton. We drove to our target's home. Nobody was in. A bottle was thrown through the glass pane in the front door. Then we drove to a large industrial estate where he ran a firm that hired out heavy-lifting cranes. We thought the 'nonce' might be hiding out there.

It was Sunday morning, so the estate was empty. We booted down his warehouse door. After a brief search, we established he wasn't there. We doused the warehouse and a few cranes with petrol, then set them alight. We sped away, satisfied with our act of vigilante justice.

Later that afternoon, we arrived back in London. We heard our other friends had gone to some sort of fête on Clapham Common. Most of us thought we ought to avoid the area as we'd stolen the car there. But Adrian said he'd drive carefully and abandon the car discreetly within easy walking distance of the beer tent. 'Relax,' said Adrian. 'No one'll notice us.'

He drove through Stockwell and up the Clapham Road. Then I spotted the beer tent on the Common. I said to Adrian, 'Just find somewhere off the main road, mate.'

At that, he swerved the car sharply with a tyre-screech, mounted the pavement with a bone-jarring bump and drove straight across the grass of the Common, scattering bystanders, before parking outside the tent's packed entrance. We all jumped out, shocked but laughing. Amid shouting and swearing from some of those who'd almost been mown down, we disappeared into the crowd.

My brother Jerry's mother-in-law got five years' imprisonment when her case came to trial. That didn't shock me. What did shock me, and my brother, was the true reason she'd shot her husband. Apparently, he'd been having an affair with his secretary. The 'child abuse' story had been invented by the mother, and her daughter had backed her up. My brother got divorced shortly afterwards.

Despite events such as this, I had actually become more responsible. The demands of work meant I had less time to get into trouble. And Debra was pregnant. In June 1987, she gave birth to our son, Vinney. We'd both wanted children and were both extremely happy. Vinney gave meaning to the long hours I worked.

His arrival also caused me to look more critically at my life and to reflect more on my behaviour. I suppose I started seeing everyone as someone's son or daughter. Previously, my people-hating attitude wouldn't allow such a fact to register. Now I could imagine the pain and anguish parents would feel if their loved ones fell victim to violence from me and my friends. Not that the beast was tamed. There are no overnight conversions to decent living. I could still feel within me that short-fuse anger and potential for violence. I just started trying a bit harder to keep a lid on myself.

Adolf rang me early one morning in mid-August 1987. He asked me if I wanted to go to the funeral. I said, 'Whose funeral? Who's died?'

He began ranting. 'Died? Died? Who's fucking died? Are you telling me you don't know?'

'I'm sorry, mate. I really don't know.'

'Rudolph Hess! Rudolph Hess has been murdered by ZOG!'

I had in fact heard on the news that Hitler's former deputy had committed suicide in his Berlin prison. I said, 'Oh yeah, I heard on the news he'd died.'

'No doubt you heard he'd "died" on Jewish TV. He didn't just die. He was murdered by ZOG. I think we should go to his funeral.'

'Right. It's in Clapham, is it?'

'Don't provoke me to anger, Bernard. It's in Germany. The Fatherland.' He said we'd have a 'top away-day', meeting fascists from all over the world. He said, 'It's bound to go off with the reds and we can have a bit of a jolly up.'

I had a few days off, but I didn't fancy spending them at an international neo-Nazi jamboree in Germany. I'd long begun to find the whole scene irrelevant. Only Adolf kept me involved. I told him that, even if I wanted to go, I couldn't afford it. He said I was lazy, useless and just like the others, who'd also turned down the suggested outing. He added that he'd expected better of someone who'd travelled to the other side of the world for the Aryan cause.

Adolf had a way of making me feel like a spineless and unreliable backslider. Foolishly, I said that if I had the money, I'd go. 'Good!' he screamed. 'I'll pay for everything. Meet me at Victoria Station at ten. Don't worry about the money. Bye.' The line went dead.

On the way to meet Adolf, I read a discarded broadsheet newspaper on the train. A story about Hess had been filed by the news agency UPI on 21 August 1987:

> Bavarian security officials and the family of the late Nazi war criminal Rudolph Hess, once deputy to Adolf Hitler, complained today that neo-Nazis are using his death to spread propaganda and stage provocations.
>
> The Hess family hid the body of the former Nazi leader, said by Allied officials to have committed suicide in a Berlin war-crimes prison Monday at age 93, somewhere in northern Bavaria after British military authorities turned it over to them Thursday.

> Wolf-Ruediger Hess, 50, son of the dead man, arranged Thursday evening for his father's burial in a family plot in Wunsiedel, about 70 miles north-east of Nuremberg – the city where Hess and other top Nazis were tried by the Allied powers after World War Two.
>
> Rudolph Hess, who spent most of World War Two interned in Britain after parachuting into Scotland with a bizarre peace proposal on May 10 1941, was convicted of war crimes at Nuremburg in 1946 and given a life sentence.

I declined Adolf's offer of money and paid for my own journey, which was a bit like buying the bullets for my own firing squad.

Sharing a long journey with Adolf – as Debra had once discovered – is like being strapped into a seat by a torturer who forces you to wear headphones through which the music of a stuck record is played at full blast.

I can't remember the ferry, the towns we passed through or even any real conversation between us. I can just recall his trying to 'explain' things about the Nazis. When my interest showed signs of fading, when the matchsticks holding open my eyelids fell out, he'd rant about my being an 'armchair Nazi', a 'conspirator' or merely 'blind to the enemy'.

Many years later, as I was doing a bit of research for this book, I read a tribute to Hess in a Nazi magazine. Suddenly, I felt transported back to that awful 15-hour journey with Adolf. It was like a dreadful flashback to some long-buried trauma. Adolf's ranting voice came once again to my ears, spitting terms like 'National Socialist martyr' and 'an immortal hero of the Aryan race':

> Nearly sixty years ago, there was a man who held the position of deputy leader of a world power. His career was at its peak. The future for his nation, for him, and his millions of supporters looked glorious. This man gave up everything: his position, his family and eventually even his life trying to save Europe from a devastating brothers' war.
>
> In a sane society, such a man would be considered the hero of his century and be awarded the Nobel Peace Prize

along with utmost praise and admiration. But we do not live in such a sane world. We live in a grotesque and twisted society under the awesome iron heel of world Zionism.

In such a hellish place, where all values have been turned upside down, a messenger of peace between Aryan peoples is condemned as a criminal warmonger and awarded with 46 years' imprisonment before being murdered by the hidden hand of the Allies' secret service.

We arrived in Cologne, still a long way from Bavaria. We spoke to a few German neo-Nazis outside the station. They said we had no chance of getting anywhere near Hess's funeral. Adolf didn't believe them. He viewed them contemptuously as liars, weaklings and 'conspirators'.

In the early hours of the morning, we caught a train to Frankfurt. We took a look around the city as we waited for our next train to Wunsiedel, near the Czech border. Adolf expressed pleasure at the amount of graffiti in honour of Hess. Most daubings read simply, 'Rudolph Hess, German hero, murdered 1987'.

We met some more German neo-Nazis. They also told us to forget about the funeral. They said the police had sealed off the town and probably wouldn't even let us leave the station. Again, Adolf refused to believe them. He suspected ZOG had paid them to dress as Nazis in order to deter true Nazis from paying homage to a great leader. He said, 'They can't fool us. We'll catch our train as planned.'

However, when we went to board it, a group of well-padded German Robocops stopped us. They asked to see our passports and tickets, then made us accompany them to the station's police office. They said they needed to check our documents. They kept us sitting there till we'd missed our train. We remonstrated, but they threatened to arrest us.

Eventually, they let us go, but warned us not to try to head for Wunsiedel. I said to Adolf I saw no point trying to continue: we wouldn't get anywhere near the funeral and, if we tried, we'd just end up being detained on some pretext. I thought he might rant at me for being a defeatist, but surprisingly he himself conceded defeat. We went on the piss in Frankfurt instead. Adolf said, 'At least we made the fucking effort. Not like the fucking others.'

Gradually, our group of friends in south London began drifting apart. Del Boy had been sentenced to five years' imprisonment after being caught at customs with a large amount of cocaine following a trip to Holland. My brother Paul sat in jail, too. He'd been sentenced to 18 months for a violent assault. Adrian 'Army Game' and Colin had finally found the only army in the world prepared to accept them – the British Army.

Adolf rang me on the morning of 1 September 1987. I thought he might have been phoning to remind me of the 48th anniversary of Hitler's stormtroopers marching into Poland. I was wrong. He said, 'I've got some bad news.' He sounded quiet and sombre. 'Adrian's dead.'

I said, 'Dead? How can he be dead?'

Adolf explained that Adrian and three other soldiers had crashed their car in Germany. Adrian and two of his friends had died. Only the driver had survived. I thanked Adolf for calling and put the phone down. I sat on my bed and wept.

Del Boy and my brother couldn't get day-release from prison to attend the funeral. Colin applied for compassionate leave, but the army refused to grant it. He walked out of the camp gate – and 17 years later has still not returned.

On the day of the funeral, a few of us agreed to meet at The Royal Oak in Stockwell. It was a fitting venue because so many of our memories of Adrian revolved around it. We remained barred, but that didn't matter a jot to us that day.

As soon as we walked in, I spotted Buzz, the brave but foolhardy barman who'd informed on Adrian, Colin, Ray and another friend and got all but Colin locked up.

'You fucking wanker,' I said. 'Get out of our sight or you're fucking dead.'

Buzz, never one to be intimidated, told me to get lost, so I hit him. Customers jumped to defend him and a free-for-all erupted. I held Buzz, trying to land punches in his face. Others tried to pull me off him, tearing my shirt and making my nose bleed in the process. A stand-off ensued. Buzz disappeared behind the bar and we decided to leave.

I had to buy a new shirt before heading to Adrian's father's house on Battersea Bridge Road, from where the funeral cortège would set off. I hadn't been back there since Adrian, Colin and I had trashed the Carlsberg salesman's flat some years earlier. As soon as I walked in and saw my friends, I had to go to the toilet to stem my tears. I felt really choked up. Back in the living room, no one knew what to say.

After a short while, someone announced, 'Adrian's here.' We all made our way outside to the hearse. The coffin containing our dead friend lay in the back, covered in flowers. The pub and several shops near his house closed. Numerous people, including a policeman, showed their respects as the cortège passed slowly on its way to the church.

Outside the church, a few of the lads broke down. Adolf rounded on them, 'Be men, not snivelling tarts.' I told him he was out of order. We began to argue and almost exchanged blows, but others intervened and we dropped the matter.

After the burial, we all headed back to Adrian's house for a drink. Before long, we were all steaming. Frank Sinatra's 'Strangers in the Night' was played endlessly, while Colin staggered around singing the song's 'Shoo be doo be doo' line at the top of his voice.

Around seven, Ray and Tony said they couldn't drink any more. Adrian's dad phoned a minicab for them. We carried on drinking. Every few minutes, either Ray or Tony would pull back the front-room curtain to see if their cab had arrived. Eventually, Ray spotted a Datsun outside with its hazard lights on. For some reason, the Datsun acted as the carriage of choice for many south London minicab drivers. The two brothers said goodbye and left.

A few seconds later, we heard Ray shouting outside at the top of his voice. We all ran out. Ray and Tony were standing next to the Datsun. A West Indian woman sat in the passenger seat. There was no sign of the driver. Ray had opened the door and was shouting, 'Please get out of my fucking cab. This is my cab. I ordered it.'

The woman was shouting back, 'Shut the door. Fuck off or I'll call the police.'

Ray replied, 'Call the fucking police. I don't give a fuck. The law's on my side. This is my cab.'

And so it went on.

Eventually, Ray tried to manhandle the woman out of the car. She resisted fiercely, slapping and punching him. Before any real damage had been done, a West Indian man ran up to the car. He said, 'Hey! Hey! What's going on? Stop it! Stop it!'

We assumed he was the driver. Tony said, 'We ordered this cab, mate, and this bitch has tried to nick it.'

'Cab?' said the man. 'This car ain't no cab and that "bitch" is my girlfriend. We've broken down. I just went to use the phone.'

Somehow, it seemed like an appropriate farewell to our friend Adrian.

CHAPTER 11

ALL TATTERED AND TORN

I'VE BEEN TOLD THAT WORD EXPERTS BELIEVE THE WORD 'HOOLIGAN' BECAME popularised in part by a late nineteenth-century book called *The Hooligan Nights*. The author, Clarence Rook, claimed to have identified the word's origins in the deeds of a south-London-based Irish criminal called 'Patrick Hooligan'. A doorman with 'an exuberance of lawlessness', this probably fictional character was said to have died in prison after beating a policeman to death. His followers, 'the Hooligans', supposedly lived 'within a stone's throw of Lambeth Walk' and were described as 'sturdy young villains, who start with a grievance against society, and are determined to get their own back'.

Be that as it may, 'supporting' Millwall became the main outlet for my anti-social urges. Being bad brings joy to those at war with 'normal' society. But being bad is never enough. You want to be the baddest. The ultimate baddies are Nazis. But high up there in the badness charts – back then, at least – sat the hooligans of Millwall FC, the 'Bushwhackers'. Their arch-rivals from West Ham United FC, the 'Inter City Firm', vied with them for top dishonours.

In November 1987, Millwall drew West Ham ('the Hammers') in one of the early rounds of what used to be known as the League Cup. By then, the competition had some ridiculous name I've forgotten. (Gonad Cup? Simod Cup? Something like that.) It had been ten years since the teams had last met. Both sets of hooligans had spent a whole decade yearning to clash again.

The game loomed like a hooligans' FA Cup final (if FA stood for 'Fuck Authority'). My south London friends talked of little else. Years earlier, a Millwall fan had died after being pushed in front of a tube train by West Ham fans. Now the day of retribution had arrived.

The night before the game, a group of us went to The Gin Palace down the Old Kent Road. Millwall supporters filled the pub with their bodies and their voices. Everyone was singing as if on the terraces of 'the Den'. The favourite song – to the tune of Rod Stewart's 'Sailing' – went:

> No one likes us,
> No one likes us,
> No one likes us,
> We don't care.
> We are Millwall,
> Super Millwall,
> We are Millwall from the Den.

A close second, also sung on a loop, to the tune of 'My Bonnie Lies Over the Ocean', came:

> He's only a poor little Hammer.
> His face is all tattered and torn.
> He made me feel sick,
> So I hit him with a brick,
> And now he don't sing any more.

I'd never been in such a charged atmosphere. The air pulsed with electricity. I could feel the static crackling in my hair. Or perhaps it was just sweat. The place seemed like a big hot-air balloon just waiting to go pop. Millwall wanted to attempt the impossible. Millwall wanted to run West Ham on their own turf in the heart of the East End. Even Hitler hadn't managed that. And he'd used bombers.

This match aroused an intensity of violent feeling I'd never experienced before. I felt sure that pure bloodlust would ensure there'd be more than scuffles and wet punches next day. I imagined this encounter ending up like a scene from the Lebanese civil war.

In The Gin Palace that night, the would-be warriors held the final tribal war-dance before the big battle. Being in a mob that strong, that powerful, is exhilarating. It offers a massive buzz. You know you want to damage the opposition, you know you won't run (even if you're scared) and you know you'll go to extremes you wouldn't normally contemplate.

The next day, still a little hungover, I caught the tube to Whitechapel with Larry 'The Slash', Ray, Tony, 'Benny the Jew' and a few others. A lot of the Bushwhackers had arranged to meet there. Only fools would have gone in a small group to Upton Park for such a game. Most of us carried knives. I had a six-inch knife which, when sheathed, looked like a wooden ruler. When around 200 of us had assembled, we went out into Whitechapel High Street, but the police refused to let us wander round the East End and herded us back onto the tube.

The word was that West Ham would be in a pub called The Horn of Plenty at Mile End. I knew the pub. It stood next to the tube station. Anticipating an ambush, we all agreed that, as soon as the train pulled into the station, we'd steam out and surprise any would-be attackers.

The train pulled into the station. The doors opened and we piled out. Onto empty platforms. 'Fuck the Hammers,' someone shouted, 'Let's do their pub!' Everyone cheered and we made our way upstairs. As we got to the ticket barrier, a huge roar from the street outside almost blasted us back down the escalators. West Ham fans stormed into the station from every direction.

I was panicking like fuck, but we surged forward. Everyone went under, over or through the barriers – and engaged in battle with the West Ham mob. It was pure savagery. We really wanted to kill each other. I grabbed one of the Hammers and kicked his legs from under him. As he fell, he cracked his head on the side of a ticket machine. I didn't give him a chance to get up. I held him by the hair and kicked him repeatedly in the head.

Somebody jumped on my back. Someone else started punching me in the face. But shouts of 'Old Bill! Old Bill!' brought everything to a sudden end. Both sides ran to escape arrest.

The police rounded us up and pushed us back down onto the platform. Soon, we continued on our way to Upton Park, home of the Hammers. When the train doors opened, we all steamed out, shouting in unison, 'Millwall! Millwall! Millwall!' We wanted them to know we'd stepped onto their home turf.

Veterans had identified the Queens Market as the most likely place for a battle. Apparently, when you walked down Green Street towards the ground, the West Ham usually emerged from The Queen's pub, set back from the road in the marketplace. However, the only people who met us there wore uniforms. The sheer number of police astonished me. Riot vans, dogs and horses supported officers linking arms on foot. Even a helicopter circled overhead.

As we progressed down the road, groups of West Ham would emerge from side streets offering violence. They hurled abuse and the odd missile. The police would chase them back down the street. The chances for confrontation began to look remote.

When we got to the ground, I noticed the airport-style, walk-through metal detectors. An 'amnesty bin' for illegal weapons stood nearby. Fans had already deposited knives, CS gas canisters, metal kung-fu stars, an axe, a butcher's hook and other weapons before reaching the detectors.

My mates walked over to a nearby bush. Pretending to have a piss, they dumped their knives. I decided to take a chance with mine. I stuffed it down the back of my trousers. The journey back to south London seemed certain to be more lively. I already had a deep red bruise forming under my eye after the fight at Mile End. I didn't want to take any more wounds home. Nor did I fancy a spell in hospital.

Coins and belt buckles kept setting off the detectors, slowing everything down. A huge backlog of fans had built up outside the ground with the game about to start. In order to push people through more quickly, the stewards started ignoring the buzzing of the detectors in favour of random searches. As I got to the front, I raised my arms in anticipation of being searched, but a steward said simply, 'OK, mate,' and let me through.

They packed us all into one corner of the South Bank. Police in full riot gear stood on either side. In the main stand to our left stood the bulk of the West Ham fans. They looked pretty frightening. Not many people bothered watching the game. Both sets of fans stood facing each other. Millwall fans chanted 'We are evil' and 'You'll get the same as Luton'. West Ham chanted 'ICF' as they threw coins and missiles.

A loud roar drew our attention to the game. West Ham had scored. We all surged forward and tried to get on the pitch. So did West Ham. I found myself being crushed against one of the barriers. Tony had lost his footing and fallen into a sea of bodies. At the front, Millwall fans started fighting the police, who soon beat them back.

The game played on under a cloud of mutual hatred. You could tell the atmosphere had unnerved the players. The referee awarded West Ham a corner in front of us, but no player wanted to take the kick. Several of them got into a huddle and argued. Eventually, one dashed over to the ball and took the quickest corner I've ever seen.

So many police now stood in front of us that it had become impossible to see the pitch, let alone follow the game. Some people started shouting, 'Millwall's scored!' Others joined them and soon we were all jumping up and down in delight, although hardly any of us had seen the goal. To everyone's surprise, Millwall scored a second time. Again, almost no one saw the goal, resulting in another delayed roar.

At the final whistle, they kept us locked in until the streets outside had been cleared. Eventually, the gates opened. A line of police officers, three-deep, greeted us. As we crossed a junction, a loud roar went up and West Ham fans ran at us from a side street. We ran at them, but the police swamped the area and prevented fighting.

A few minutes later, we were standing in a tube heading out of the East End. But we knew the threat of violence hadn't passed. Everyone was trying to guess the most likely place for a battle. Mile End? Whitechapel? Or London Bridge? The latter seemed most likely: a 'neutral' venue with few police around. This meant if a fight kicked off, no one would have an excuse to run.

Around 200 Millwall congregated at London Bridge Station. People were saying that ICF 'spotters' had been seen ringing the main mob on their mobiles. An 'off' seemed inevitable. We walked out of the station and down the concourse towards Borough High Street. Suddenly, a mob of about 150 ICF came round the corner. They spread out across the road and shouted, 'Come on Millwall, come on Millwall.' As they did so, they held their arms apart in boxing pose and started running towards us.

I was at the front with Benny, Ray and Tony. I couldn't have run off, even if I'd wanted to. We surged forward, and were pushed, in the direction of the advancing ICF. I could see that several had armed themselves with knives, scaffold tubes, bottles and bits of wood pulled from a nearby skip. A loud bang made me glance to my right. One of the ICF had fired a flare gun. The glowing missile zoomed towards us, but then climbed steeply over our heads. I searched the advancing faces for my opponent. A tall, thin man in a leather jacket bore down on me. He was the one. Bang, bang, bang. Before I'd even had time to get one punch into him, he'd whacked me three times in the head.

I grabbed his hair and tried to pull him into me, so I could get some punches into his face and head. But he knew his stuff. He twisted his body and punched me hard in the mouth. Blood poured down my chin and onto my chest. I knew if I didn't do something drastic I could lose badly. I pulled the knife out of my trousers. I stabbed him once in the upper arm. He let out a scream. Then I stabbed him again in the side, just above his waistband. His instinct was to try pressing his hand against the wounds, but he didn't know which one to press. He did a funny sort of turn, then fell to the tarmac.

'Cunt, fucking cunt,' I said as I kicked him in the head a few times. Then I turned towards his friends with the knife still in my hand.

With blood pouring out of my mouth, and a blood-stained knife in my hand, I can see now why I had no takers. I lunged at a half-caste man, but he backed away, screaming, 'Put the knife down! Put the knife down!'

The shrieking of police sirens ripped through the air. Everyone started legging it. Everyone, that is, apart from the eight or ten bodies lying on the ground.

My friends had all survived unscathed, bar a few cuts and

bruises. We hailed a black cab and asked the driver to take us to Kennington. I didn't want him to know where we were from in case the stabbing later became an issue. At Kennington, I dropped the knife down a street drain.

It was around this time in the late '80s that I put the BNP leader John Tyndall in a headlock at the meeting in Arnos Grove. Since then, my involvement in Nazi activities had pretty much ceased. I'd come increasingly to find the whole scene laughable, a ridiculous waste of time.

Most of my south London mates felt the same. Only Adolf remained a 'true believer', but his cranky, paranoid, conspiracy-obsessed eccentricity merely underlined for me how the far-right would never make the leap into the hearts and minds of ordinary white working people. I didn't express my views to Adolf, partly because I didn't want to be ranted at for several hours. But, all the same, I hadn't exactly converted to the Anti-Nazi League. I had no intention of standing up tearfully in The Royal Oak to repent my Nazi sins and to pledge undying loyalty to *The Guardian*.

Millwall achieved promotion to Division One (now called 'the Premiership') for the 1988 season – the high-point of their recent history. For decades, their hooligans had fought on the terraces of lowly clubs like Leyton Orient, Crystal Palace, Hull and Cardiff. Now, the Bushwhackers had a chance to take on hooligans from the country's top clubs like Manchester United, Arsenal, Liverpool, and, of course, West Ham. They could finally put beyond dispute their unofficial status as the country's number one 'firm'.

Hooligan south London buzzed with expectation. Most pub conversations in my circle at this time seemed to revolve around plans for 'jolly ups' to games at the big clubs, whose grounds had seemed so unreachable for so long. For the first game, Millwall drew Birmingham-based Aston Villa – a chance for a crack at Villa's highly rated 'Steamers' firm. I decided to return with my new tribe to my old West Midlands hunting ground. Benny, Ray, Tony, Larry and I took the iron horse to Birmingham New Street Station. We travelled with around 50 other Millwall, largely from Peckham and Brixton. Most were travelling for the hooliganism rather than the football.

We arrived around ten in the morning and decided to split into small groups so as not to attract police attention. Once clear of New Street, we'd meet at a pub near Digbeth Coach Station. As my little group ascended the escalators into the Bull Ring shopping complex, we saw a few teenagers watching us. We assumed they were 'spotters'. I knew Birmingham well, so I could guide people away from areas of possible ambush.

In the pub at Digbeth, the Millwall fans began arriving. None had encountered any trouble, though several said they'd been followed by 'spotters'. As we stood having a chat and a drink, a missile smashed the pub's front window, showering people in glass. Outside, we heard the chanting of 'Villa! Villa! Villa!'

We ran out onto the pavement and found ourselves being pelted with bottles and stones. Those at the front began to run at the 75-strong Villa mob; those behind followed. We hadn't even reached the Villa fans when those at the rear started running. Soon, they'd all taken to their heels. Many of them ran onto the dual carriageway. Vehicles swerved or screeched to a halt. The blowing of car horns accompanied the chaos. The remaining Villa fans disappeared into shops and side streets. None of us caught any of them. Only world-class sprinters could have managed that feat.

Outside the ground, Millwall fans fought running battles with the police. Larry, Ray and I ended up being arrested after a scuffle. Because of my Midlands accent, they locked me up initially with Villa supporters. These supporters knew I was Millwall, but no one said anything. By that stage, our common predicament had united us, and our differences had been forgotten. It didn't matter what I said to the police, though, they wouldn't accept I was in the wrong cell. Only when I was charged, and could show the desk sergeant the Millwall tattoo on my arm, did they move me to the same cell as my friends.

Magistrates later fined us all a hundred and fifty pounds for public order offences.

In early 1989, Millwall played Liverpool at home. Everyone had been waiting for this game. At Anfield earlier in the season, 100 of us had stood in the road outside the famous Kop end waiting for the Scousers to come out. When they saw us, they initially ran at us, but when we ran towards them, they shot back into the Kop. The humiliated Scouse hooligans had sworn revenge at the return match at Millwall.

Before the game, I met up with my mates for a drink in The Brockwell Tavern. About an hour before kick-off, we went outside to a minicab office and ordered a cab to take us to the ground.

A black African driver came out and led us to his car. He noticed five of us and said, 'I can only take four.' I said I'd 'give him a drink' if he took us all. It hardly seemed worth taking two cabs. He insisted he'd only take four. I tried reasoning with him politely, but for no reason he quickly got really shirty, telling me if I asked again he'd take nobody. I didn't like his aggressive attitude and told him to calm down.

He started walking back to the office. Over his shoulder he said, 'Fucking walk.' I put my hand on his shoulder to attract his attention. He spun round with a small penknife in his hand. I said, 'What the fuck are you doing?' He didn't answer. He just stabbed me twice in my left upper arm and ran into the office.

I genuinely couldn't believe what had happened. I stood there speechless and in shock. My mates ran into the office behind him and steamed into the four or five drivers sitting in a waiting area. I ran in, too, and looked for my assailant, but he'd disappeared.

We bashed everyone in there and trashed every phone and piece of furniture. I never did see that man again. I dearly wished I could have set Dougie on his trail. We walked down to Brixton and got a cab from there. My wounds weren't serious, though one of them should have been stitched. I didn't even bother going to hospital as too many questions would have been asked.

But the incident did have quite an effect on me. It scared me. Although I'd been stabbed on two previous occasions, this stabbing made me realise I was as vulnerable as everyone else. In a few months' time, I'd be 29 years old. Debra had been talking about having another baby. I felt I wouldn't be around much longer if I continued running round the country behaving like a juvenile delinquent. I was certainly slowing down, but unfortunately I hadn't yet stopped.

I felt intrigued when Adolf told me that Patrick Harrington, one of the country's best-known far-right 'faces', had been in contact. Harrington, as a member of the National Front, had achieved national publicity in 1984 when some of his fellow students at the Polytechnic of North London tried to stop him attending lectures. He'd gone to court to secure his right to be taught. The mob of far-left demonstrators who'd tried to block his path had been pilloried in sections of the media as 'red fascists'.

Harrington's choirboy looks and his quiet, reasonable manner had impressed many on the far-right. They saw him as a future leader, possibly capable of delivering electoral success. In the mean time, the National Front had split again. The BNP had been founded in 1982 after one such split – leader Tyndall was himself a former NF deputy leader. Now came another major split. This meant that for a while two National Fronts, one led by Harrington, vied for the hearts and minds of right-thinking people. Harrington had got in touch with Adolf because he hoped to build up support for his 'new' NF. He wanted to meet up for a drink with Adolf 'and friends'.

We all rather liked Patrick Harrington, who was certainly no Patrick Hooligan. He came across as easy-going, modest and intelligent, the sort of bloke your mother would describe as 'a nice boy'. He assumed the current right-wing groups had left us all disillusioned. He thought his 'new' party might reawaken our interest and set our hearts beating with hope for an Aryan future. He said the launch of his new NF would be held at an exclusive hotel in Victoria. He invited us along to see what we thought of his manifesto and ideals. We told him we'd go. He seemed pleased. I suppose the problem with all politicians is they think that a yes to one answer means you're going to say yes for ever more.

In the end, about six of us went to the launch: Adolf, Ray, Colin, Benny, my brother Paul and me. The hotel, a spit from Buckingham Palace, exuded wealth and class. Huge, crystal chandeliers complemented the thick, red carpets. We stuck out like the sorest of sore thumbs. Party workers greeted us at the door to the 'conference room'. They thanked us for coming and politely asked for a donation. We laughed and politely told them to bollocks. We barged our way past and sat in the second row facing the podium.

We distinguished ourselves as the only yobby types there. The other 25 or so people in the room were largely elderly 'old major' types, the sort who'd retired back to England after a life spent running the colonies, only to discover the colonies had arrived before them. Even the notorious aristocratic fascist Lady Birdwood had brought her blue rinse along. The other celebrity far-right 'face' was an Italian whom Adolf called 'Bob'. He'd allegedly taken part in the Bologna railway station bombing. The anti-fascist *Searchlight* magazine was always writing about him. Benny referred to him as 'Adolf's wop friend'.

The launch bored us shitless. Harrington wasn't much of a speaker and, in Adolf's eyes, his manifesto made him little more than a Tory. After the speeches, we ate what remained worth eating from the buffet and went to leave. Harrington came over and asked us what we thought. We told him what he needed to hear. He invited us to a 'social evening' at a West End pub.

We guessed we'd be able to secure a few free drinks, so we went along. We sat alone at the bar for 15 minutes. We thought no one else had turned up. But Harrington arrived and whispered that the actual event was being held in a private room upstairs. At the entrance, party workers told us admission cost twenty pounds, 'which includes a buffet'. We ignored them and bundled in. The room contained the elderly majors from the hotel plus a group of middle-aged, leather-clad bikers from Milton Keynes.

These sort of events were always lousy. If a black singer came on the sound system, people would shout, 'Jungle music! Nigger music! Turn it off!' Barbra Streisand? 'Jew! Turn her off!' The DJs, unable to play 'undesirable' music, didn't have much left to select. You'd end up feeling imprisoned in a First World War RAF-officers' mess tea party.

We sat drinking their lager and eating their buffet for an hour or so. The party workers looked on resentfully. Harrington came over and asked us to make at least a small contribution. Please. We told him we didn't have any money.

We didn't see Harrington again for a little while. Then a parliamentary by-election was announced in the Vauxhall constituency, part of our south London patch, for 15 June 1989. Harrington decided to stand as a candidate for his 'new' NF. The other NF faction also put up a candidate. Everyone on the far-right took sides – and feelings ran very high. Harrington came canvassing in our favourite local, The Royal Oak in Stockwell. He went down very well with the mainly Irish customers ('A noice lad, a very noice lad'). He could hardly fail with a name like Patrick Harrington. I guessed, like most of our little group, he had a bit of Irish in him. In fact, he informed the charmed customers that his grandmother was Irish.

He also stressed his party wasn't anti-Irish or anti-Catholic, unlike the 'old' NF, which had once referred to the Irish as 'bogwogs' and demanded their repatriation along with all the other immigrants. Harrington even coloured some of his election leaflets green. Somebody told us his mother read tarot cards. We used to joke with him that she knew the election result already, so canvassing seemed pointless. Possibly believing that we owed him for two buffets, Harrington approached us once more to ask us to show support at the poll count at Brixton Town Hall. He said it'd be shown live on television. He warned us there might be trouble, so we decided to go.

On the night of the count, around 20 of us congregated at Brixton Hill, a five-minute walk from the town hall. We arrived there via two 'redirection' points. We walked down the hill and entered the hall to be met by half a dozen policemen who warned us that any problems would be dealt with 'swiftly and severely'. Harrington looked excited to see us. Perhaps it was just relief, because the other NF faction's supporters had got there first and, we heard later, already abused him verbally.

Our choirboy 'leader' gave us all a T-shirt bearing the words 'NF' and his party HQ's telephone number. He said, 'Get yourselves in front of the TV cameras as often as you can. We need people to see the phone number.'

As soon as we put on the T-shirts, and thereby clearly identified ourselves as Harrington's supporters, members of the other NF faction glared and sneered, but they lacked the bollocks to take us on. We closed in on those pointed out as having been particularly abusive to Harrington. A bit of pushing, shoving and swearing followed. It looked like it was going to kick off. Screaming Lord Sutch and a sidekick from his Monster Raving Loony Party tried calming things down, but when the fists started flying they and the other candidates ran towards the thin blue line.

The police restored order swiftly, but hardly severely. They neither arrested nor ejected anyone. Screaming Lord Sutch came back and stood next to us with his arms folded, as if he intended maintaining order. No one was sure if he was having a laugh or being serious, so I told him to fuck off. Or else. He mumbled, 'Take it easy, boys,' then disappeared swiftly back into the crowd. Within minutes, fighting had broken out again between the factions. Again, the police restored order. This time, they said if we misbehaved again we'd be arrested.

The TV presenter told the viewers (who could view me wearing my NF T-shirt), 'The last count should have been taking place uninterrupted, but there've been a couple of unpleasant and violent scenes. In the first, a member of the official National Front engaged physically in the front row with the Revolutionary Communist Party newspaper, attempting to grab the camera.

'And then there was a violent fist fight between the actual candidate for the official National Front and the chairman of the other National Front, that's the new National Front party.

'And now things are at last a little calmer, and I hope they'll stay calm for the rest of this count. That is, of course, the politics of the fringe – the extreme fringe.'

As the evening wore on, the tensions subsided a little. People began wandering around alone. One of Harrington's supporters literally bumped into members of the old NF near the counting tables. He was a geeky suit-wearer, so someone in the old NF got brave and levelled him with a punch to the head.

Another scuffle broke out. Although my little group and I hadn't been involved, the police ordered us all to leave the hall. As we walked out, Lord Sutch stood behind the police and shouted, 'Bloody fascists! Bloody Nazis! Go on, get out! Get out!'

Several of us started shouting, '*Sieg Heil! Sieg Heil!*', while giving the Nazi salute. We waited outside to see if the old NF would come out, but they didn't. So after half an hour we retired to the pub.

Out of the 28,806 votes cast, Harrington secured 127 of them (and a black eye). This represented 44 votes (and a black eye) more than the candidate for the old NF, who got 83 votes, but only 21 more than Screaming Lord Sutch, who secured 106. A far-right victory at the polls seemed some way off.

Some months earlier, Debra had become pregnant for the second time. In November 1989, the birth of our daughter Karis delighted us both. The time had come for one of my new starts. I know my attempts to change myself may sound half-hearted, but each time I really did try to start anew.

I decided I'd have to make the break with south London. I started looking for work in Essex. Colin, still wanted by the army for being absent without leave, had left England to live in Sweden. No doubt he'd wanted his own new start. He had a girlfriend and a job out there, but he still turned up for the occasional weekend in London. I could hardly blank an old friend who'd travelled all the way from Sweden. So whenever he came to town, we'd meet up for a drink. In January 1990, I was in south London having one such drink. Ray had also joined us in The Heaton Arms, Peckham Rye. We kept out of our usual haunts, because Colin remained on the run.

Colin was staying at his father's house in Stratford, east London. At around 10.30 p.m., he said he had to go. Ray asked him how he'd be getting back.

He said, 'I'm going to get the tube to Stratford.'

I'd noticed a group of very large men, probably in their 40s, standing nearby, but I hadn't paid them much attention. They must have overheard our conversation.

That day, Millwall had been playing their arch east London rivals West Ham again, this time at home. I hadn't bothered going: I'd wanted to stay out of trouble. I can only assume that when Colin mentioned Stratford in the East End these probable Millwall supporters thought we were West Ham.

Ray went home first. At closing time, Colin and I left the pub. I was walking just slightly in front when I heard a loud thud. I turned to see Colin lying on the ground. Four or five men – the group of 40 year olds from the pub – stood over him with baseball bats. I ran to help him. They knocked me unconscious. A witness told police that as I lay comatose on the ground, my assailants had smashed my knees with their bats. Someone had been shouting, 'Cripple the bastard! Cripple him!'

I awoke in King's College Hospital, East Dulwich. I had stitches in my head. Both my knees had swollen to twice their normal size. I asked after Colin. A nurse said he'd been hit in the face between his chin and nose with the baseball bat. The blow had broken his jaw and a cheekbone and knocked out several teeth, pushing them flat underneath, and above, his tongue.

I had no money on me. I didn't know if it had been lost or stolen. I told the nurses I was going home. They found this amusing, because my injuries meant I could barely sit up. However, I crawled out of bed. The nurses remonstrated with me, but I kept on hobbling down the corridor and out onto the street. Blood covered my clothes. It was about eight in the morning. I'd been unconscious for 36 hours. I'd never been in so much pain. I scrambled onto a bus full of commuters. I said to the driver, 'I've just come of out hospital, mate. I've got no money. I've got to get to the tube.' He didn't say anything. I sat down. Without any kind of ticket, I managed to get the tube and then a train to Basildon.

I must have looked like an escaped lunatic sitting there, covered in dried blood and disorientated. I thought I'd made it home without a ticket, but two stops before Basildon an inspector got on. He asked for my ticket. I said, 'Look, mate. I've had a bad fucking day. Leave me alone. I'm not in the mood. Go away.' He did.

I've since had five operations on my knees. I underwent physiotherapy every week for almost two years. In 2003, I underwent another six months' physio when a muscle in my right leg ceased functioning. It still doesn't work. I continue to suffer from arthritis and other conditions related to the injuries sustained in that attack.

I've returned to that pub with my friends a few times, but I've never found those responsible. In wartime, I suppose the attack would have been investigated as a 'friendly fire' incident. I still dream of catching up with the hooligans who attacked us. I even hope that someone reading this book might possibly identify our assailants. Then, of course, I'll finally be able to make a citizen's arrest and claim a reward from Crimestoppers.

CHAPTER 12

DISCO DAVE

IN MARCH 1990, I STARTED WORKING AS A DOORMAN AT A NIGHTCLUB CALLED Raquels in Basildon. I'd just turned 30 and wanted to earn a bit of extra money with a job that kept me closer to home.

In the early days of my new job, I'd have at least two fights a night. These weren't usually gentle scuffles with harmless drunks. Our valued customers didn't tend to observe the Queensberry rules when brawling. If they hadn't brought along their own weapons – knives, machetes, knuckle-dusters, coshes and axes – they'd use whatever came to hand: heavy ashtrays, bottles, glasses, chairs and tables. The dance floor was as often the venue for pitched battles as for dancing. Fractured skulls, broken bones and comas were what customers often took away from the club. Ears, eyes and parts of noses were what they sometimes left behind.

Bouncing troublemakers down three flights of stairs and throwing them into, then out of, the doors didn't always end the trouble. The aggrieved revellers, especially if part of a gang, would sometimes call for reinforcements and try to storm the place.

The door staff with whom I worked just couldn't get on top of the violence, partly because they allowed a small number of local villains to intimidate them, and partly because the head doorman didn't encourage them to intervene. It was as if the sheriff and his deputies had locked themselves in jail while the Crazy Gang took over the town.

I felt this stance put everyone in danger: staff, doormen and decent customers alike. I raised the subject more than once with the head doorman. Discussion dissolved into dispute. Our differences festered for several months before culminating in his walking out. He told the manager he could no longer work with me.

The following day, I took over the door. I immediately set about replacing most of the local doormen. Over the next few months, under my leadership, the new team ruthlessly established a rough sort of order over the once-prevailing anarchy. The foundation stone of my new approach was that violent people should be dealt with violently. We, the doormen, had a stash of our own weapons, which we used without compunction.

People soon began to joke about the three ways of leaving Raquels: on foot, by taxi or in an ambulance. In fact, a fourth existed – out the back, head-first down the concrete stairs. We reserved this exit for the most badly behaved customers. Some nights, there seemed more ambulances outside than taxis.

The matronly woman who ran the cloakroom was Jewish. Before I started working at the club, some of the other doormen – all white and non-Jewish – had begun light-heartedly taking the piss out of her. She'd ignored them. When I arrived, and more customers began turning up for their cloaks in a badly beaten state, she started complaining to both the manager and his area superior about what she saw as our excessive violence. We regarded her behaviour as 'grassing'. The piss-taking became more personal and vicious. Doormen would leave pork sausages on her counter, ask for directions to Auschwitz and wail the Yiddish exclamation 'oy vay, oy vay' whenever she spoke.

One evening, a doorman brought to the cloakroom a grey, Second-World-War German officer's trenchcoat. To it, he'd pinned a metal Wehrmacht eagle clutching a Nazi swastika. As he handed it over and received his ticket, he said to her, 'We'll be back for this – and you – later, you kike grass.' She collected her own coat and handbag before walking out. She never returned.

Around the same time that I took over the door, the club got a new manager. Usually, it's the manager's job to get on well with the council and police. Then they all blame the head doorman for any trouble. But the manager and I hit it off, so the usual 'good guy, bad guy' scenario couldn't gel. Soon, the council and police hated us both.

Not all of the customers were violent villains. Many were just ordinary freaks. One character I grew to like was an awesomely thin creature in his late teens or early 20s. Around 6 ft and with lizard-like features, he'd gulp and stutter violently when he tried talking. We named him Disco Dave.

On Mondays, we used to hold an under-18s night, which attracted 300 potential and actual juvenile delinquents from the local estates. We wouldn't sell them alcohol. It didn't make any difference. They'd just get pissed beforehand. Like their sociopathic parents, these kids would then indulge in brawls, beatings and drunken gropes. One night, we got called to a disturbance on the dance floor. As I approached, I noticed a heap of around ten writhing, spitting kids. They appeared to be attacking someone who lay on the floor beneath them. We dragged the kids off one by one to find a bleeding man at the bottom. Disco Dave had entered my life. Apparently, he'd taken off his shirt to expose his gruesomely underdeveloped body. A group of youths – who may have been eating at the time – objected. Disco told them to fuck off, and they'd steamed him. I cleaned him up and suggested he go home and come instead to the adult nights, as a few years had now passed since he'd been under 18. He said he didn't have enough money to attend the adult nights or to get home. I agreed to give him a lift when the club closed.

He waited for me patiently. Every time I tried talking to him he became engulfed in violent gulping and stuttering. In the end, silence seemed the best policy. I sent him to sit in the back of my car to prevent idle chat. On the way to his house, the police stopped me. Not an unusual event: they liked sitting on my case. When I saw the flashing blue light, I told Disco to let me do the talking, because I wanted to get home at a reasonable hour. The policeman walked up to the driver's door and asked me the usual questions. I said, 'I've been to work, and I'm going home, and – before you ask – he's fuck all to do with me. I'm just giving him a lift home.'

The officer then asked Disco for his details. The request

provoked a nervous crisis. Despite superhuman efforts, Disco couldn't squeeze out an answer. He gulped, stuttered, spat and blinked for so long that in the end the policeman said, 'It's all right, mate. Forget it. Off you go.'

I suppose I adopted Disco Dave as a sort of club mascot. I knew he had no money, so I used to let him in free. I could see this made him feel important. One day, I told him that in the future he should ignore the long queues, march straight to the front, walk past the doorstaff, cashier and those searching and, if ANYBODY said ANYTHING, he had to say, 'My name's Disco Dave. I don't pay. And I don't give a fuck.'

Nothing more. Nothing less.

One evening, the company directors and other VIPs visited the club. They were all standing around the reception area when Disco walked in wearing trainers, which the management had banned in an unsuccessful attempt to filter out the riff-raff. One of the directors looked at Disco, stared at his forbidden footwear, glanced at me and stood waiting for me to say something. I just shrugged my shoulders.

The director decided to intervene. He said to Disco, 'I'm afraid you can't come in wearing trainers, Sir.'

Disco looked straight at him, gulped and, with the pride and arrogance of a bullfighter, stuttered out the words, 'My name's Disco Dave. I don't pay. And I don't give a fuck.'

He then marched past the director and all the doorstaff and disappeared upstairs. The director said, 'Who on earth is that?'

'Don't ask,' I said. 'He's a fucking nightmare.'

When we went upstairs later, we watched Disco dancing on a raised podium with his shirt off. He looked in need of urgent psychiatric assistance.

Indirectly, he'd helped us rebuff the charge that we'd become too violent to customers. Indeed, the director thought we ought to impose our authority a bit more firmly. He hadn't liked our completely hands-off approach to a stuttering and skeletal representative of the undead who'd pushed his way into the club without paying.

One day, the manager told me he had a friend due for release from prison. Would I be able to employ him on the door? The man's name was Maurice and he came from Bristol. He'd broken a man's arm with a baseball bat during a road-rage incident.

The manager said, 'But he's not a violent man, Bernie. Honest.' I said half-jokingly, 'If he ain't violent, he's no use to me.'

One Friday night, I watched as a big black car pulled up outside the club. The driver's door opened and a big black man got out. Decorated generously with gold jewellery, he strolled majestically towards the club, avoiding undue exertion of his muscular frame. I thought, 'Pimp.' Lamentable racial stereotyping, I know. In fact, Maurice had just arrived. I shook his hand, gave him a hundred pounds (as cash is usually what you need most when you walk out of prison) and showed him round the club.

To be honest, his skin colour didn't present a problem for me. But I feared it might for many of the customers. Basildon isn't known for its commitment to multiculturalism. Not many blacks live there. The few that do often end up being driven out. Many of the white residents have their roots in the East End. They'll tell anyone willing to listen that they only left their beloved Bow Bells to escape the blacks and Asians. Some Nazis even dreamt of setting up in Essex an Aryan 'homeland' – a whites-only separatist state.

I liked Maurice. Although quiet and reserved, he feared no one and would fight all-comers. After working with him for a while, I mentioned that I needed a tenant for my flat in south-east London. He confided that he had a few West Country women working for him in the capital as prostitutes. I suppose this made him a lamentable racial stereotype after all. I agreed to let some of his working girls rent the flat. Since the road-rage incident, he'd also been banned from driving. I let him use my licence. Without really realising, I'd become good friends with a black man.

Despite spending my nights beating manners into the locals, then sleeping till mid-morning, I still managed to go to the odd Millwall game on a Saturday afternoon, but not usually as a Bushwhacker. I even took my infant son Vinney along to a few.

My friends seemed to be growing up a bit, too. I spoke more on the phone with Adolf than with the others, who'd all become a bit resistant to his nutty Nazi ways. I was probably the only one of our circle still willing to listen to his political rants for more than three minutes.

Adolf kept me informed of developments in the world of the far-right. He continued to invite me to meetings and to send me Nazi magazines. So I knew that, by 1990, the National Front (new and old) had almost expired, devoured by the usual splits and in-fighting. The BNP had become the Great White Hope, though not for Adolf, who regarded them as left-wing Tories. He often sounded disillusioned and gave the impression he was biding his time till the emergence of a new Messiah who'd lead us to the Aryan promised land.

In early 1991, at a BNP election rally, a new security team was formed to protect the party leadership. I assumed leader John Tyndall wanted to avoid being strangled in public by strangers. The team was composed mainly of football hooligans from the London clubs Tottenham Hotspur, Millwall, Charlton and West Ham. They called themselves the 'East End Barmy Army', which was a bit puzzling because Tottenham's in north London, Millwall's in south London and no one knows where Charlton is. Only West Ham is east. They were meant to be purely for defence, but before long they went on the offensive, attacking red marches and meetings. The East End Barmy Army formed the nucleus of what later became the most feared and dangerous British Nazi grouping of recent times, Combat 18.

In August 1991, 'Mad Bomber' Tony Lecomber asked Adolf to bring his 'mates' to a BNP demonstration being held in Bermondsey in London's Docklands. The demonstration's target was a planned march through the area by the National Black Caucus, a group campaigning for the rights of blacks. For around two years, I'd avoided taking Adolf up on his political invitations, but it just so happened that, on that day, Millwall were playing at home. I planned to go to the match with Benny, Ray and Tony.

Bermondsey is only a stone's (or bottle's) throw from Millwall, so we told Adolf we'd combine the two events for a day out. We used to call our outings 'jolly ups' and this promised to be a double serving of jolly. We made our way to the Rotherhithe Road in Bermondsey to await the marchers. I hadn't been in such a hyped-up atmosphere since the first Millwall versus West Ham match I'd attended years earlier.

Now members of those rival sets of hooligans had joined together in the East End Barmy Army. They stood there poised for attack, along with members of the BNP and NF. Many of the area's white residents had also joined the throng. This 'black' march in a 'white' area was regarded by many of them as 'anti-white' and 'provocative'. A mob of about 400 of us stood waiting.

The trouble started before the marchers arrived. Millwall's Bushwhackers started hurling bricks, bottles and coins at the line of police standing behind barriers. Then the marchers appeared. A cry of rage went up and everyone surged forward, smashing down the barriers. We were chanting 'Kill! Kill! Kill!' and pelting the rapidly retreating police with missiles. The marchers stopped moving as the police surrounded them. We all headed for a nearby park in the hope of attacking from behind. A police riot van tried to block our route. Missiles rained down on the van. The driver slammed the vehicle into reverse and drove almost blind down the street to escape.

Once inside the park, we armed ourselves with whatever we could find – bottles, lumps of wood, stones, the metal inserts of bins. Then we charged the terrified marchers again. Police reinforcements swamped the area. Suddenly, a policeman announced through a loudhailer that the march had been cancelled and that we should all disperse. The BNP organisers didn't want the day to end just yet. They also took to their megaphones and whipped the mob up once again for a final effort. We regrouped and charged at the marchers, who turned and began running up the street. Later, one of the marchers said to journalists, 'We were lucky to get out alive – that was our only success.'

Exhilarated by our victory, we turned on the police. A group of Met motorcyclists were punched, kicked and pelted with missiles before they sped away. An Asian photographer was singled out from a group of journalists to be kicked and beaten. A car containing two black people was turned over onto its roof. In a small shopping centre, an Asian shopkeeper was beaten up and another had his shop looted.

For about ten minutes, the police seemed to have disappeared. And a marauding mob can do a lot of damage in ten minutes if no one's there to stop them. Eventually, the police returned and began hunting us down. They arrested some stragglers at the rear. Everybody else dispersed into the maze of back alleys.

Publicly, the BNP condemned the disorder. Adolf sent me their paper, *British Nationalist*. The editorial read:

> The BNP continues to advocate that lawful political action is the correct method for opposing the evils of the multi-racial society that the rulers of Britain have created, but as long as those rulers do not respond to the people's wishes by bringing their hideous experiment to an end, the kind of street warfare we saw in Bermondsey is inevitable.

Adolf resented the 'criticism'. He said angrily on the phone, 'Typical Tory bollocks from Tyndall.' He thought the BNP leaders were taking liberties in rousing the rabble, then condemning them for what they'd been roused to do.

Around this time, I'd developed a sideline involving 'jobs' set up for me by an intermediary known as 'Fatman'. He weighed about 22 st. Hence the nickname. These jobs involved destroying property, threatening people and beating them up. The victims had usually fallen out with business associates, friends, partners or neighbours over business, money, love or the position of the garden fence. Whatever the reason, someone was willing to pay good money to have his (or, quite often, her) revenge.

Despite my 'new start', I needed a decent income, so I was prepared to accommodate a degree of lawlessness to suit my needs. A cynic might say that, with each of my 'new starts', I didn't become a better person as such, I merely found new outlets for my badness. I wouldn't agree entirely with such a cynical assessment, but, at the same time, I wouldn't squirt the cynical assessor with ammonia for saying it.

Customers would arrange the job with Fatman. They never knew who I was or how to contact me. This protected me from being grassed up if the police became involved, as they sometimes did. If customers unwisely gave them Fatman's name, he'd say he'd sold the debt on. We did work all over the country – and even once in Switzerland.

Our clients ranged from solicitors to drug dealers, with all sorts in between – market traders in Manchester, property developers in Bristol, Smithfield Meat Market people in London. On busy days, I'd have up to 20 jobs to do, and I did this work three to four days a week in addition to my nightclub shifts. Yet my main job remained my position as head of security at Raquels.

By September 1993, I felt that to bolster my position I needed to form an alliance with a strong 'firm'. That was how I ended up going into a partnership that would have a profound effect on my life. The person I shook hands with was Tony Tucker, who ran a large and well-respected door firm. He used his control of security at clubs to give dealers, at a price, exclusive rights to sell drugs on the premises.

Tucker started sending me men from south and east London. Sometimes, he'd need to find work for doormen whom the management at other clubs no longer wanted: perhaps they'd bashed someone half to death; maybe they'd forgotten to wear a bow tie. Other times, Tucker just liked to act as a one-man employment agency for bodybuilders. Nine times out of ten, I'd tell him to send them along. Then next day a Mr Universe would stick his head round the door and say, 'Bernie? Hi, my name's . . .'

The first two men to come to see me this way were two East Enders, Ian and Greg. Both were black. Now three of my eight doormen were black. It was the first time in my life I'd been forced into such a close working relationship with black people. And at first I didn't feel that comfortable.

Perhaps my years steeped in racism caused my discomfort. Or maybe three was a crowd. Perhaps, in the back of my mind, I feared they might try to take over. Whatever the reason, I remained wary of them for some time. I even bashed Ian once, because I thought he was laughing at me. But gradually I grew to like and trust them (as far as anyone trusts anyone in that world). In times of danger, they proved their reliability and loyalty.

In late 1993, I got a call from a doorman who said his mate Gavin needed work. Apparently, Gavin had been sacked from a club in Ilford after sending a customer to hospital. The doorman said he'd already rung Tucker on Gavin's behalf, but had been told there was no work. This struck me as odd, because I'd already mentioned to Tucker that I needed an extra doorman. I suspected he had another reason for saying no. Doorman politics is worthy of academic study. The microcosm of the door is a catty little world built on bubbling jealousies, stifled resentments and long-borne grudges. People won't speak to each other for years for quite petty reasons. Perhaps someone sweated on their towel in the gym – or tipped over their nail varnish.

Indeed, many bodybuilders are better manicured than Barbie. If you could calculate which groups spend the most on sunbeds, leg-waxing and hairdos, you'd find a toss-up between call girls, bodybuilders and bored housewives with rich husbands. I rang Tucker and asked him about employing Gavin. He said he didn't really like the guy, although he couldn't, or wouldn't, give a reason. In the end, he said, 'It's up to you, Bernie. If you need someone, then take him on.'

I hated all that doorman politics. One week, someone was in favour, the next, he was a grass, a bottler or a wanker. I like to take people as I find them, not as other people describe them or as they're 'generally known'. So I rang my contact back and told him to send Gavin along.

When I got out of my car outside Raquels that Friday evening, I noticed an Asian-looking bodybuilder locking up his car. I was always very vigilant when entering and leaving the club. I felt that was the point at which a doorman was most vulnerable to attack from people seeking revenge.

The Asian man walked towards me and said, 'Are you Bernie?' I said I was. He stuck out his hand and said, 'All right, mate. I'm Gavin.' I thought, 'Fucking hell. A shopkeeper. He'll be annihilated.'

Basildon's the sort of place where Asians travel round in ambulances. Maurice, Greg and Ian were regularly called 'black bastards' when they turned people away; I was called a 'northern bastard'. So it seemed safe to assume that an Asian doorman – a rare breed in any event – would take endless stick.

During the evening, I asked Gavin why certain people seemed

so set against his getting a bit of work. He explained that Tucker had once turned up at a club where he was working and hadn't wanted to queue, pay or show any sort of respect to the doormen. That would have been typical of Tucker. He'd walk to the front of the queue and, when asked for money, look at the doorstaff as if they were mad. Tucker had ended up being bashed. He'd lost a bit of face – an unforgivable outrage in the world of the door. As a result, he didn't want to give work to anyone who'd been part of the door firm that bashed him.

Despite my initial reservations, I liked Gavin from that first conversation. Quiet and uncomplicated, he meant what he said and said what he meant. His catchphrase with leery customers became, 'What's your problem, mate?' Then he'd usually try reasoning with them. If they remained unreasonable, he had no hesitation in creating new customers for the NHS. He didn't care for reputations – and could certainly fight. Indeed, he turned out to be one of the best doormen I ever employed. In a short time, he became the man I relied on most when war broke out. And, perhaps most remarkably, away from Raquels he became my best friend.

One evening, two skinheads with tattoos on their heads and necks came to a bar annexed to the club. They arrived with four non-skinhead friends. I could see them looking at Gavin, then making remarks and laughing. They started doing the same to me. One of them stood behind me, aping me. I turned round and grabbed him by the throat, pushing him backwards as I did so. He fell back and hit his head on the corner of a small glass pillar, which shattered – as did his tattooed head.

Gavin heard the sound of breaking glass and ran from the other side of the bar with a bottle in his hand. He told me later he thought I'd been attacked with a glass. He saw my 'attacker' on the floor, but couldn't see the gash at the back of his head. Gavin whacked his bottle a few times over the skin's already-skewered skull.

Then we both pulled him up and dragged him to the doors. His mates seemed too stunned to do anything. We threw him into one of the glass doors, which also smashed, cutting his upper arm. He kept struggling a bit, so we beat him before throwing him down the stairs. His mates followed him meekly out, only shouting abuse when they'd got safely outside.

About half an hour later, customers near the exit doors began screaming and shouting, 'Fire! Fire!' Gavin and I ran to the stairwell and saw flames leaping up from the bar entrance. I told the manager and staff to deal with the fire. Then Gavin and I ran out through the flames into the street.

We found the skinhead with the sore head standing there with a red petrol can in his hand. Perhaps the earlier beating had slowed his reflexes because, although he looked surprised to see us, he didn't immediately run – a significant mistake on his part. I held an Irish hurling stick in my hand. I ran across to him. He dropped the petrol can and said, 'It wasn't me. It wasn't me.' He turned to run, but I hit him across the back with the hurling stick. He fell to the ground.

Gavin began kicking him in the head with his steel boots. The skinhead begged us not to beat him any more. Gavin stamped on his head and I hit him so hard across the back with the hurling stick that the latter broke. He lay there unconscious.

We picked up the petrol can and doused him with the remaining petrol. The other skinhead, who'd run a short distance away, began screaming, 'Please don't burn him! Please don't burn him!'

We told him to come to us and promised we wouldn't do anything. He wasn't daft. He stayed where he was. We gave the impression we were about to light the fire. The skinhead became hysterical. In the end, we threw down the petrol can and walked back to the club. The fire had been put out.

As we passed through the club's crisply baked entrance, Gavin said, 'If there's one thing I hate, it's those National Front-type skinheads. I detest them. They used to hang round where I live, giving it, but when you give it them back they don't want to know.'

'Yeah, I know,' I replied shamefacedly. I wanted the ground to swallow me up. I found myself going red. I could feel my cheeks giving off more heat than the smouldering carpet. I felt ashamed because Gavin – one of the most fair-minded and tolerant people I'd ever met – had become my friend and, unknown to him, I'd been the only type of person he actually hated. I never did tell him about my past. I couldn't bring myself to explain how I'd once been so deeply immersed in such a small-minded movement.

A week later, the skinhead who'd run away came to the club's front door, pissed out of his head and asking for 'that fucking Paki'. Gavin and I dashed downstairs to the dissatisfied customer. Gavin said, 'What's your problem, mate?'

'You, you Paki cunt,' said the skinhead. 'You're going to get this.'

He took out an axe from the inside of his jacket. But before he could use it, I'd squirted him in the face with ammonia and Gavin had slashed him across the head with a blade. We threw him outside amid a flurry of kicks and punches, then slammed the door shut. The skinhead lay howling outside in the gutter. Eventually, he got up and skulked off. We received regular death threats and warnings on the grapevine, but the skinheads never came back.

The town had plenty of wannabe Nazis. Some even tried getting elected to the local council. Around six months later, I heard a knock on the front door of my house late one evening. I opened the door to find 'Mad Bomber' Tony Lecomber canvassing for a local BNP man. I hadn't seen him for several years. I'd heard that after serving his sentence for the hobby-bombing that had almost killed him and Adolf, he'd received another three years for attacking a Jewish teacher whom he'd caught peeling off a BNP sticker on the tube.

I'd always liked Lecomber, so I had a chat with him, because I didn't want to be rude, but I made plain he was wasting his time knocking on my door. He wouldn't be getting anything out of me, neither money nor vote.

In July 1994, a mountain of a man called Pat Tate came out of prison after serving four years of a six-year sentence for robbery. Tucker soon recruited Tate as an enforcer for his rapidly expanding drugs empire. Tate had grand ideas. He believed 'the firm' should import drugs direct from the Continent, rather than deal with middle men. He said in prison he'd met several interesting people who'd supplied him with international contacts.

'The firm' soon began importing large shipments of drugs – and earning large amounts of cash. Tucker, Tate and their sidekick-cum-driver Craig Rolfe lived like kings, but behaved like animals. Excessive cash led to excessive drug-taking, which led to excessive violence.

The three of them got away with murdering one man by disguising the killing as a self-inflicted drugs overdose. Then, in March 1994, a 24-year-old man died after taking an Ecstasy pill that had been imported by 'the firm'. Having got away with murder, Tucker, Tate and Rolfe must have thought they could get away with anything. Foolishly, they began robbing rival 'firms' of large shipments of drugs. I could see that some, if not all, of us would probably end up in jail or an early grave.

I didn't have anything to do with importing, or robbing, drugs. My job was head of security at Raquels. However, in this role I did turn a blind eye to drugs being sold at the club – if the dealers had the firm's permission to do so. I began to think about quitting. It was time, I suppose, for another new beginning, another new start. Then a dramatic event accelerated my decision-making process.

In November 1995, Raquels and 'the firm' were catapulted into the headlines when Tucker, Tate and Rolfe's imported Ecstasy claimed a second life. Leah Betts collapsed while celebrating her 18th birthday at her father's house. She died a few days later. The tablet that killed her had been bought at the nightclub.

I told Tucker I was leaving Raquels and quitting 'the firm'. I wanted no part in murder or the deaths of young people. Tucker and Tate threatened to kill me. I don't know if their drug consumption led them to make empty threats or whether they did genuinely intend murdering me.

I'd never find out, because less than three weeks later the blood-soaked corpses of Tucker, Tate and Rolfe sat slumped in a Range Rover parked down a remote farm track in Essex. Each had been shot three times in the head with a shotgun.

This event demonstrated the inadvisability of robbing other drug barons. They're not usually the sort of people who'll take you to the Small Claims Court.

For a while, I became chief suspect, but I'd had nothing to do with the murders, and the police soon knew I was innocent. However, for me those events brought to an end my criminal way of life. I'd never been a drug dealer, but my role in charge of security at Raquels meant I'd acted as a cog in the machine that delivered drugs to those who chose to take them. I turned my back decisively on that past when I quit 'the firm' and became a prosecution witness at the trial of the man accused of supplying Leah Betts with the Ecstasy tablet that killed her.

For my troubles, I received death threats from cowards trying to salvage some sort of gangland 'respect' in the hope that 'the firm' might maintain the reputation its deceased leaders had earned. The police advised me to move house. I had to uproot my family and live with panic alarms connected to a police station.

The pressures of living under such circumstances created problems between Debra and me. Our relationship suffered. We both knew we couldn't continue as we were. As well as the problems at home, many of my so-called friends distanced themselves from me. They feared those loyal to the murdered trio might seek revenge, especially as many believed I'd played a part in their execution. Only Gavin, Ian and Greg kept in touch with me during that difficult time. This involved some risk for them, because they remained working in the unforgiving world of the door, where I'd become about as welcome as a Fenian in an Orangewoman's front room.

CHAPTER 13

CUCKOO KLUX KLAN

MY DECISION TO ASSIST THE POLICE WAS MY WAY OF TURNING MY BACK ON CRIME and everything else rotten in my life. I knew my criminal associates would have nothing more to do with me. I'd be free to start a new life without the violence and misery in which I'd immersed myself for too long. I felt I owed my children a better life.

I decided too that I would, where I could, put my previous experiences to good use in the hope of somehow atoning for my appalling behaviour. In the first instance, I assisted with a documentary and wrote the book *Essex Boys*, about the drugs trade and gang violence.

I also made a self-incriminating statement to the police about my efforts to pervert the course of justice on behalf of Lisa and Michelle Taylor, two south London sisters convicted of the vicious 1991 murder of 21-year-old Alison Shaughnessy, then controversially freed on appeal after a 'miscarriage of justice' campaign run by me. I've told this story in my book *The Dream Solution*.

I'd long felt embarrassed by my past involvement with the Nazis. For almost three years, my closest friends had been black, my best friend an Asian. Only a few years earlier, I'd have regarded someone like myself as a 'race traitor'. All the same, I'd undergone no blinding 'road to Damascus'-type conversion to the cause of anti-fascism. I hadn't started shaking with fervent faith in multiculturalism. I wouldn't be begging the government to let in another few million asylum-seekers. But I'd changed significantly nonetheless: I'd gradually learned to judge people as individuals. The idea of hating (or even liking) someone merely because they belonged to a particular racial group had come to seem ridiculous. I'd sometimes tried to persuade myself that, because I'd never had much grasp of fascist ideology, I'd never been a 'real' Nazi anyway. But I had to face the fact that, though I might never have read a word of Hitler's *Mein Kampf*, I'd actively supported 'the Movement'. I decided the best way to ease my conscience would be to find ways to undermine that same 'Movement'.

I'd known for some time of plans to introduce into Britain the notorious American-based white supremacist group the Ku Klux Klan. An American Klan member had moved to Wales in the early 1990s. He claimed to have been appointed 'Grand Dragon' of 'the British Knights of the Ku Klux Klan'. He'd been visited by the overall American boss, the so-called 'Imperial Wizard'. Sadly for the British Klan, its would-be leader was then exposed as a fugitive from justice and a convicted child molester. The Klan suspended its plans to expand its franchise in Britain.

The Klan was founded in the southern states of America in the late nineteenth century, supposedly to campaign non-violently for the rights of whites. But Klan members soon started spreading terror among blacks with a wave of murder and arson. Blacks were lynched, and their homes torched, by men wearing slit-eyed, peak-hooded white robes. Their calling card was often a burning cross.

The fundamentalist Protestant Klan expressed hatred for Catholics, Jews and Freemasons, as well as blacks. Mainstream America views Klan members as backward, Deep South, inbred rednecks – the sort of people who go to family events to pick up dates.

In late 1995, I heard that the British Knights of the Ku Klux Klan had reorganised themselves and were planning a new recruitment drive. I discussed this with the *News of the World* journalist Gary Jones, with whom I'd become friendly after helping him with a story about a critically-ill boy for whom I'd been trying to raise funds a few years earlier. He suggested the best way to counter them would be to infiltrate them. He felt that, with my far-right background, I'd have a better chance than a journalist of succeeding.

At the back of most Nazi magazines are addresses of like-minded extremists in other countries. I directed my first letter at a PO box number in North Carolina in America's Deep South. I asked if they knew of any 'real right-wing groups' in Britain, as I was tired of 'liberal faggots' like the BNP and wanted 'to do more than talk'.

Within days, I received a handwritten letter from a woman calling herself 'Breeze'. Her group called itself 'Air, Trees, Water, and Animals' (ATWA). They sounded more like Greens than white supremacists, but I thought the name might be some sort of front to mislead snoopers. She asked me a few brief questions about myself and suggested I join.

Around a week later, another letter arrived:

Hi Beaver,
Good you joined the team. I would like you to send me a postcard of that beautiful land over there. And would you please sign the card Beaver. I'll let you be Beaver ok? Whatever you can do for our earth, big or small all counts as our team. I myself don't eat meat except a few times when I eat with people who didn't know and the meat is mixed with whatever like Chicken casserole or spaghetti. And we try to buy recycled things, cant always, we just do our best at whatever we can do ok? There is people in our team that do eat meat but don't kill – hunt animals, even kids pick up cans and sell them and paper and we have cleaned up lakes and parks and we have done petitions on different things that hurts ATWA our earth, our air, water, trees, animals. So, whatever you can do, we thank you and who loves earth will thank you and you'll thank yourself.
　Sincerely,
　Breeze.

The nutcase Nazis I'd met tended to call themselves 'Beast' and 'Breadknife', not 'Beaver' and 'Breeze'. I decided to put my demands more explicitly.

Breeze's response to that letter seemed more promising. She said she wished she had the money to fly me over 'to some white power, Klan and other rallies'. She asked if I could put up ATWA's flyers in 'occult papers and places'. She also wanted me to send $10 to join and $25 for a tape and photo 'of the great Charlie Manson'.

I was stumped. I knew absolutely nothing about the occult and very little about Manson. I'd always thought of him as some sort of drug-crazed hippy serial killer from the free-love '60s. I'd never linked him to White Power and the Klan. I sent my subs and the money for the tape and photo.

This prompted a letter from another fruitcake:

> I was given your address by Charlie Manson and I assumed that you were supposed to get the tape list because that is what I was doing with Charlie. All the tapes are done totally be Charlie except for a few voices from the friends of his (very little), inside the prison. A.T.W.A. is the way to shorten and say all the living on earth, of earth. It is to say . . . leave the Life the way God has it . . . air trees water and animals; all the way alive. Charlie has said A.T.W.A. is the body of all religion. And it is his King . . .

Charlie Manson sounded more like Dr Doolittle on crack cocaine than a white supremacist. I felt myself becoming sidetracked from my Klan mission, but I was curious to discover what, if anything, linked Manson to the White Power extremists. I began reading up about him and soon saw that pattern of extreme childhood trauma followed by war on 'normal' society that I could trace in my own life and in the lives of many of the disturbed people I knew.

Born in Cincinnati, Ohio, in 1934, the illegitimate son of a teenage prostitute who abandoned him, Manson never knew his father. Brought up in homes and reform schools, he soon graduated to prison. Armed robbery, assault, homosexual rape, forgery and pimping ensured he spent a large part of his teens and 20s behind bars. He spent his incarceration taking drugs, learning steel guitar and studying magic, Satanism, hypnotism, the Bible and cult mind-control.

Soon after his release in 1967, aged 32, he came to regard himself as the reincarnation of Jesus Christ. Manson – the Son of Man. He gathered around himself a group of largely female disciples, whom he called 'the Family'. Between bouts of group sex, acid trips and car theft, he preached that the world was coming to an end. Based partly on his reading of the Bible's book of Revelation, he predicted war between blacks and whites. The blacks would win, but, after a few years, they'd realise they lacked the intellect to rule and would ask Manson and 'the Family' to take over.

Wannabe pop star Manson took his term for the coming revolution, 'Helter Skelter', from a song by the Beatles. He believed the Fab Four to be the Four Horsemen of the Apocalypse, communicating with him through their songs. In the space of a few months in 1969, he incited his followers to murder at least nine white people in and around Hollywood. The victims, often murdered in a bestial and sadistic way, included the pregnant Sharon Tate, actress wife of film director Roman Polanski. Manson wanted the murders to be blamed on blacks, thus provoking a race war. He was sentenced to death, later commuted to life imprisonment.

I expressed a lot of interest in Manson to Breeze. I wrote more personalised letters, talking about my loathing of the police and normal people. Slowly, she began to open up, talking about Manson, blacks, the Klan and her criminal associates. One of the latter, 'Lord Spider', had just been arrested for shooting someone.

The more 'personal' I made my letters, the more personal she made hers. The picture she painted of herself was hardly glamorous. She was 46, had grandchildren, was grossly overweight and owned not only handguns, but a Kalashnikov. She said she'd never been to England (except in 'out-of-body travel') and asked if I thought she was 'coming on' to me. She described herself as a pagan high priestess 'for our white race'. She told me to write to Manson directly. I sent him a brief letter, playing on my membership of ATWA. Manson wrote a reply on red card. He'd scrawled his words over a drawing he'd done of himself:

HEADMAN

The head deadman said the head deadman don't need no
head man – I hate what was said man. A little secret can
hold a big thought. What I tell you is not what you would
tell – even if you think its dumb – don't tell.

    Charles Manson.

He sent three more short letters. I gave up trying to make sense
of the drivel:

I will write when I can, I'm not smart, try ATWA PO211
Alpaught CA 93201. I know you in the will of our god and
I do have a lot of respect for you and your command.
There is so much to it, I wish I had a telephone . . . Air
Trees Water and Wild Animals, one world for one god one
mind one money one will one one. A LOT of people use
that for other reason but the real of that wheel is the earth
will die unless you take it and give it who it wants . . .

    B. OMAHONEY. Before England trees were god, then
from somewhere someone came to Scotland, Ireland, with
a cross – I'm all before that and the granes that are in
forever – rest on my alter stone – I use the word my-I-me
. . . I've known a lot of OMahoneys in prison and they were
good as bad and bad as good, rocks of sort but rocks do
make so they were hard rocks bla bla. I've always been steel
and good whisky also.

    Charles Manson.

The news that my namesakes had apparently been filling up
prisons in America, too, didn't surprise me. I never heard from
Manson directly again. I wrote him a few more letters, but he
didn't reply personally. He delegated one of his disciples to do so,
but she made less sense than him. In the mean time, Breeze had
sent me her phone number. I rang her. She sounded surprisingly
'normal', at least in comparison to her letters. I said I'd had some
problems understanding her and Manson. She said they
deliberately wrote in babble to confuse whoever might be
monitoring the mail.

I pointed out that, as they encrypted no code in the letters, the recipient ended up as bewildered as everyone else. She didn't seem to get my point. She mumbled something about 'the Feds' listening to her calls, then rang off. Finally, after a bit of wrangling – I think she was holding out for another donation – she gave me the address of a Klansman called Juss. She described him as a friend of Manson's.

Juss seemed to warm to me, even making me an honorary member of the Klan in Stone Mountain, Georgia, where he claimed to be 'Grand Kleagle' (that is, chairman) of the local branch. He sent me an 'Invisible Empire' membership card and advised me of its benefits: 'If you're ever in the southern states and the Highway Patrol stop you, show your Invisible Empire Membership card with your licence. The cops will leave you alone.' I was soon inundated with flyers asking me to pledge money to White Power causes.

Eventually, Juss gave me an American address for the 'British Knights of the Ku Klux Klan'. I had to write to a PO box in Bethlehem, Philadelphia. My letter must then have been sent back to England, because I received an application form in an envelope with an English postmark. A Klansman on a white charger, carrying a flaming torch and wearing the distinctive peaked-hood robes, decorated the top of the form.

Apart from the usual 'name, address, date of birth' particulars, they wanted to know where I worked, my bank-account number, my National Insurance number, my place of birth and several other ridiculously intrusive details. They also wanted two passport photos.

I didn't like giving the Klan such information, so I made up most of it. I knew they just wanted to give would-be recruits the impression of an impenetrably secure organisation with the resources to vet applicants thoroughly. The same theatre of the paranoid made them base themselves in America, even though the Klan isn't outlawed in the United Kingdom. Yet, shrouded in secrecy and taking precautions that would drive most people away, they hoped to recruit their own anti-foreign legion.

I completed the form and sent it back to the American address. A few weeks later, I got a call on my mobile from a man with a Birmingham accent. He said, 'Mr O'Mahoney?'

I said, 'Yes, that's me.'

'This is the Ku Klux Klan.'

I said, 'Yes, I sent you a form.'

'Oh yeah, I know.'

After a pause, he said, 'Eh, I was ringing to see if you, eh, wanted to join.'

I told him I wanted to join. That was, after all, why I'd sent in an application form. An initiation ceremony was planned for the following week. I asked him where and when. He said, 'You don't need to know that.'

'Well, how am I going to get there then?'

'No, I mean you don't need to know that at the moment. Meet me outside Burger King at New Street Station in Birmingham next Saturday morning.'

'What time?'

'I'll confirm the time nearer the date. Till then. Bye.'

He rang off. My deceased former colleague Tucker hadn't put this much planning and secrecy into importing pallet-loads of cannabis from Holland. And the Klan weren't even doing anything illegal. To top it all, I noticed that my anonymous, security-conscious Klan caller had left behind his number on my mobile.

I rang Gary Jones at the *News of the World*. Not knowing the location of the ceremony prevented us setting up audio or video recorders in advance, and having to meet at a redirection point would prevent us doing it on the day. Gary said he'd find a way of hiding the equipment on me.

More problematic was Gary's wish to accompany me to the initiation ceremony. He had no time to undergo the long-winded, transatlantic vetting procedure. And, given the Klan's paranoia, I couldn't see how they'd allow a complete stranger to tag along. But Gary insisted.

On the Thursday before the planned Saturday meeting, I rang the Klansman who'd called me. 'Hello, mate,' I said. 'About this meeting Saturday.'

'What meeting?' he said. 'Who are you and where did you get my number?'

'You rang me,' I said. 'Your number came up on my phone

and I'm calling you back about Saturday. My name's O'Mahoney.'

He seemed to relax, 'Oh, right. Hello, mate. What's the matter?'

I reassured him I remained keen to join, but said I had trouble arranging transport. However, I had a friend who had a car and, even better, he too wanted to join, although he hadn't yet sent in his form. I said he'd be willing to pay on the spot any membership fee, as well as making a donation.

The Klansman said, 'It's £10 to join, then we expect £2.50 each month for Klan funds.'

I said my mate would be willing to pay six months' subs in advance as proof of his commitment.

The Klansman almost stuttered with excitement: 'That's brilliant, mate. Bring him along. The more of us the better.'

It all seemed so easy that I decided to push things a bit. I said my friend had business in Birmingham the next day, Friday, and perhaps we could all meet up for a drink in the evening before the ceremony on Saturday.

The Klansman said, 'I could meet you for a couple of pints, but no more. I'm a bit skint.' I told him not to worry about money. I said my mate could put everything down on his company expenses.

Gary and I travelled to Birmingham the next morning. We booked into a hotel, from where I rang the Klansman, whose name I still didn't know. He told us to meet him outside Burger King near the taxi rank at New Street Station. He had my passport photo, so he knew what I looked like.

On the way there, Gary emphasised that if anything untoward happened we were, in classic *News of the World* style, to make our excuses and leave, rather than get into a confrontation. As we approached Burger King, I saw two men standing outside. They could have been anything from early 30s to late 40s. One was an overweight stump with beer gut and moustache; the other had a shaven head and goatee beard.

Mr Moustache nodded recognition. He stretched out his hand and said, 'Join the Klan and help us rid Britain of niggers.' I recognised his voice from the mobile conversations. His words confirmed my earlier intuition that I was dealing with a fool. Serious people don't talk in such a theatrical way.

Mr Moustache introduced himself: 'My name's Nigel. I'm the Grand Kleagle of the Realm of England Knights of the Ku Klux Klan.'

I said, 'I'll just call you "Nige", if that's all right, mate. It's much easier.'

Everyone laughed, but I could tell Nige thought I might be taking the piss. In an effort to regain some ground, he told me he worked as a bouncer at a nightclub in nearby Willenhall. I didn't know it. I imagined the usual sweaty little groping parlour for council-estate toerags. However, I'd been in prison with a member of a well-known Willenhall crime family and I name-dropped, adding that he'd taken me there once to celebrate our release. I said, 'Some of the doormen are black, aren't they?'

Nige didn't answer the question. He was finding conversation with me difficult. He took refuge in being abusive again about 'niggers' and 'coons'. His goatee-bearded mate, a bodybuilder, sensed my impertinence and introduced himself as 'John, head of Klan security.'

As if to defend Nige for working with blacks, he pointed out that, whichever walk of life you found yourself in, you came inevitably into contact with them. He said, 'You can't escape them. They're like a cancer in society.'

We went into Burger King and sat down at a table. Nige said others would meet us there. I introduced myself and then introduced Gary as 'Arthur Owen'. Head of security John asked Gary a few trivial questions and, despite the fact that Gary hadn't sent off all his personal details, said he'd be allowed to take part in the initiation ceremony next day.

With the 'vetting' over, Nige began preaching, as if he feared we might now be having doubts about joining. He said the Klan was growing fast, attracting members from the BNP 'because they don't think they're hard enough'. He said the BNP was all talk and no action. He explained his political philosophy: 'There are two forms of protest – direct action and violence, and debate. Right now, we want more direct action . . . We're not here to mess around. You've got to be serious and committed.'

John joined in to give some examples of how we could spread the Klan message: 'They have nigger shoots in America where the KKK hunt blacks in forests. We should do that here . . . We could burn the mosques here. There's one which holds 2,000 people. I'd like to see it burn. I know a lot of them sleep there overnight.'

Nige still seemed unsure if he'd convinced us to cough up our membership fees. Perhaps to stop us thinking we were dealing with a group of sad, middle-aged losers, he said, 'We're getting a younger membership all the time.' He said they'd put up posters at schools all over the area encouraging kids to join. And, perhaps to emphasise the adventure-holiday aspect of membership, he said he'd been on military exercises at a secret Klan training camp in Portsmouth: 'We learn all sorts of combat techniques.'

Within a short time, various misfits turned up to join us: a retired tube driver, a clothes-shop worker and even someone who claimed to be studying music at university. The clothes-shop worker handed round photos of American Klan members holding various weapons. He boasted he'd recently been involved in an attack on anti-fascist students. He said, 'I like a scrap. I got seven stitches in one fight.'

I whispered to Gary, 'He'll be getting more if he carries on.'

Then a stereotype of a sexual deviant, complete with dirty mac, sat down near me and asked if I worked out in gyms or 'wrestled'. The way he said the word 'wrestle' made me think it might be a code-word for some sort of homosexual activity. I said, 'What do you mean, fucking "wrestle"?'

Realising he'd offended me in some way, but not quite sure why, he said something about my reminding him of someone he knew. That annoyed me even more. I stared at him. I could imagine him hanging around gyms, sniffing discarded jockstraps and taking an inordinately long time in the communal showers. He mumbled an apology and moved to another seat.

My new comrades included a leather-clad skinhead with a spider's web and Union Jack tattooed on his face. He said proudly he'd just come out of prison for killing someone with a scaffolding pole. I've known several people who've killed people and, to be honest, none of them ever said they were proud of that fact. It's usually one of the last things you learn about them. But this idiot was telling strangers that he'd served four years for manslaughter. He claimed he'd clubbed his victim to death to protect a friend who was being beaten. To me, he didn't look like he could kill half an hour waiting for a bus, never mind another human being. I began to wish he'd visited me and Gavin at Raquels on one of our occasional but popular skinhead-bashing nights.

Although several of us hadn't yet been properly initiated, Grand Kleagle Nige talked as if addressing a committee meeting of stalwarts. He asked for the treasurer's report. Gary and I sat listening disbelievingly as 'the treasurer' began reading the accounts. Printing had cost so much, booking venues had cost so much, stationery so much, and so on, leaving a grand total of £16.50.

I nearly choked on my french fries. This terror group couldn't afford a decent box of fireworks, let alone the weapons they'd need for the race war they dreamed of. I realised now why Nige had waved Gary through without the proper vetting. He'd been dreaming of almost doubling the group's funds with a windfall payment of six months' subs.

Nige moved to break up the meeting. He said he'd ring us in the morning to tell us when to return to Burger King. From there, we'd be taken to 'the Klavern' for our initiation into the fearsome Ku Klux Klan.

CHAPTER 14

BEDSHEETS IN BIRMINGHAM

THE FOLLOWING DAY, ENGLAND FACED SPAIN IN THE EURO '96 FOOTBALL championship. I hoped to be back from the initiation ceremony before the mid-afternoon kick-off.

My brother Michael and his wife Carol, who lived just down the road, came to visit me at the hotel. I got some beers in, hardly nervous about the task ahead.

Nige rang me late morning. He told me to meet him at Burger King in two hours. Gary and I hid microphones on ourselves and concealed a camera in a sports bag, hidden under some T-shirts and boxer shorts. The camera would transmit pictures to a broadcast team nearby. So even if the bag were seized, or left behind, we'd still have the pictures. However, we knew if the Klan searched the bag thoroughly, we'd be rumbled. I decided that, if they tried, I'd feign offence and try to bluff my way through.

To my surprise, around 20 would-be Klan members arrived in dribs and drabs at Burger King. Several of them looked like they'd just secured day-release from the local psychiatric unit. We didn't all sit together. Grand Kleagle Nige would nod at people as they arrived and exchange a few conspiratorial words. After a while, he asked us to follow him.

We left Burger King and made our way to the Fiveways roundabout, passing the scene of the 1974 IRA pub bombings, then turned left into the main shopping street, which was packed with Saturday shoppers. Under the guidance of the Grand

Kleagle, our group of white males entered the foyer of the respectably plush Britannia Hotel.

Head of security John told us to go to the third floor. The Klan had booked a suite for a 'football presentation'. The suite contained a main room for the ceremony and a smaller reception room where we initiates had to wait in single file. The cost of booking the suite had probably caused the shortfall in branch finances.

We lined up. Gary and I stood in the middle of the queue. Nige and his goatee-bearded sidekick entered the main room, presumably to put on their frocks. I got a quick glimpse of others wearing the distinctive Klan bedsheets before the door slammed shut. Then I heard the sound of chanting. The jockstrap-sniffer who thought I might be a 'wrestler' stood in front of me, sweating and visibly excited.

Then the door opened again. A Klansman in robes stood there. He said, 'Enter.' Each man was searched as he stepped forward. I didn't want Gary to go first and then be trapped alone inside if something went wrong, so I stood in front of him. The Klansman beckoned me forward and began to frisk me. I held the camera bag in my hand. He asked to look inside. I opened it and said, 'Hold your nose, mate. There's two days' worth of pants and socks in there.'

He looked briefly into the bag, but didn't search around inside. It was a good job my 'wrestling' acquaintance hadn't been doing the searching. I'd probably have needed help prising his fingers off the bag's soiled contents. I was nodded through into the main room. At the far end was a table, behind which sat three chiefs. A crucifix rested on the table. The two walls on either side were lined with hooded Klansmen and decorated with banners from both the Klan and Combat 18, the new Nazi bad boys on the block.

I put the bag on the floor, pointing the camera towards the proceedings, which were now being beamed back to the *News of the World*'s outside-broadcast unit. I joined the other initiates standing at the back of the room. Gary also survived the search.

My name was called and I walked to the table where the three chiefs sat. I was asked who I was. I said, 'You just called my name.'

Then one of them asked me about my religious background. I'd been brought up Catholic, but I knew the Klan hated Catholics as much as it hated Jews and blacks, so I said, 'Church of England'.

Grand Kleagle Nige said, 'We don't like them. They give money to coloureds.' He said their 'Kludd' (which I later discovered meant 'chaplain') could teach me their 'faith', which I gathered was an extremist Protestant version of Christianity with all the bits about loving your neighbour taken out.

I was then asked in which 'area' of Klan activity I saw myself becoming involved. 'Security' seemed the obvious answer, as I could see it was currently rather poor. I replied, 'Security.' I then had to repeat a few sentences of religious drivel before being asked to stand down. Gary went next and underwent the same procedure. He told me later that he'd volunteered to help out with publicity.

When Gary had finished, he came to stand at the back with me. Now we waited to swear an oath of allegiance. As the next candidate started to be questioned, one of the Klansmen at the side of the table stepped forward and said sternly, 'Could every non-Klan member leave the room immediately.'

I looked at Gary and looked at the bag, but before I could say anything the Klansman added, 'There's no need to take your stuff. This will only take a moment.'

Once we'd all left the room, a Klansman slammed the door shut. Gary and I moved away from the other recruits. Gary whispered, 'I think they've sussed us.'

'Me too,' I said. 'What d'you want to do?'

'Let's get out of here.'

We walked out of the suite into the main corridor. The lift stood about 50 yards away. We decided against using it, and headed instead for the stairs. As we got there, the door to the Klan's suite burst open. I turned to see hooded figures running into the corridor. Raised voices shouted, 'Where've they gone?' Then someone screamed, 'There they are!'

Gary looked at me, laughed and said, 'Remember, Bernie. No trouble. Let's get out of here.'

We ran down the stairs. Soon, we could hear the Klansmen jumping down behind us. When we reached the bottom, we burst through a fire door into the packed reception. Everyone stopped to look at us. We composed ourselves and walked towards the main exit.

As we reached the door, the pursuing Klansmen, some still wearing their bedsheets, raced into the reception area. Several women started screaming. One of the Klansmen shouted, 'Back, back.' They all turned and disappeared back up the stairwell. Those without bedsheets covered their faces with their hands.

Gary and I jogged and laughed all the way back to the hotel just in time to see England beat Spain on penalties. I felt good about what I'd done. I felt embarrassed to think I might once have joined the Klan for real.

In one Klan newsletter, I'd seen Nige's 'Klavern' described as 'the biggest and best in the Midlands'. I had difficulty imagining the smallest and worst.

The next day, Gary rang Nige in the hope of getting a quote, but received only threats. Nige said, 'We've got a top ten of people on our hit list and you've made it. We'll get you.' Gary told me that Nige had also threatened me.

I didn't like what I heard. I don't like being threatened, particularly by sad deviants who hide under bedsheets. So I rang the Grand Kleagle myself.

Nige sounded surprised to hear me. I said, 'Have you been threatening me?' He didn't answer my question. I asked him if he wanted to meet to sort things out man to man. Again, he didn't answer my question. Instead, he began mouthing off about our use of covert recording equipment, which he said was illegal and for which he was going to report us. He ignored my offer of a 'straightener' (that is, a bare-knuckle fight).

I admit that at this point I did get a bit frustrated. I said I was going to arrive unannounced at his council house and stove his head in. I may also have given him the impression I was going to lynch him with his bedsheet and stick a burning cross up his arse. I thought he'd hurl similar abuse at me. I was therefore a little surprised when he started bleating about his girlfriend and their little baby. He said if I was threatening him, then I was threatening them, and he was therefore going to ring the police.

I almost laughed. The leader of a group which intimidates,

threatens and attacks innocent people wanted to run to the police because someone had spoken harshly to him on the phone. I called him 'a fucking tart' and replaced the receiver.

A week later the *News of the World* printed the story under the headline, 'WE EXPOSE EVIL KLAN'.

The hoods and robes are chillingly familiar. Menacing symbols of hatred and fear. Of burnings, beatings and brutal murder.

This is a meeting of the dreaded Ku Klux Klan. A gathering of evil racists hell-bent on wiping what they call 'coloureds' off the face of the earth. Our exclusive picture of these white supremacist devils at 'prayer' comes moments after they initiated a killer into their ranks.

It was taken secretly at a Klan conclave in Birmingham. Not Birmingham, Alabama, in the racial hotbed of America's Deep South where the Klan has traditionally struck terror into black communities.

But Birmingham, England.

For today we reveal how this vile sect has:

GAINED a strong foothold in our country with IRA-style small cells growing nationwide;

SPREAD its tentacles to school gates as it searches for new, impressionable members;

JOINED forces with the violent and fiercely racist Nazi group Combat 18 and

SET UP a secret military camp to train members for racist attacks.

We also UNMASK one of the beasts who leads the British Ku Klux Klan, a smiling thug who lives in a housing estate among West Indians and Asians.

A thug whose first words to the *News of the World*'s undercover reporter were, 'Join the Klan and help us rid Britain of "niggers".'

Our painstaking and dangerous investigation in which our reporter was initiated into the KKK penetrates the very core of the feared sect which guards itself night and day against discovery.

The details were spread over two pages, including grainy pictures from the ceremony and a photo of Nige without his bedsheet. I was pleased the story had been given such a good spread, but I felt a bit uncomfortable, because indirectly the article boosted the morons. It took them as a serious threat, rather than the ridiculous halfwits I knew them to be. The article ended with the words:

> Their leader, who bounces at a nightclub in Willenhall, is known to West Midlands police.
>
> The thug, who bragged he would never be exposed, made death threats when our reporter contacted him yesterday.
>
> 'We've got a top ten of people on our hit list and you've made it,' he yelled. 'We'll get you.'
>
> Now we are making our dossier of evidence on him and his Ku Klux Klan henchmen available to the police. Last night Gerry Gable, editor of international anti-fascist magazine *Searchlight*, praised our investigation.
>
> 'The KKK are active everywhere,' he warned. 'If anybody thinks the Klan is a joke, a political fancy-dress party, they should look at their criminal records. People should be very worried.'

The article, and the footage of the ceremony broadcast on the television news, caused a commotion, particularly in the Midlands. Police chiefs, bishops and talk-show hosts all had something to say. MPs even raised the matter in the House of Commons.

A few days later, a plain, brown envelope arrived at my mother's address in the Midlands. I'd never lived there. I was living 150 miles away. Inside was a calling card from the British Knights of the Ku Klux Klan with the words 'Always Watching'. I was furious. As far as I was concerned, these pricks were threatening my elderly mother by letting me know they knew where she lived.

I rang Grand Kleagle Nige again, but his number was now unobtainable. I considered dropping in on him, but I couldn't be sure he'd be there. One news report had said he'd gone into hiding. And I didn't want to have to pass on a message through his girlfriend and baby daughter.

I rang Adolf. He had numerous contacts within the far-right and I wanted him to pass on a message. Adolf wasn't pleased to hear I'd helped turn over a part of 'the Movement' for ZOG's press. He thought I deserved some grief, but he didn't like the idea of my mother being threatened. I asked him to let it be known that I wanted a straightener with the bastard who'd sent the calling card. I'd go to a place of his choice and I'd go alone.

Adolf rang me a few days later. He said the response hadn't been favourable. He'd spoken to a senior Klansman in Birmingham who was in denial. I sent a written offer of a straightener to the British Knights of the Ku Klux Klan's PO box in America. I told them to publish it in their 'rag'.

A few months later, a genuine rag landed on my doormat. It was a magazine which looked like it had been knocked out on granddad's typewriter, then photocopied at the local newsagent's. The Klan had sent me a copy of their members' and supporters' newsletter, *Always Watching*.

My face glared out from the cover. They'd used my passport photo to decorate an article headlined, 'WE EXPOSE EVIL REPORTER SCUM!'. The article, written by 'the Imperial Wizard', was riddled with simple spelling mistakes:

> The picture on the right is of a sick freelance reporter who goes under the name of 'PATRICK BERNARD O'MAHONEY'. Mahoney along with sidekick *News of the World* reporter Gary Jones who also goes under the name of Arther Owen tried to pass themselves off as Klan Kandidates at a Klavern meeting in Birmingham.
>
> However they did not get as far as they make out in their fairy story article about us in the *News of the World* and they were NOT initiated into our Order.
>
> It was thanks to quick thinking of our Security Staff who spotted the ilegal recording equipment and they were then quickly expelled from the Klavern.
>
> Cowardly Mahoney made death threats on my Grand Kleagle and his family by telephone which encluded my

Grand Kleagles baby daughter. Of course the police are now involved on a local level to monitor any futher threats made on the Grand Kleagle, his family and any other of our members. Together with this I have installed Nighthawks to keep watch over the Grand Kleagle and his family.

If you do make a move Mahoney we will be waiting for you, you gutless cowardly scum.

It is unfair to envolve the Grand Kleagles ex-girlfriend and baby daughter as they have been apart now for some time.

The Imperial Wizard said I'd already tried to infiltrate other Klan groups. Indeed, he'd be putting my name on the Internet to warn other comrades of 'theses gutter-sniper's':

So Mahoney I would not bother trying to join any other groups as the game is up my son. You will have to find another way of earning your 'Thirty Pieces of Silver'.

This reference to my 'thirty pieces of silver' showed me they knew I'd once genuinely been a part of 'the Movement'. They saw me now as a Judas, a betrayer – as indeed did Adolf – not just a reporter who'd done the dirty on them.

The article attacked Labour MPs who'd threatened to jail Klan members. Apparently, Gary Jones and I were the real criminals deserving imprisonment, because we'd used recording equipment illegally and allegedly threatened to kill a woman and her baby.

The Klan article continued:

Next the 'Bishop' of Aston joined the band-wagon by saying 'that it's sad to see that there are these evil men in society who wish to destroy the multi-blended faiths that we enjoy in Birmingham.' Well Bishop I sugest you read your Bible mate. It makes it quite clear about the dangers of race-mixing.

Also Bishop what about the Evil Reporters that made death threats on a baby, is it because she is white that you are not botherd about her well-being? You make me sick.

'They profess they know God, but deny him by their works' – Holy Bible.

The truth is if anybody understands the cultural needs of the ethnics groups, then it is the Klan and National Socialism. We preach racial love, NOT racial hatred. It is the above MP's and so-called church leaders that are trying to destroy all races by their policy of forced race-mixing. It is the un-Godly race-mixing that we hate and NOT the colour of a persons skin.

The Imperial Wizard then thanked the *News of the World* for 'the free advert', claiming to have gained more members and hundreds of enquiries as a result. He finished with an effusion of thanks worthy of an Oscar ceremony:

Once again I would like to thank the Grand Dragon, Grand Klaliff, Grand Kludd, the Grand Kleagle, Grand Knighthawk and Great Nighthawk and the Exalted Cyclops (Hinckly Klavern) who have been fantastic in their help and supportive actions in concern to the above.

He ended his rant with a supposed quote from 'Adolph' Hitler: 'That which does not destroy us, makes us stronger.'

I turned to the rag's letters page to see if they'd printed my letter offering a straightener. They hadn't. However, they'd printed several letters slagging off the *News of the World* as the *Jews of the World*. I had the impression the letters had been written by the same person. Surprisingly, one of them gave a faint nod to multiculturalism:

Dear Sir,
I have read the very biased *News of the World* Article.

As a Pakistani Muslim and someone who knows you from my school day's, I just Know that what Gary Jones has printed about you is just not true.

I always knew your views and had respect for them as you did for mine.

However I am sure that your brothers and mine share

the same fight against Zionism, Capitalism and Communism.

Mr M.

At the back of the newsletter, which had devoted so much space to my supposed threats, the Imperial Wizard reprinted an article from Northern Ireland's *Sunday Life* newspaper. It had been sent in by 'Our Ulster Klan Comrades'. The billy-boy bully boys had sent hatemail to a local anti-racism campaigner. The envelope had contained a poster showing a bedsheet-wearing Klansman with the printed words, 'Ku Klux Klan – Closer Than You Think'. They'd handwritten the words, 'Now in Ulster'. I was reminded of the words of Gavin, my Asian mate from Raquels: 'They don't mind giving it, but when you give it them back they don't want to know.'

CHAPTER 15

MUMMY SAYS I'M HANDSOME

And a word of thanks to our comrades of the NSA and the Editor of *The Order* magazine who have helped in exposing the reporter scum despite the fact that Charlie and Will are having their own problems with ZOG at the moment together with some other comrades that have not long been arrested for so-called alleged anti-race laws.

THE IMPERIAL WIZARD'S LAST WORDS WERE MEANT TO REMIND ME THAT, BY infiltrating the Klan, I'd also invoked the wrath of Britain's newest Nazi bogeymen, Combat 18. The 'NSA' stood for the National Socialist Alliance, a loose network of British Nazi groups, dominated by Combat 18 (C18); *The Order* was its magazine; and 'Charlie and Will' were C18's notoriously violent leading personalities, Charlie Sargent and 'Will' Browning (usually only reds called Browning 'Will'. Among his mates he was 'Wilf'.).

Combat 18 had emerged after I'd stopped supporting 'the Movement'. Only the occasional phone conversation with Adolf, and the Nazi magazines he continued to send, had kept me in touch with the far-right scene. In 1992, the BNP had sought to harness some of its more violent fringe elements such as the 'East End Barmy Army' – the alliance of London football hooligans formed in part to protect BNP leaders and events. But the violent, direct-action hardcore didn't want to be harnessed. Instead, they formed Combat 18. The number 18 represented Hitler's initials: 'A' being the first letter of the alphabet, 'H' the eighth. For their logo, they chose the skull-and-crossbones insignia of the Waffen SS's Death's Head Division.

Indeed, C18 presented themselves as the Death's Head Division of the British Nazi movement. They'd have run the concentration camps if the National Socialist government of their dreams had come to power. In the mean time, they existed to carry out physical attacks on anyone they considered the enemy. Their stated aim was to start a race war.

At first, C18 remained nominally loyal to the BNP. But after the party secured its first-ever council seat in Millwall in September 1993, tensions grew between a political party seeking electoral success and a gang of Nutzi hooligans seeking street warfare. C18 started attacking members of the BNP. Indeed, in a short while, the BNP had more to fear from C18 than from the reds.

Articles in C18's magazine containing extreme and illegal incitement to racial hatred brought things to a head. The magazine declared that C18 wanted:

> . . . to ship all non-whites back to Africa, Asia, Arabia, alive or in body bags . . . to execute all queers . . . to execute all white race-mixers . . . to weed out all the Jews in the government, the media, the arts, the professions. To execute all Jews who have actively helped to damage the white race and to put into camps the rest until we find a final solution for the eternal Jew.

This viciously crazed anti-Semitism (from people who'd probably never met a Jew in their lives) had become a hallmark of the magazine. One issue contained a report of a visit to Sachsenhausen concentration camp in Germany by a group of C18 supporters. It read:

> Why is it after 50 years people still go on about the so-called Holocaust? We know it's a load of bollocks and so must anyone else with half a brain. Yet still we're bombarded with films and documentaries about those poor little Jews. Not a day goes past without some hook-nose kike weeping on our TV screens, 'Oy vay, oy vay. I lost my

daughter, oy vay. I was gassed six times and my wife she's a table lamp.' Is there no end to this dribble? Of course not. Because all ZOG's TV channels are controlled by the Jews. It doesn't matter that there weren't six million Jews in the whole of German-occupied Europe or that most of these so-called gassed Jews fucked off to New York, Israel and Whitechapel before there was any smell of danger.

The writer said that a CI8 'team of experts' had examined the ovens at Sachsenhausen: 'On further investigation we found that you couldn't cook a cheeseburger in them, let alone six million stinking Yids.' The conclusion was there was no way that six million Jews could have been gassed: '. . . and even if they were, who gives a fuck because next time we're gonna incinerate every last stinking one of 'em! No fuss! No mess! Just pure cyanide.'

In December 1993, the split between C18 and the BNP became official. BNP leader John Tyndall issued 'a notice of complete repudiation of Combat 18', declaring that group to be 'a hostile organisation' guilty of divisive behaviour. He added that BNP members had to sever all links with Combat 18, whose leader Charlie Sargent, a football hooligan with aspirations, then wrote:

> Those involved in the struggle now have a straight choice between the failed policies of Tory nationalism or the ideology of Adolf Hitler. The two groups cannot work together. One must be crushed . . . It is now your decision. Do you follow Tyndall or National Socialism?

Putting his fists behind Adolf Hitler and National Socialism was an emerging rival to Sargent: Wilf Browning, known as 'The Beast'. He'd made a name for himself attacking opponents with screwdrivers. He gave a good beating to Adolf's mate and senior BNP figure 'Mad Bomber' Lecomber, who, from the outset, had been suspicious of, and hostile to, C18.

Sargent continually preached the need to 'incite the niggers and Arabs' in the hope of lighting 'the touch paper to a fire so powerful that ZOG will never be able to put it out'. In September

1995, he told a meeting in Holborn, central London, that if everyone in C18 killed two people, then 400 would be dead within a week. The scale of the killings would shock the nation and ignite the race war.

Shortly afterwards, Sargent claimed the credit for engineering the riot that brought England's football match against the Irish Republic to a premature end at Dublin's Lansdowne Road. He told a journalist, 'We didn't care if England won or not. The lads was only there for a good fight and to teach the IRA bastards a thing or two, and to try to screw up the so-called peace talks.'

According to the Klan, Combat 18 were now on my trail too. I soon received a copy of Issue 16 of their magazine, *The Order*. My passport photo occupied the whole of the front page with the words, 'Not so clever now, are you!' Inside, an editorial written by 'Andy Saxon' said:

> Our cover page shows intrepid *News of the World* reporter Patrick O'Mahoney, AKA Gary Jones, the man behind the recent so called exposé of the alleged members of the British Ku Klux Klan in Birmingham. This red hack took gutter journalism to new depths with his two page spread on the BKKK. We at *The Order* hope that he understands that we do not take kindly to our own kith and kin being subjected to such vile smear stories!!!!!!!!!!!!!!

They didn't scare me. They obviously knew my address. If they had a beef with me they should have popped round for a chat, not slagged me off in their semi-literate magazine. I wouldn't be losing any sleep over them.

On the other hand, I wouldn't be forgetting the tossers either. I vowed to continue monitoring their activities – and to exact my revenge when the opportunity arose.

One amusing coincidence I noticed in the issue of *The Order* which had slagged me off as a 'red hack' was the mention of a new 'Irish' group. The editorial said:

> A new development with the cause which is warmly welcomed is the formation of British-based Irish racialist

group, The Shamrock Legion. Full details of this group will appear in Issue 17. With more Irish living in mainland Britain than actually in Ireland, the potential for this group is huge. We at *The Order* will be doing everything we can to help our Irish brothers start up.

I'd been in an unofficial 'Shamrock Legion' for years with my south London friends.

Through my own experience in Tucker's gang, I could see the cracks beginning to appear in C18. They were posturing bullies with inflated egos, just like Tucker and his henchmen.

C18 had moved into the Nazi music scene, which, by all accounts, was surprisingly lucrative, generating around a hundred thousand pounds a year for Sargent and his clique. In much the same way that Tucker's gang (of which I was part) beat, bullied and terrorised its 'business competitors' in the drugs field, C18 trashed rivals' concerts, intimidated rival promoters and took control of CD and merchandise distribution. And just as Tucker's gang had linked up with Continental counterparts to import drugs, C18 linked up with European Nazis to distribute its musical wares.

But, as with Tucker's gang, C18 soon came to a gruesome end. Only six months after I'd appeared on the front page of *The Order*, C18 broke apart. Incredibly, leader Charlie Sargent was sentenced to life imprisonment for the murder of Wilf Browning's mate, Chris Castle, who was stabbed in the back with a nine-inch blade. Sargent didn't stick the knife in himself – he incited someone else to do the deed. From what I heard, Castle wasn't even heavily involved in 'the Movement'. He was just a good mate of Browning, and a popular and well-liked person.

Shortly before the murder – but nothing to do with it – the police had thwarted a C18 letter-bomb campaign, involving devices sent to, among others, Sharron Davies, the Olympic swimmer married to a black athlete. Her crime? Race-mixing. The devices had been sent by a supporter in Denmark, himself the product of a mixed-race relationship: his mother was Danish and his father, with whom he'd lost contact, was an American of Japanese descent. The would-be letter-bomber, who was arrested and imprisoned, also had a half-sister with a Pakistani father. In England, Wilf Browning was arrested in connection with the thwarted campaign, but wasn't charged, despite evidence of his extensive contact with the man who'd posted the bombs. At Charlie Sargent's trial, Sargent claimed that Browning had wanted to turn C18 into a proper terrorist organisation. Most incredibly, it was revealed at the trial that Sargent had been stabbing C18 in the back for some time. He'd been a long-term informer for the political police, the Special Branch. Sargent had tipped them off about the Danish letter-bomber, but his main job had been to keep his handlers briefed about C18's links with Loyalist terrorists in Northern Ireland. This led to claims that, from its inception, C18 had been little more than a so-called 'pseudo-gang'.

'Pseudo-gangs' or 'counter-gangs' are a well-tried British intelligence counter-terrorist ploy involving the setting up of groups that can be attributed to the enemy in order to discredit that enemy. Such pseudo-gangs draw in extremists, cause splits in the wider movement and make sure everyone goes nowhere. A C18 'Information Bulletin' released before Sargent's trial described him as an 'arch-traitor', a 'poison dwarf', a 'misfit', a 'dickhead' and a 'cretin'. It said:

> How on earth did we ever listen to Sargent? He's just such a mug . . . Sargent purposely split every movement he's been involved with and that's a fact!!

The BNP's new leader, Nick Griffin, later wrote that the state had created the 'Combat 18 pseudo-gang' in order 'to disrupt the BNP through lies, intimidation and physical violence against key officials'. Griffin admitted that C18 had seriously damaged the party for two to three years. Indeed, he failed to add, Griffin owed his new position to one of C18's indirect successes – the toppling of my old sparring partner, the BNP leader John Tyndall.

Adolf told me that his mate Tony Lecomber had planned to take over from Tyndall, but that the Cambridge-educated Nick Griffin had convinced him that his criminal convictions would ensure that the media had a permanent, ready-made smear to use against him. This would 'taint' the leadership and prevent him ever being able to lead the party to electoral success. Adolf said Griffin had promised Lecomber a leading role in the party if he dropped his own leadership ambitions and supported Griffin's, which he did, urging branch activists to support Griffin. 'Mad Bomber' Lecomber became the BNP's 'national organiser'.

One C18 faction regrouped under Wilf Browning and published the magazine *Strikeforce*. On the foot of each page, they printed the logo, 'Trust no one'. In Issue Two, published in spring 1998, they detailed the astonishing story of their former leader Charlie Sargent. Under the headline, 'End of the road for the 5 ft toad', the article began, 'After years of grassing, lying and outrageous treachery, Charlie Sargent's Special Branch career finally came to an abrupt halt as he was sentenced to life imprisonment at Chelmsford Crown Court on Wednesday 21st January 1998.' The article explained the sordid battle for power between Browning and Sargent that had led to the murder. It read:

> It's ironic that Sargent was shown mercy by Wilf, who felt embarrassed for the fat mug after seeing him crying when confronted about his bullshit. Both he and his gutless brother Steve were offered the chance to sort it out like men, but they both bottled out. Instead, we had the spectacle of the two misfits sitting around their Chelmsford flat, heads facing the floor, not having the courage to admit what they had been saying behind Wilf's back, not having the guts to go outside and sort it out, either by fists or knives. Wilf openly laughed at Sargent about his interview where he said that he challenged people who slagged him off to a knife-fight to the death. Well, he was given the chance, but he bottled it. As Wilf said to him, 'You're pathetic. Look at yourself. You're meant to be the big terrorist leader.' So there you have it: this fat trembling coward was shown mercy because he was so pathetic. So what did he do? He plotted the death of Chris Castle, then tried to use the police to put Wilf out of the game.

The article ended with an unsubtle threat for their one-time Führer:

You've been exposed for what you are Sargent and we promise you this: whatever lifer jail you go to, your statement will follow and everyone will know what you are YOU FAT BACKSTABBING GRASS! . . . What he did was disgusting, cowardly and is unforgivable. He overstepped the line: he will have to pay the price for his treachery, but for the time being he will languish in jail.

The foot of the article was decorated with a drawing of a gallows and the words, 'IT AIN'T OVER TILL THE FAT MAN SWINGS'.

Disillusionment at discovering they'd been led by a man who was simultaneously grassing them up must have provoked some soul-searching. For in the same issue, someone wrote a very perceptive assessment of the whole Nazi scene. The article – apart from its nods to the good old days of the Third Reich – could have appeared in the anti-fascist *Searchlight* magazine. Unsigned and titled, 'They ain't alright just because they're white', it read:

I've been involved in the so-called 'right-wing' for a number of years now, but when I step back and look at our so-called Movement, especially more recently, I can't help saying to myself, 'Why am I surrounded by so many "misfits"?' I'm sure that, if you are honest, you would have to agree with me.

The writer said that most of the so-called 'right-wingers' around today wouldn't have been fit to dig latrine pits for the Waffen SS, yet they claimed to represent the white race and declared themselves to be 'the so-called vanguard'.

The problem now is that since the war the pro-white groups have been desperate for the numbers and will accept absolutely anyone just because they're white and call themselves racists. It doesn't matter what sort of lowlife they are as long as they are 'our way'. Obviously, not everyone is scum in our movement, so let's take a look at the sort of people attracted to it.

1. The genuine idealists: these are few and far between. It's refreshing when you meet people who genuinely believe in the cause and are normal decent people.

2. The cowards: these unfortunately make up the bulk of the 'right-wing'. Blokes who are nothing by themselves, join up to be part of a gang, give it the right large one when they are at a nationalist event, sticking the boot in when the numbers are on our side, but in reality are the sort of blokes who would watch a couple of spades push in front of them in a queue and do nothing about it, just look away. You all know the sort: without the beer for 'Dutch courage', they're nothing.

3. The inadequates and losers: again, the 'right' is full of these types. They join because no one else will have them. They don't fit in with any 'normal' groups of people, so they turn to the group that accepts anyone – the 'right-wing' – where they have instant friends and drinking buddies and, because there are so many other inadequates, they fit in perfectly.

4. The faggots: because of the nature of the Movement, which is comprised of a lot of young blokes, queers tend to be attracted to it for devious reasons.

5. The sickos and weirdos: these are the sort of freaks who believe in the Hitler = Evil equation that is spread by the media, and because they want to be 'evil' they latch on to us. These types are usually involved in 'Satanism', cults, paedophilia, you name it. Luckily, these are small in number, but always prove to be the most embarrassing when they are exposed in the press and we are all tarred with the same brush. These types aren't National Socialists: if they hadn't infiltrated the 'right-wing' they would be in some sort of cult. Our enemies love deviants such as these, often encouraging them to join us.

6. The drunken bums: these sort of blokes are in their element in the 'right-wing' because most of it is just a big drinking club.

So there it is. You may not want to hear it, but it's true. The 'right-wing' accepts ANYONE – it has NO standards. We set ourselves up as though we're better than everyone else and talk about the general population as though they're scum and we are somehow above them. Well, the truth is that percentage-wise we most probably have ten times the number of scumbags in our movement than exist in the so-called 'non-racist' general population.

The writer said 'the Movement' had either to clean up its act and introduce some standards or carry on being a freak show for society to laugh at.

Personally, I don't want it to be the latter and I doubt if you do. So, it's up to the decent activists to give the freak show a wide berth and clean up our movement – dump the misfits, let 'em join the NSM!

The NSM was the 'National Socialist Movement', which had become the refuge for the wing of C18 that remained loyal to Charlie Sargent. It had about eight members, including Sargent's brother Steve. It described itself as 'the political wing of Combat 18'. In fact, it had been formed originally by another fruitcake of my vague acquaintance called David Myatt, who was an unusual Nazi in that he had a posh accent, a long ginger beard, pebble glasses and a tweed flat-cap.

I met him once at a paper sale in Brick Lane. I thought he'd mistakenly come to stand on the wrong side of the police barriers, because he looked more like a tree-hugging leftist than an Aryan stormtrooper. Indeed, Adolf regarded him as 'a deviant' and whispered that 'a naive young northerner' such as myself should steer well clear of him. Under no circumstances, said Adolf, should I accept an invitation from him to view his stamp collection. Myatt later resigned from the NSM after an anti-fascist group exposed his links with Satanism. I understand he's since abandoned Nazism – and converted to Islam.

The same issue of *Strikeforce* carried an article about the so-called 'Mardi Gra' bomber who'd been planting explosive devices at branches of Barclays bank and the supermarket Sainsbury's since late 1994:

> Although the 'Organised Crime Group' has proved successful in dealing with groups and organisations thanks to its heavy use of informers and agents, it has up until now failed to stop the lone 'Mardi Gra' bomber. The 'Mardi Gra' bomber is ZOG's nightmare: he is intelligent and capable of making bombs and booby traps; he works ALONE and it seems he is totally autonomous; he strikes at random and without warning.

The article concluded with the observation:

> We at *Strikeforce* don't know the 'Mardi Gra' bomber's political orientation, his race or his motives, and we don't condone his attacks on stores where innocent shoppers could be hurt, but we have to agree that he is very effective and his 'modus operandi' is proving to cause ZOG a few problems. Look at the trouble he is causing, yet he is a one-man cell. Imagine if there were fifty White Resistance 'Mardi Gra' Bombers. Think about it!
>
> So the moral of this story is:
> 1. Don't let your granny go shopping in Sainsbury's.
> 2. LEADERLESS RESISTANCE DOES WORK!

In fact, the 'Mardi Gra' bomber was caught in April 1998 while the magazine was at the printer's. He turned out to be a reclusive white man in his 60s called Edgar Pearce. His motivation had been financial, not political. He'd demanded ten million pounds to stop. Pearce was jailed for 21 years in April 1999.

In that same month, London was terrorised by another 'lone-wolf' bomber. On 17 April, a bomb exploded in Brixton, south London. Shoppers were blasted with hundreds of nails; 42 people were injured. A 4-in. nail embedded itself in the brain of a 23-month-old boy; two people lost eyes.

When I first heard news of the bomb, I thought Adolf might have planted it. I knew Brixton had no political or military significance for Irish terrorists. But to the far-right, the area represented the black face of Britain. Adolf had been present 14 years earlier when Tony Lecomber's bomb had detonated in his car in nearby Clapham. And I couldn't help but think that Adolf might have had something to do with this one.

A week later, another bomb exploded in Brick Lane in London's East End, an area with a large Asian population. It injured six. The third and most devastating bomb exploded the following Friday in Soho, the hub of London's gay scene. At the Admiral Duncan pub, two people died instantly, one of them a pregnant woman. A third person died in hospital. A hundred and thirty-nine were injured; four people lost legs. Callers allegedly from Combat 18 and a hitherto unknown group, the White Wolves, claimed responsibility.

A short time later, the police announced the arrest of a single, 23-year-old London Underground worker from Farnborough in Surrey called David Copeland. At a press conference after his arrest, the police ruled out Copeland's links to the Nazi groups who'd claimed responsibility. Most journalists, who didn't pay close attention to the Metropolitan Police Assistant Commissioner's phrasing, assumed he'd said that Copeland had no links whatsoever to extreme right-wing groups. That was my reading too. In fact, the Assistant Commissioner had only said that Copeland had no links to the groups who'd claimed responsibility for the attacks.

The police presented him as someone 'working alone for his own motives'. These words seemed to rule out political motives. I didn't believe this. My friends and I had never officially joined any Nazi groups either, but we'd still worked for 'the Movement'. I knew from Copeland's choice of targets that he had to have a fascist background, even if he'd worked alone in devising and carrying out his bombing campaign.

In the week following the press conference, I rang Adolf. He'd been greatly excited by the bombs and, like me, had guessed immediately that Nazis stood behind them. In fact, Adolf had already heard on the grapevine that Copeland was a member of the National Socialist Movement, the refuge for the discredited Sargent faction of Combat 18, slagged off by the other faction as a dumping ground for 'misfits'.

I hadn't forgotten Sargent's threat to me in the editorial of *The Order* or that he'd posted my photo both on the Internet and on the magazine's cover. I remembered his words, 'Not so clever now, are you!' I thought, 'We'll see who's fucking clever. I'll have the last – and longest – laugh.'

Although Copeland had been working alone, without help from his NSM comrades, I knew those comrades would be delighted at what he'd done. By hoaxing Copeland, the new National Socialist hero, I hoped to remove a little bit of their delight – and get a little bit of revenge in the process. I decided in that moment that David Copeland would become the target of my next letter-writing campaign.

Over the years, and quite by accident, I'd developed an unusual sideline in writing to 'nonces' – the sex murderers of women and children – usually in a bid to get them to confess to crimes they'd denied. I'd had some extraordinary success.

I'd written to the Yorkshire Ripper posing as a blonde barmaid called 'Belinda Cannon'. Over a few months, he'd answered every question I'd asked him – from his favourite colour to why he'd wanted to commit mass murder, signing his letters 'with big juicy hugs'.

Parallel to my correspondence with Sutcliffe, I'd also written to another nonce, Richard Blenkey, who'd been charged with sexually assaulting and strangling a seven-year-old boy. Our correspondence had lasted a year. Initially, he'd said he intended pleading not guilty. Then, remarkably, three weeks before his trial he confessed to me in a letter that he had indeed murdered the boy. The prosecution produced the letters at the trial – and Blenkey immediately pleaded guilty. He got a life sentence with a recommendation he serve at least 20 years. The father of the victim publicly thanked me for having saved the family the ordeal of a trial from which the murderer might easily have walked to freedom.

I was named in national newspapers as the person who'd 'forced a child-killer to confess'. By the time of Copeland's bombing campaign, I'd had similar success with another child-killer.

Now it was Copeland's turn. The main purpose of my hoax

would be to coax from him details that might damage him at his trial. And getting one over on Sargent and the NSM would serve as an added bonus.

When I wrote my first letter, I knew nothing more about him than what I'd gleaned from the media – single, 23-year-old London Underground worker from Surrey. In addition, as he'd bombed a mostly gay pub, I assumed he might be heterosexual, though perhaps not a practising one, as it had been reported that he didn't have a girlfriend. I decided to supply him with the female company he obviously lacked.

I didn't need the police's description of him as a 'loner' to know he'd turn out to be a bit of a loser. Inevitably, there'd be some serious disturbance in his background, something that had probably destroyed his childhood. Inevitably, also, whatever had wounded him as a child would have left him with a deep-seated grievance against the world – and the belief he had the right to hit back violently.

I had to create a female character who'd appeal to him. I drew on my experience of what tended to make young Nazis tick. Far-right magazines sometimes featured photos of blonde women wearing stockings, suspenders and Waffen SS regalia. They'd often be bound, gagged or in some other way restrained, that is, vulnerable and helpless. I knew my character had to be young, attractive and, most important, vulnerable. In her vulnerability, she wouldn't be a threat to him. He could feel in control.

I settled for a slim, blonde secretary called Patsy Scanlon, a naively curious 20-year-old English rose. I created her name from my mother's maiden name, Scanlon, and my own first, albeit abandoned, Christian name, Patrick, the name of my hated father which I'd dropped when old enough to choose. 'Patsy' is also an American slang word for a sucker.

I always tried to tailor my letters to suit the tastes of my targets. Usually, I'd start with a barely formed character, then wait to see how my 'penfriends' responded. What did they want? A lover? A friend? The character would be moulded, chameleon-like, to become whatever the target required.

I knew I had to write the letters in a way that forced him to do the talking. That way, nobody could later accuse me of entrapment. I wanted him to brag about planting the bombs and to detail his Nazi beliefs and background – something the police had seemingly failed to unearth.

I kept my first letter brief, its tone inspired by the sympathetic social workers and probation officers who'd sometimes offered me plausible excuses for my own vile behaviour. I made Patsy overflow with warmth, goodwill and the desire to understand. Patsy said she didn't believe everything she saw in newspapers or on television about 'monsters' and 'evil people'. To her, everyone did things for a reason and everyone remained innocent until proven guilty.

I made Patsy come across as a bit of a bubbly airhead. I mentioned, for instance, the suntan she'd got during a disappointing holiday in Spain. I also wanted him to imagine her in a bikini on holiday. No pictures of him had yet been published, so Patsy asked him to describe himself.

Copeland wrote for the first time from Belmarsh Prison in south London on 30 May 1999. It was exactly one calendar month since his third and last bomb had torn apart the Admiral Duncan pub and its customers:

Dear Patsy,
Thank you for your letter and im sorry to hear your holiday to Spain wasn't all that, why didn't you go to Ibetha it would of been a lot better, things are a bit better hear as I have been moved out of the Madhouse and put in the HSU, this is better as there are a few more things to do such as go up to the Gym, watch telly play cards Great 'uh'. Im 5'8 23 with brown hair, blue eyes athlectic build. My mum says im Handsome but dont they all. I like music and some sports not football, my other interests are Politics and History boaring I no. Its good to see you are a 'thinker' as you pointed out some interesting points in your last letter, a thinker is someone who thinks not just believes what you hear on the T.V. so I will enjoy writing to you. My lawyer has just received all the paper work concerning my case and when I get hold of a copy Ill probably spend the next few weeks going through it all

which will be a tedeus task. Thats all for now and Ill wait until you write back.

Dave.

Copeland's prose highlighted the failings of the British education system. His spelling was appalling. However, the content pleased me. He showed real enthusiasm for 'Patsy'. I assumed she represented the first female attention he'd had for a while.

I wrote back immediately. I underlined Patsy's vulnerability by expressing her fear that other inmates might get hold of her address. I wanted 'Dave' to protect her. I also wanted him to keep the address – and our correspondence – secret. Following my exposure during the child-killers' trials and subsequent publicity, other prisoners had been warned off me and my letter-writing by defence lawyers and prison officials.

An artist's sketch of Copeland had appeared in the papers: I asked him whether it offered a good likeness. I wanted him to know that Patsy, young and naive as she was, had a healthy interest in the physical.

On 4 June, he wrote back:

> Dear Patsy,
> Thank you for your letter it was much needed at the time as I was in a terrible mood. You cheered me up. You do not wish to worry as your address is safe with me and no other inmates will see it, I promise. I am courious to know exactly what the tabloids have been saying about me, im pretty shore it is all bad but I would still like to know. Things ain't been to good here as I am on Health Care (Madhouse) under 24 hour servailance they say it is to keep an eye on me, but personaly I do not believe this. The drawing in the tabloids doesn't look anything like me so my lawyer says. Sorry if I am complaining to much but there is nothing to do in here but complain and wait for my Trial. This is the third letter I have written and i do not know what else to put in it so ill finish now and hope you'll write back,
> Dave.

I hadn't got his second letter. I noted Copeland was no longer in the High Security Unit (HSU). He'd been returned to 'the Madhouse'. No doubt, his second letter had gone astray in transit. The fact that he'd written three times in less than a week compensated for its loss. I felt confident I'd hooked him. I replied swiftly, but I didn't want to bombard him with questions, nor did I want to make statements to which he just said yes.

I hoped Patsy would make him feel relaxed, so that in time he'd open up completely and tell her what he'd done and why. I wrote about her plans to go to a friend's wedding in Camberley, not far from where he'd lived in Farnborough. I hoped the location might prompt him to reminisce about his home and family.

He replied on 7 June:

Patsy,

How are you, sorry you didn't recieve my last letter, I did send you one the same day as I recieved your last letter, it doesnt matter as I didn't say much in it anyway, I got those press cuttings so sent and the made interesting reading, so your going to a party in camberley It seems strange your friend getting married so young as your only 20 yourself, thes days not many people even bother, Patsy, your address you gave me seems strange It has no numbers, is it your work address, I don't blame you if it is, Things in hear ain't to bad most of the other inmates are OK 1 or 2 don't like me but the leave me alone, I haven't been gang raped so thats a good point, Im studying the bible at the moment, and strangly it makes very good reading, all the things which the Government run church say is the total oppersite off what God supposedly says, he says that Slavery is good, Mixed racing is bad, Queers deserve to die, black people are off mud and have no sole and are not of his creation, all this things are bad in the Government run church no wonder why he plans to wipe us out soon, are you religious, Patsy patsy could you send me a photo off yourself maybe one off you on holiday in Spain as I find it hard to write to you as you are just a letter not a face. Ill stop writing know and hope you'll write back soon.

    Dave.

God's arrival in our correspondence fazed me for a short while. I hadn't considered Copeland might be a religious, rather than Nazi, nut. Then I remembered the Bible-quoting Ku Klux Klan Nazis. But thoughts of God didn't completely fill his mind. He wanted a photo of Patsy 'on holiday in Spain', which I assumed was his way of saying, 'in a bikini, please'.

I knew I'd have to send him a bogus photo eventually, but I planned to delay for a while. He'd have to earn it by revealing more about himself. I asked him if he'd met the disgraced former Conservative minister Jonathan Aitken, who'd also changed his address to Belmarsh Prison. I'd read that Aitken, too, had found God.

I felt confident enough about Patsy's hold over him to ask an explicit question about his political beliefs. But I knew I had to be careful: although hooked, Copeland occasionally wriggled. His paranoia had already raised questions about Patsy's address.

He wrote on 11 June:

> Dear Patsy,
> Its good to hear from you and I didn't forget about you, That Tory Aitken you asked about is in the Hospital wing so I didn't get to see him, Its just bad luck i was moved out a few days before he got here because there was alot of things about the Torys and himself I wanted to ask him, never mind, so how are you, have you lost your suntan yet the one you got when you went to spain, Im locked up most of the time and wont get a chance to sunbathe. Its good really as its bad for you and makes you age a lot sooner, I can't really Tell you much about my political beliefs 'if i have any' for one my letters are censored and anything I could write could predurdice my case (2) Im scared I could offend you and you could stop writing to me, I find it hard to write to you as all you are is a letter not a face, It would be easier if I new what you looked like so maybe you could send me in yur next

letter a photograth of your self maybe one on your holiday to spain, you dont have to if you don't want to, but it will be easier to write to you, Ive been recieving some of the paperwork concerning my case so most off the time i spend going through it all, Im reading a good book at the moment its about the spanish Inquisition. Like you say it may not be that factual but it will give you an insight into what happened, Ill stop writing now and if theres anything persific you would like to know please ask.

Dave.

His caution in replying to my question about his political beliefs didn't surprise me. I knew he wouldn't divulge everything at once. I didn't think he had real concern about the censors: he'd already scribbled words of hatred about blacks and gays, even if he'd done so under the guise of offering Bible instruction. I could detect a bit of flirtatious games-playing – 'I'm not telling you, but . . .' He wanted to tantalise Patsy with his secrets. Yet he also feared the effect his secrets might have on her.

I'd encountered this before in my correspondence with the child-killers. So vile were their crimes that they feared rejection from their new 'friend' if they told the whole truth. My strategy had been to convince them their new 'friend' was so open-minded and understanding that they could tell everything. While I was wondering how to get to the heart of Copeland's political background, the *Daily Mirror* provided the short cut. The paper printed a photo of Copeland taken at a BNP street demonstration in Stratford, east London.

The party had at first denied that Copeland had ever joined them. Yet he'd been pictured close to the BNP's then leader, John Tyndall, who had a bloody nose after a brush with political opponents. In fact, Copeland had briefly been a member of the BNP. He left after finding it 'too democratic'.

The BNP's new leader Nick Griffin wrote in the party's *Spearhead* magazine that he thought the shadowy hand of the state lay behind Copeland's bombs. His conspiracy theory suggested that the explosions had been timed to coincide with the BNP's European election campaign. The resulting carnage was to be used as the basis for a smear campaign against the party. He added:

> It appears to be common knowledge among journalists that the man charged with the bomb attacks was not a loner, but a member of the political wing of the state-controlled or infiltrated Combat 18 at the time of the bombings – and a group with nothing to do with ourselves. Only poor Joe Public does not know.

In my next letter, I referred to the photo in the *Mirror* and asked Copeland if he knew Tyndall. I also asked him for his views on royalty, especially Princess Diana. I wanted to know if he admired anyone in the public eye. I returned again to his suspicions about my address: I made Patsy sound hurt, truly hurt, that he appeared not to trust her.

He replied on 20 June:

> Patsy,
> How are you, Ive got all your letters now and am sorry for asking about where you live but I seem to get alot of people who are not who they say they are, you must feel angered and think I don't trust you but I ashore you I do, so how are things wear you are sometimes it sunny and hot, but most of the time it's dole, but we live in Britain so what can we expect, it sounds lovely where you live all those green fields its better than living in a concrete Gunjle riddled with vermin, I did not Mr Tyndall the Person in the paper whos infront of me all bloodied up, I was a member of the BNP for a very short time, I joined more for my coriousity, I expected a bunch of yobs but was surprised to find a group of dedicated ordinary people who gust wanted to return Britain to a morally and richous country again, but due to the Zionist media they portrade this group as a bunch of rasist yobs, I didn't much care for Diana, being politicly correct all the time borders on the lines of stupidity, Send me a selection of photos. I say this as I feel like I now you well but I can't picture what you look like, I havent got anyone

special in my life at the moment no doubt if I had she would have deserted me by now but thats how shallow people can be, ill stop know, write back soon.

Dave.

I discovered after his trial that 'Mad Bomber' Tony Lecomber had also been at that BNP demo in east London. At the time Copeland met him, Lecomber was one of the BNP's two east-London organisers.

Only three weeks had passed since Copeland had first written. His relationship with Patsy had blossomed. He seemed to be skipping along the path of romance. He was making my task easy, but I needed him to open up more. I decided to drop him for a few weeks – something I tended to do when my 'penfriends' chose not to talk about their crimes.

In prison, your cherished lifeline to the outside world is the mail, especially if you're in solitary confinement, unable to make phone calls and not getting many visits. Torment comes when someone special suddenly stops writing. You don't know what's going on: you can't pop round to check and you can't ring up to find out. Some prisoners work themselves into a frenzy as they wait anxiously for the next letter. They become desperate for a renewal of contact – and massively grateful when that special person returns to them. I hoped Copeland would be one of those.

CHAPTER 16

MY LITTLE SOLDIER

I WAS SURPRISED WHEN COPELAND DIDN'T WRITE.

I'd been so sure he'd be desperate to discover the reason for Patsy's silence. I thought perhaps I hadn't excited his fantasies enough. I decided to sexualise Patsy a bit more, though subtly. I had to avoid making her come across as a slut. She had to remain virginally innocent – healthy, fresh and vibrant, waiting for a strong Aryan man to guide her.

I thought of those propaganda films from Nazi Germany of blonde maidens exercising in fields, stretching their young limbs for Hitler. I imagined such images might appeal to Copeland. I began to develop Patsy as a back-to-the-land type. A real English rose.

In my next letter, I wrote that she'd just spent a few weeks with her parents on their farm, helping out with the harvest. I imagined Copeland in his solitary cell thinking of Patsy gathering hay on a sunny day in the green fields of England (or possibly Hitler's Germany). I guessed his imagination might supply other 1940s images: soldiers driving past in their lorries waving at the girls, Spitfires (or possibly Messerschmidts) zooming overhead. Then, at the end of the day, the slow drive back to the farmhouse on the back of a tractor, sweating but happy, ready for a warm bath and a good night's sleep in a skimpy nightgown.

I avoided mentioning Patsy's political beliefs. I knew from my years of experience with Adolf how easy it was to upset a political nut. A trivial remark could spark a furious outburst. I expressed

246

interest in his religious beliefs. I said that, although not particularly religious, Patsy had started reading the Bible again after his comments about God's views on mankind. I also said Patsy would like to visit him or at least speak to him on the phone. In fact, given the security around him, I knew only close family members and legal representatives would get such permission. I felt the situation might change. If he got permission to phone, I'd arrange for a female to take the calls at my home. But I'd always find an excuse to avoid visiting him.

I told him I hadn't received his last letter and that I'd written several times over the previous few weeks. I tried to convey a young woman's sense of disappointment at his seeming lack of interest. He replied on 8 August:

> Dear Patsy,
>
> Sorry you haven't heard from me but I did reply to your last letter, it must of got lost in the post (well thats what the screws would say) things hear are OK the same old boring crap, Im getting a new laywer as the last one was obviously working for the Pigs, but hes like a leach so ive just used him for things, im up to court tommorrow same old rubbish, no dout ill be in the news, how are you bye the way, it sounded like fun stacking those hay things but I wouldnt like it as I get hay fever you said you would like to visit me hear, ill arrange it from here as because of my security status theres a lot of paper work but ill sort it out don't worry, maybe in a few weaks, its good to hear that you are reading the bible even if you are not religious it can help you and guide you on to the right path, as it makes common sence, My parents are fine now and they'll becoming up to see me shortly, ill stop writing now and look forward to hearing from you or Seeing you soon,
>
> Dave.
>
> PS hears some verses in the bible you might want to read.

He'd written out 25 references. I worked my way through a copy of the New International version. Copeland's verses came largely from the Old Testament. They contained three main themes: first, that the Jews are the Chosen People (although a passage from Revelations referred to some people who claimed to be Jews, but weren't); second, that Jews should not be unfaithful to God by marrying foreign women (that is, women from neighbouring tribes); third, that homosexuals should be executed.

Leviticus, chapter 20, verse 13 reads, 'If a man lies with a man as one lies with a woman, both of them have done what is detestable. They must be put to death: their blood will be on their own heads.' A few verses later, the book lists others who – God apparently tells Moses – must be put to death: adulterers, men who sleep with their daughters-in-law, people who have sexual relations with animals and – most worrying for me – those who curse their fathers. In that case, execution and eternal doom awaited me too. This chapter of Leviticus also says that God orders the stoning to death of 'mediums and spiritists'.

I quickly wrote several other letters. I used different dates from previous weeks when I hadn't written. I didn't think he'd notice the postmarks didn't match. I hoped the letters would arrive together. Then he might think the authorities were conspiring to thwart the relationship. This belief could only strengthen his bond with Patsy.

At the time I was writing to Copeland, I was having to deal with a developing crisis in my own life. Paul Betts had appeared on television to call me a bastard and to blame me for the death of his daughter Leah, who'd died after taking an Ecstasy pill bought at Raquels by one of her friends. He based his conclusion on the fact I'd turned a blind eye to drug dealing at the club. I regarded his allegation as ridiculous, like someone blaming a pub landlord for getting him convicted of drink-driving. I was sorry for Leah's death, but she, as an 18-year-old adult, had chosen to take drugs at her father's home (15 miles from the club) knowing the risks. And even her moralising father didn't deny that she knew the risks. Leah took the pill that killed her in her own upstairs bedroom with her parents downstairs.

The publicity created by Paul Betts's allegation led to my children being taunted at school by fellow pupils who called me a 'murderer'. I wrote an open letter to him, urging him to confront me on live TV, so we could debate who might really be responsible for Leah's death, but he declined my invitation.

This strain added to already existing tensions in my relationship with Debra. After a prolonged period of turmoil, we decided to split. We sold our house in Mayland. Debra found a house near her mother's. I went to live in a flat near Basildon.

Patsy told Copeland she'd moved to Basildon. I knew he was desperate for a photo, so I had to acquire one from somewhere. I didn't want to send a photo of anyone I knew. Instead, I wrote as a would-be customer to a marriage agency offering Russian brides to British men. They sent me a large envelope crammed with photos. The only problem with the woman I chose as the best Patsy was her brown hair. I'd earlier described Patsy's as blonde. I decided to take the risk: if Copeland noticed the discrepancy, I'd say Patsy had dyed her hair – an innocent girly pastime.

The woman in the photo looked good, but not knockout. She came across as warm and friendly, but meek and eager to please. I made out Patsy had hesitated in sending him her photo because she felt insecure about her looks. She thought she looked a bit geeky. I enclosed a newspaper article and mentioned the many articles on the Internet praising him. I failed to point out that this praise could only be found on Nazi websites, a few of which had voted him 'Aryan of the Month'.

On 12 August, he wrote:

> Dear Patsy,
> I thought I better write again as know I have recieved all your letters, they all came within about 4 days of each other, I allso recieved your photo and you don't look geeky at all, if you don't mind me saying, you are very attractive young lady, but didn't you say you were blonde once, never mind, I got that newspaper article you sent it was very interesting, please send me all the stuff on the internet about me as im curious to know what it says, so youve moved to basildon it must be a change from Mayland, I left home when I was about 20 and i never wen't back, It feels strange being famous (for all the wrong reasons) people wanting your autograph people wanting to slit your throat,

well thats life isn't it, Ill write more often cause I know its just the screws holding up your letters.
     Dave.

In my next letter, I said Patsy had now read all his Bible references, but they'd left her confused, because, while God did seem hostile to homosexuals, Patsy hadn't been able to find His description of blacks as people of mud having no souls.
     He replied on 22 August:

> Dear Patsy,
> How are you, things hear are as normal, waiting to go back to court, the courts have been messing me around and won't let me change lawyers, so ive decided to do my case, how are things with you, settling in to your new home, lots of wild parties i bet, those references I gave you are just a guide, the problem is there are houndreds of different bibles thes days, most of them have had all the good bits taken out, the Jews are mostly to blame along with the degenerates, anything good about me on the internet, if there is send me a copy Im still waiting for the screws to clear you for visits, when they do ill sort out a visit, don't worry about any one saying anything, if someone does say your my sister or something, its a bit of a ordeal though, Metal detectors, searches, a good rub down from lesbien screws, what do your friends think about you writing to me, or don't they know, anyway ill stop writing know and wait to you write back,
>   Dave.

The idea of 'lesbien screws' might have frightened an innocent like Patsy, so I didn't write back at once. On 6 September, he wrote without my having replied to his earlier letter.

> Dear Patsy,
> How are you and how are you doing haven't heard from you for a bit, Probably just the screws holding up my mail, though I would right so you didnt think I would forget about you, so how are things, settling into your house OK,

anything good about me on the internet, Ive finally got back visiting forms so you can come and visit, It would be easyer if you sent me your new phone number so I could call to book a visit, anyway thats all for now, take care and write soon.

Dave.

I said Patsy had found it hard to write back immediately. She'd been frightened by his description of the security procedure she'd have to undergo. His comments had made her realise what a dangerous place prison could be. I said she had particular anxiety at the thought of her intimate parts being manhandled by a butch lesbian. In the future, such a prospect would provide a good excuse for not visiting him.

A few months after moving back to the Basildon area, I bumped into a woman called Emma Turner, whom I'd first met at Raquels. We'd always got on well and we began to see each other regularly. Before too long, I gave up my rented flat to move in with her.

Since the end of my catalogue of court appearances in connection with the events of 1995, I'd found a full-time job driving a tipper lorry. I was soon offered a managerial position – and a post in Peterborough, Cambridgeshire. I didn't want to move away from my two children. Being able to see them every other day had lessened the trauma of being separated from them. Instead, I chose to drive to Peterborough every day, leaving the house at 4.30 a.m. and returning around eight in the evening. The rewards of going straight weren't overwhelming.

I gave Copeland my new address in Basildon. On 17 September, he wrote:

> Dear Patsy,
> How are you, sorry I scared you about the security, I was properly in a funny mood, anyway it doesnt matter if you write, phone visit as long as I hear from you in some way im happy, So have you moved again, Is there any more stuff on the internet about me, I am up to court next week so there might be anyway thats all for now, Take care
> Dave.

I downloaded more material from the Internet: his public image clearly obsessed him. I wrote that Patsy felt impressed by the number of people who seemed to admire him: he had to be a very special person to arouse such devotion. However, my trawl through the Internet dredged up some bad news for him. The BNP – of which he'd been briefly a member and which he'd earlier praised to Patsy – now said he ought to be hanged for his crimes.

I wasn't surprised. In recent years, with an eye on winning elections, the party had tried to develop a more respectable image. They still spat the rhetoric of hatred, but when dupes like Copeland acted on that rhetoric they rushed to distance themselves. I knew that behind closed doors the average BNP member would be raising his can of Special Brew to Copeland. But, publicly at least, the leadership couldn't support his 'war effort'. I imagined Copeland in his cell receiving my news – the soldier being told his mission had been pointless. Copeland replied on 4 October:

> Dear Patsy,
>
> How are you, thanks for your letter and that internet stuff you sent me, the BNP are a bunch of twats, they dont realise that most British people are just walking Zombies with no mind of there own, I feel sorry for these people so content with nothing, I don't class you as one of thes, I have your picture up on my wall and sometimes ill look at it and play with myself, ive been in prison for six months and ive had to learn to masterbait, I lye on my bed at Night and think about you I think things, scenarios, fucking you, another inmate noticed your picture on my wall and said I was a lucky Guy, if all this didn't happen I would of nether met you, so thats one good thing thats come out of this,
>
> Dave.
>
> PS Could you send me some more pictures of yourself, Thanks

I really laughed when I read his words. The big Nazi who pitied other people's empty lives lying on his cell bed masturbating in front of a photo of an imaginary lover. I knew I had to use Patsy's sexual allure to keep him hooked, but I didn't want to provide him with props for masturbation. In the past, with my other 'penfriends', I'd always boxed around sex, trying to avoid writing anything too explicit, while indicating that my imaginary character had similar sexual interests.

I decided in this instance that Patsy would have to act shocked. I'd developed Patsy as a nice young woman with traditional values. Such a woman would hardly respond warmly to an incarcerated nail-bomber's pornographic fantasies. I was experiencing what I'd experienced before: a character forms as you write, and gradually this imaginary person has certain views on certain things.

I didn't give Copeland too brutal a ticking-off for his premature advance. I didn't want him to think of Patsy as a frigid ice-maiden who'd remain permanently cold to him. She'd repulsed that first crude grab, but he needed to know that if he persisted he might eventually get more than a peck on the cheek.

I wrote that, while Patsy felt close to him and wanted their relationship to continue, she'd been hurt and upset by his strong language. This had come at a time when her devotion to him had caused a rift within her family: they didn't approve of her writing to him. Then all Patsy's other little hurts came pouring out – how she felt Copeland had doubted her in the past, questioning her address and so forth. He wrote back swiftly:

> Dear Patsy,
> How are you, and what have you been getting up to, sorry my last letter up set you, I don't know why it did I wasn't trying to, if I did, I am sorry,
> Anyway im back up in court on thursday, im not looking forward to it, all those people staring at you, being the center of attension, thats not me im a bit shy,
> Sorry to hear that you writing to me has caused rifts in you private life with your family, thank you for standing by me I know how hard it can be for you,
> Ive never douted you patsy, Qut the oppersite, you have been a piller at my side during my incarceration, and I

253

appresiate this alot, Anyway sorry I might off hurt you, I
didn't mean to, write back soon.

Love Dave.

For the first time, he'd ended his letter with 'love'. Again, I
decided to stop writing for a little while. I hoped he'd torture
himself with the thought he might have scared Patsy off. I always
bore in mind the adage, 'treat them mean, keep them keen'.

In a short time, I'd expanded considerably the haulage business
I managed in Peterborough. It took up more and more of my
time. My working day grew even longer, to the point where my
job began to affect my relationship with Emma. Her mother had
recently been killed in a tragic accident and, when I wasn't at
home, she felt isolated and lonely.

On top of everything, when we went out to relax in Basildon
I'd sometimes be confronted by unwelcome ghosts from my
Raquels past, one of them being a small-time drug dealer with a
grandiose self-image called John Rollinson. This gnat, who likes
to call himself 'Gaffer', has described himself publicly as the most
dangerous man in the country, proving at least that he's got a
sense of humour.

I'd heard he was unhappy that I'd named one of his drug-
peddling friends at the Leah Betts trial. He'd then told lots of
people he was 'after' me and was going to 'do' me. One evening,
Emma and I went to a nightclub in Basildon called Jumping Jacks.
When we entered the club, I found myself confronted by a scruffy
degenerate calling me a 'fucking cunt'. It took me a little while to
realise that this was in fact Gaffer. His appearance had changed
drastically since I'd last sniffed his body odour. His ravaged face
now bore cruel testimony to the perils of a lowlife existence spent
popping pills and sniffing coke.

To cut a long story short, he squirted me in the eyes with
ammonia. As I stood in front of him, temporarily blinded, he had
the best chance he was ever going to get to 'do' me. He failed to
take it and, as I prepared to sink my double-bladed, 12-inch
combat knife into his head, he screamed hysterically and ran away.

The incident had been partly captured on CCTV cameras, and
I was arrested and charged with threatening unlawful violence

and possessing an offensive weapon. The charges were eventually dropped, but this minor incident on top of everything else made me realise that to escape the shadows of 1995, Emma and I would have to leave Basildon. We decided to move to Peterborough, where I continued my correspondence with the nail-bomber.

Copeland wrote again. He, too, had a new address – Broadmoor Special Hospital for the criminally insane.

> Patsy,
> How are you, I haven't heard from you in quit awhile, I hope I didn't scare you off in my last letter but it's the way I feel, Ive been moved to broadmore, this place is mental, I dont think ill be staying hear long thou, If you want me to phone tell me in your next letter and ill do so, it would be so good to hear your voice and would cheer me up, so what you up to in peterborough, this place is full of lunatics, one off them is hear for killing sheep then shagging them, its so easy hear, but I can't wait to get back to belmarsh back to doing hard time, Its because of who i am, a soldier, someone who thrives on hardships, I sit hear and think about what we could of done together, so many exciting things I could teach you, make you feel alive, not the boring things ordinary people get up to, but dangerous things, ill hope I will hear from you soon,
> Dave.

I noticed he hadn't signed this letter with love. Perhaps he felt he'd been too mushy in his last letter: he was, after all, a soldier. In my next letter, Patsy returned to her cheerful and exuberant self. Her only worry was that she wasn't going to enjoy Christmas. I also acknowledged his move to Broadmoor by saying Patsy feared for his safety with all those dangerous lunatics around him. At the same time, Patsy started referring to him as 'my little soldier'.

Patsy said she hoped her letters cheered him up. She added she wanted to write more intimately about her feelings, but feared having her words read by strange men in the censor's office. She needed to feel sure any words of intimacy would be read by him alone.

On 3 December, Copeland sent a traditional Christmas card with a jolly Father Christmas on the front holding a tree and presents. Inside, he wrote:

Dear Patsy,

How are you doing, I am doing fine, Your right your letters do cheer me up in these trying times.

Sorry to hear your not going to enjoy christmass, it's Better when your young,

Look to the future and the millenium, as next year is going to be a lot different to this one, I promise you,

Being assessed is a horrible concept, being in someones power, I wish I was in your power Patsy having to do what you say sounds like heaven,

Ill be back in court by next January and then back to belmarsh, this place isnt scary at all its full of divs, I know how you feel about writing your feelings down on paper for some pervert to read in the censor's office,

Anyway try and enjoy yourself at christmass,

Until we meet,

Love Dave.

I noticed that 'my little soldier' had returned to the 'love Dave'. He'd even added two little hearts. The following week, on 12 December, he wrote again:

Dear Patsy,

How are you, Just a quick letter to let you know im alright, Im thinking about what Christmas present im going to send you, I though ill get you a nice watch Tick tock tick tock something that will remind you of me, I don't need much in hear maybe some nice photos of you, I know you would like to send me some bad photos but they won't let me have them (Bastards), Im still trying to get your number cleared hopefully it wont be to long, Your letters are the only thing that keeps me going in hear, they drive

me mad knowing I can't talk to you, hold you, make love to you, pleasure you, teach you, anyway thats all for know, thinking of you,
    Dave.

I felt our correspondence had fallen into a rut. I had to get him to stop writing as some sex-starved soldier from the front. I needed to get him bragging about his murderous exploits. His bomb-timer joke ('tick-tock-tick-tock') pointed to his pride in his achievements. I felt sure he wanted to talk about what he'd done. Or did he? I began to wonder if he might be playing mind games with me, holding out morsels, then snatching them away. In my next letter, I made clear that with his reference to 'bad photos' he'd delivered yet another blow to Patsy's modesty: she wasn't some porno slut. Yes, she'd indicated she wanted to write to him more intimately, but she'd only meant about romance and nice things and who he was and what he'd done. I sandwiched the criticism between slabs of praise and respect. He replied on 20 December:

Dear Patsy,
Sorry about my last letter but you must realise that its driving me Mad not being able to see you,
    I was thinking the other day that we could of bean a bonny and Clyde having so much fun, I hope you are ok and are looking forward to the millenium.
    How are things with you, do you Enjoy Peterborough, what sort of things are you getting up to, will you be seeing your family or just a few friends at Xmass, I wonder if you have got my present yet, it should be there soon,
    Things here are no good, I can't believe that I have fooled all the doctors, Anyway, take care of your self, I hope to hear from you soon,
    David

His response gave me a better Christmas present than the one he was promising (and which never arrived). Fooled the doctors? I knew instantly he'd written something he'd come to regret.

I guessed that no one at his trial would dispute the fact that he'd planted the bombs. What might be in dispute, however – particularly as he'd been sent to Broadmoor for 'tests' – was whether he'd been of sound mind when he did so. If he hadn't, then he could be convicted of manslaughter due to diminished responsibility, rather than murder. In the past, a child-killer had torpedoed himself by telling me ('the only woman I've trusted in years and years') that he thought he had an excellent shot at some sort of insanity plea, even though mentally and physically he was, as he said, 'fit as a fiddle'. He'd wanted to go for insanity because he knew he'd then have a far easier time inside – and be released much sooner.

I guessed Copeland might be thinking similarly. As someone who'd been in jail awaiting trial more than once, I felt I knew which mental stage he'd reached. When you're first imprisoned on remand (and you know you're guilty), you're depressed. Then comes hope. Usually aided by your lawyer, who highlights legal loopholes, you begin to convince yourself you'll beat the system. Then – usually a week or so before your trial – reality gobs on you. You consider the evidence – and realise you haven't got a chance. I could see Copeland was cocky, sure of himself, going through the period when he believed he might get away with murder. His reference to Bonnie and Clyde, the glamorous gangster couple from 1930s America, gave a hint to the real motivation for his crimes – recognition and fame. The nobody wanted to be a somebody. 'Bonnie and Clyde' had inspired a well-known film. I didn't think 'Patsy and Dave' had quite the same ring as a potential Hollywood blockbuster.

Before I'd had time to reply, I got the following letter:

> Patsy,
> Please do not write to me while I am in broadmoor, the reasons why I will explain to you when I get back to Belmarsh early next year, You have done nothing wrong so don't worry,
> Dave.

Copeland wasn't a total fool. He must have realised he'd made a mistake with his earlier letter – and in a panic had sought to end his correspondence with Patsy, the holder of his secret. I imagined him sweating before every session with the doctors he'd supposedly 'fooled'. Was Patsy to be trusted?

I'd reached a crucial stage in our correspondence. I decided once more to alter my strategy. In order to keep him writing after such a damaging admission, I needed to ease his fears. Patsy would have to submit to some of his desires. I'd always tried to imply Patsy thought he was a real man, unlike the wimps she tended to meet in the offices where she worked. I'd made Patsy admire him as a man with beliefs – and the willingness to act on them. Perhaps I could develop the Bonnie and Clyde idea. Patsy could tell him how, if only she had the nerve, she'd like to do exciting things with him too. He needed to know she wanted someone like him to teach her the things she needed to learn. I felt perhaps I'd overplayed the 1940s good-girl role. Patsy had to become a little less innocent. I believed I knew him well enough now to prod and provoke him into reopening the correspondence.

I sent my next letter to Broadmoor, ignoring Copeland's instructions. In it, I told him Patsy regarded him as her boyfriend. I said how much she yearned to have him on the outside to protect her. She'd been to a New Year's Eve party where she'd been bothered by an Asian-looking man, quite possibly a Pakistani, who'd made improper advances, even though she'd told him firmly she had a boyfriend. I laughed as I imagined the Aryan of the Month's rage at the idea of his 'girlfriend' being harassed by an Asian. I hoped Patsy's little soldier would soon march back to her side.

CHAPTER 17

MADLY IN LOVE

Patsy,

   . . . Sorry to hear about that dirty, stinking sub human paki was bothering you on New years eve if I was there that paki wouldn't be bothering anyone anymore,

    Roses are red,

    Violets are blue

    All I do

    Is think of you

Sorry about the poetry but sometimes its easyer to express how I feel about you,

    Anyway hope to see you soon

    write back

    Dave.

This letter, written on 9 January 2000, marked his return to Patsy. He tried to explain his last letter:

> You have done nothing wrong its just sometimes me being in hear and you out there depresses me and not being aloud to see you makes me so angry sometimes, please write as your letters do cheer me up.

From his next letter, I could tell that life inside had started to oppress him: '. . . this place is a joke so are the Doctors they think there clever but they are as stupid as the fools in hear.'

He added: '. . . please write back soon and just tell me what you have been up to.'

He hungered for details of Patsy's life as a free person. When you're stuck in a cell, you think continually of the outside world. The little freedoms ordinary people take for granted become tantalising fantasies. So I kept filling my letters with the mundane details of Patsy's daily life: walks in the park, visits to the pub, trips to the cinema, shopping in Sainsbury's.

I made sure Patsy came across nearly always as cheerful and exuberant: always thinking of him, always sympathetic to the plight of her brave little soldier alone among the lunatics. I guessed that someone with the self-importance to believe he had the right to blow people to bits would need to feel at the centre of his little woman's world.

On 28 January, he replied:

> Dear Patsy,
> How are you, and what have you been getting up to, No dirty Pakies been bothering you I hope,
>
> Im Still trying to get your phone number cleared but they just keep on mugging me of with the same old excuses, Im am back in court today. Not me personally thou Just a hearing, Ill be back personally in a few weeks so listen to the news I should be in it.
>
> Things hear are as boring as usual, Someone keeps writing Kill on the walls, what he writes isn't disturbing but the fact he writes it in his own shit is, this is what the place is like,
>
> I think about us every night you know how, I think of us being together, doing such exciting things, illigal and dangerous. I wonder when we will finally meet, soon i hope Anyway thats all for now,
> Dave.

Bewitched by the character he and I had created, he seemed to spend his time in rapturous fantasy, imagining exploits with his enchanting admirer. I'd already secured one significant admission from him: I hoped more would follow.

He wrote again two days later on 30 January:

Dear Patsy,

How are you, I thought id write again as I can't get you out of my mind, all i do is dream about you and when we shall finally meet which would be after my trial hopefully, It wouldn't cost that much on the train

Anyway what have you been up to, hows your Job going in Peterborough, things hear are the same as usual, waiting for my trial having conversations with a bunch of halfwits your letters are the only sane thing left in my life right now and I always look forward to hearing from you

I had my mum and brother visit me the other day, it was good to see them but I wish it was you sitting opporsite me holding hands under the table?

What sort of music do you like Patsy, I got a screwdriver album sent in the other day by a friend on the out, Its really quit good full of racist chants, maybe not your cup of tea, Promise me Patsy you will never forget about me as you are ·the only good thing left in my life.

In the morning the sun
might shine
and I know that one day
you'll be mine
You know your really the best
I can't wait to nuzzel your breast.

Sorry about the poetry but I like writing to you, Anyway thats all for know.

Love Dave.

PS Whens your birthday?

His poems were as crude as his bombs. My strategy of making Patsy more passionate and less innocent had borne fruit. I'd begun signing letters 'with love and lust'. At last, Copeland had found, or unwittingly created, the woman of his dreams.

However, I was glad he thought the music of the Nazi band Skrewdriver (about asylum-seekers being burnt in their beds and the like) probably wasn't Patsy's cup of tea. She'd never expressed racial prejudices, if only because I doubted whether many innocent country girls burnt with hatred for blacks and Asians.

He replied on 2 February:

> Dear Patsy,
> how are you and what have you been up to, sorry my letters are short but its hard to write a few lines while im on thes drugs, you must know I'm on thes drugs for no reason.
>
> So anyway how are you, has there been anything good on the internet about me and do you still get crank calls from others on the web, becareful and dont tell anyone that you write to me as they may not be who they say they are . . .

In an earlier effort to make Patsy seem real, I'd mentioned she'd received a few crank calls after posting her own details on a Nazi website in order to download material about him. I'd wanted to underline Patsy's vulnerability and her desire to put herself in danger for her man. I'd also hoped to provoke him into talking about any Internet contacts he might have had with Nazis.

I said Patsy had no interest in casual relationships. But, just to fray his nerves and to try to capture his explosive side, I sent her to more parties, although I gave him the opportunity to restrict her freedom. Patsy asked him if he minded her going to parties without him.

On 4 February, he wrote:

> Dear Patsy,
> . . . Sorry if in my letters I don't mention things you ask, I just sit down and write to you, spilling my mind out on the paper, Its frustrating for me as well not being able to phone you as since writing to you I have become madly in love with you, having you on my mind all day and night but we'll just have to be patient,
>
> So your moving again, sounds loverly where you live all those wide open spacies, im a country boy at heart, don't worry about going to parties As long as you are happy thats all that matters to me, have a few drinks for me when your

263

there, things are the same as usual, got another black
lunatic on the ward now but they keep him locked up,

I agree with you that Casual relationships are a waste off
time to many aids victims walking around.

So your getting your hair changed you must send me in
a photo of your new apperence so when we finally get to
meet ill know who to look out for, you could shave your
hair of and it wouldn't bother me you'll still be the same
old patsy . . .

I did feel a twinge of unease at his declaration of love, but I
couldn't forget what the bastard and his bombs had done. Nor
could I forget the threats from his sad comrades. I knew what I
was doing was cruel. But so was blowing up women and children.
The X-ray picture of a huge nail embedded in a child's skull always
came to mind when I felt tempted towards compassion for
Copeland. I could only feel something for him when I
remembered that he, too, had once been a child.

Deep down, I knew his expression of 'love' represented nothing
more than an attempt to enclose his imagined enchantress in a
firmer embrace in case she might be tempted to slip from virtue
at one of those parties. He'd tried to portray himself as tolerant
and trusting, but he'd slipped in a warning – the link between
casual relationships and AIDS. In other words, 'Go to your
parties, but death will be the price of a drunken fling.'

I played things down. I told him to be realistic and not to let
his imagination run away with him. I said he didn't know Patsy
well enough to love her – he'd never met her and he hadn't even
spoken to her on the phone. I suggested that when he met her in
the flesh, she might turn out very different from what he
imagined. Very different indeed.

I tried to milk him for information about his Nazi friends – the
friends that Scotland Yard had seemed at first to think didn't exist.
I'd been following the debate about him on the Nazi websites:
people questioned whether he'd ever been a member of the BNP.
Some suggested he was a police agent who'd carried out the
bombings to discredit the far-right. I told him about these
discussions. I also asked him to send photos. I wanted to see his

favourite image of himself. I held out the possibility of sending more photos of Patsy in exchange.

He replied on 10 February:

> Dear Patsy,
>
> How are you and what's been going on down your way? Things here are the same as usual.
>
> I'm back in court on the 28th of this month which I'm not looking forward to. Being the certre of attention is not me. Some people might enjoy this but not me. Everyone's eyes are fixated on you all the time, but I'm strong and can handle this.
>
> It was funny to hear that people are arguing about me being a member of the BNP. I must admit that I was a member for about three months and didn't take it seriously. I went to a few meetings . . .

It crossed my mind that someone who didn't like being the centre of attention shouldn't have embarked on a bombing campaign that gripped London in fear for three weeks. And if Patsy had wanted to be sarcastic she might have asked why, if he didn't enjoy being scrutinised by the public eye, he kept begging for news of what was being said about him. But these were questions a woman like Patsy wouldn't have dared raise. Instead, I made her stress again he shouldn't fall in love with her, because she couldn't say for sure she loved him. She could only say she cared about him deeply.

To boost his ego, and give him hope, I added that Patsy felt so confused about her feelings that she spent a lot of time crying about him. 'Crying with laughter' would have been nearer the truth.

On 12 February, he wrote:

> Dear Patsy,
>
> How are you, and what have you been doing lately, I got your last letter and was saddened about you crying, It made me happy in a way that someone cares for me, you are right saying I sounded low, this place can really get to me, the

only thing that keeps me going is you and your letters

Im sorry if I say that I love you but its what I feel and I cant hold it back, you are all I have at the moment and im not prepared to loose you, sorry if I sound all mushy, but in the future you'll be able to visit me and get to know me alot better, the only side you know is of the media, im alot different to how they say i am, its hard for me to wright this as I am a bit shy but it feels that I known you forever,

Im not very good at writing letters thats why I only used to write to you once a week but know I write at least 2 times as im frightened I might loose you, I had my mum come and visit the other day, I feel sorry for her, as she has to put up with alot,

At night I stare at that photo you sent and wonder what would of happened if I didn't do what they say i've done, the only good thing is that ive met you, write back soon,

Love Dave.

I'd been resisting his love onslaught, if only because I had no interest in his feelings for Patsy, only in what made him and his bombs tick. However, what he'd written astonished me. He seemed to be saying he could have been redeemed by the love of a good woman. I suspected that, like my other 'penfriends', he hadn't had much love and affection in his life. His words contained a powerful hint of regret, not regret for his victims, of course, just regret that he'd now never be able to build a life with the woman he believed he loved.

In other letters, he'd shown how he loathed 'normality' (probably because, I suspected, he'd been denied it as a child). Yet, like me, deep down he craved it. Patsy sent him a Valentine's card, even though I guessed he probably associated St Valentine's Day only with the legendary gangster massacre. He forgot to send Patsy one.

He wrote to apologise on 18 February, 'I must confess that I forgot about it and didn't send you a card, there must be thousands off people explaining this to the ones they love right now.' He added:

. . . this place is a joke im told im a patient but im treated like a criminal, like some garden variety thief,

Its strange that you want to know me and why I did what I did I believe in fate and that we were meant to meet someway or another in our lives, and that we were supposed to have some sort of a relationship

Does any of your family or friends know you write to me, I wonder what there reaction would be, maybe they would want a autograph?

Perhaps the drugs made Copeland think people might want his autograph on anything other than a suicide note.

CHAPTER 18

BUNCH OF QUACKS

I HADN'T DISCUSSED WITH COPELAND HOW HE INTENDED PLEADING AT HIS TRIAL. There'd been rumours, floated in newspapers, that, despite the evidence against him, he planned pleading not guilty. Journalists suggested he wanted to use the trial as a platform to put across his Nazi views. But I felt sure he'd take the insanity route.

The television news on 24 February 2000 confirmed my guess. Copeland had appeared at the Old Bailey to enter a preliminary plea of guilty to causing the three explosions, but not guilty to murder. Instead, he admitted manslaughter due to diminished responsibility. He wanted the jury at his forthcoming trial to accept he was mad, not bad.

According to the news reports, as Copeland pleaded not guilty to the first murder, his victims' relatives began shouting and sobbing. Cries of 'shame' and 'send him down' greeted his other pleas. Copeland's barrister told the judge his client suffered from schizophrenia, delusions and emotional disorders that justified the diminished-responsibility pleas. The prosecution still wanted to convict him of murder. The judge set a date in June for the trial.

It was clear to me that Copeland wasn't mad – at least not in the legal sense. He seemed a lot saner than many of my friends, including Adolf. I'd received a letter from Copeland in which he stated he'd fooled the doctors. But, more than that, his other letters showed him sane enough to know the difference between right and wrong – and sane enough to choose between the two. When I'd started the correspondence, I'd hoped to get him writing about bombs and murder. But he'd avoided those subjects in case the censors found something to use against him. He didn't realise the correspondence as a whole could be used against him. With every letter – mundane though the content often was – he produced more evidence of his legal sanity. I felt I had almost everything I needed to nail him. I knew I just had to keep him writing. The more letters he produced, the better.

In his next letter, written on 8 March, he told Patsy about his day in court:

> Dear Patsy,
>
> How are you and what have you been getting up to, I was up in court the other day and gave my plea, there was so many people there it was weird, I feel alot better for saying I was guilty, a few people gave a few sneers but that is understandable,
>
> Patsy I am no monster but some kind of terrorist, someone who puts them selves forward for what they believe in, on a good note least you know what I look like after my photo was splashed over the papers and TV, least now I dont have to get my mother to send you one, It was strang for me waking up a having a nurse give me a paper with my photo on the front, im still waiting to see you with your new haircut, ill stick to my wall with my 1 and only photo of you so that you can watch over me, anyway that's all for know.
>
> Love Dave.
>
> WRITE BACK SOON

Copeland had no remorse. He was enjoying his infamy. I didn't regard him as a terrorist waging war for his beliefs. I suspected his motivation sprung from a more deep-seated and personal source.

Patsy offered support. She advised him to think through the options. She could see how, with his manslaughter plea, he could stay in a special hospital like Broadmoor where he could be helped over any problems he had. Then, once they deemed him 'cured', he could be released.

Also, Broadmoor was a hospital, not a prison, so conditions

were much better – and there'd be less risk of his being attacked. He'd get through and Patsy would be at his side. Patsy said there wouldn't be much chance of their having a relationship if he got sent to prison.

Copeland wrote again on 13 March:

Dear Patsy,

How are you and what have you been getting up to thes last few weeks, Anything good on the Internet about me ill be surprised if there isn't

Anyway some good news know, the doctors here have agreed to let me phone you after all this legal bullshit is over it could be over by the end of march thats if the prosecution agree to acept my plea if not it won't be until June either way its not that long and well be finally able to meet for the first time, its a bit nerve wracking for me as im a shy person so no dout you will be doing most of the talking

The weather has change hear in the last few days its starting to become summer, I cant stop imageing you wearing all thos tight summer cloths it really turns me on flashing your long legs in the sunshine maybe when you come up to visit you can wear some

How did I look when my photo was splashed across the papers was I the person you imagined or did I come across as someone different,

My mums coming up to see me tomorrow, I feel sorry for her as my grandparents as ill and her son is locked up in hear it must be very stressful for her any was thats all for now write back soon,

Love Dave.

He faced a trial at the Old Bailey for triple murder, yet the most nerve-racking event on the horizon was his first meeting with Patsy. It was obvious the bastard had no remorse, but I asked him if he did, although I avoided making him feel guilty about what he'd done.

When violent misfits like Copeland are made to feel guilt, or to confront their wrongdoing, they tend to react by shouting and lashing out – I know, because that's how I used to react. Copeland needed excuses: nothing could be completely his fault. I played on the fact that what he'd done had had such a distressing effect on his own life.

On 22 March, he wrote:

> Dear Patsy,
> How are you, and what have you been getting up to, Ive just bean reading your last letter and your right I wish I had never though the whole idea up, but its useless living in the past so I must get ready for the future which doesnt look good at all, the only thing I have to look forward to is your letters they really do pick me up,
> Anyway not much has been going on in hear same old crap day in day out all I seam to do is sleep watch telly and read but hopefully soon they let me phone you and that will be something to look forward to,
> It was a sad day the other day one of the patients hear just died he just gave up living, it must be this place getting to him as few days before he seemed quiet well, anyway thats all for know
> Love Dave.

His tone of disillusionment didn't surprise me. He'd gone to war in the cause of fascism – and now his former comrades in the BNP claimed they wanted to hang him. His actions hadn't had the desired effect. Now that the white race hadn't come forward to thank him, Patsy represented all he had to look forward to.

I kept him well informed about what was being said on the Internet. I even found some pages about him written in Hungarian. I deduced that the writer sympathised with Copeland from the swastikas decorating the pages. The only words in English read 'Man of the Year'. I didn't download anything from this website: I didn't think Copeland would want me to send him pages he couldn't read. But I did mention the site to him. I also tried to find out more about the patient who'd died. Copeland's expression of sadness at his passing had surprised me. He replied on 29 March:

. . . I don't like writing why I did what I did because my letters are cencerds but what I can tell you is that I didn't Start out to kill people that was a product of what I was trying to achieve . . . Please send me anything about me on the internet especially that stuff from Hungary even thou its written in hungarian . . . Weve been writing to one and another for nearly a year know but it seems ive known you all my life is it the same for you . . .

In fact, I did feel like I'd known Copeland all my life, because most of the people I'd known were violent nuts just like him.

Before I had a chance to reply, another letter arrived a few days later. He'd written it on April Fool's Day:

Dear Patsy,
How are you doing, and what have you been getting up to since the last time you sent your letter, Nothing much has been going on hear so this will be just a short letter Tell you the truth im not very good at writing letters, looks like ill be going to trial on the 5, June 2000, it won't be a proper Trial it will just be a bunch of Quaks (DOCTORS) giving there opions, so it will be very boring, Why don't you come along and sit in the Gallery, I will be looking out for you if you decide to do so, If you do don't tell anyone why you're there, You could get lynched, on a brighter note its only 2 moths away from my trial so I will be able to phone you and get to know you better, thats all for now Love Dave.

His impending trial didn't appear to bother him. He seemed to look on it as an inconvenience he wanted out of the way. He'd obviously resigned himself to the fact that, even with a successful insanity plea, he wouldn't be leaving his cell for a very long time.

He wrote again on 4 April:

. . . this place isn't as bad as I make it sound I got a few good friends but they will be moving on soon, I get a visit of my mum, dad and brother once a week, I must be lucky

272

> to have a family that will stand by me in this time of
> trouble, Soon as my trial is done and dusted am going to
> do a few courses in chemistry and physics and maybe
> History . . .

I doubted whether his custodians would allow him his courses in
physics and chemistry. Copeland still hadn't talked about the
patient who'd died. I was intrigued to find out why the death had
seemed to trigger sadness in a murderer who'd shown no remorse
for his victims.

He replied on 10 April, '. . . that patient that died wasn't a
friend of mine I was quit pleased as he was a child molester . . .'

Having realised he wouldn't talk about his crimes, and
learning of his insanity plea, the mundane became paramount.
Many 'insane' criminals claim they have blackouts and so forth.
So every detail they recall can help indicate their sanity. I asked
him to write about his childhood. Did he have a favourite age
and memory?

On 18 April, he wrote:

> . . . You asked me what was my favourite age it must be 14-
> 15 years thats when your starting to become an adult but
> your still a kid and you can get away with stuff as your still a
> child I couldnt say what was my favorite memory ive had so
> many but it looks like I wont be getting any moor while being
> locked up in hear o'well thats life im affraid so many people
> live such boring lives getting up for work every day dieing
> with no one to miss them thats not the life for me . . . I dred
> to think what they will say about me after my trial has ended,
> all those lies and half truths, You said in your last letter that
> you though you were getting old, im 24 in a few weeks and
> I know how you feel . . .

His desperate keenness to know what people said about him
fascinated me. What most worried him about the future was the
'lies and half truths' people might tell about him. He feared the
truth about him would emerge. I guessed 'the truth' about him
would be unsavoury and he wanted to prepare Patsy for a shock.

I made her reassure him she'd only believe what he told her himself. On 1 May, he replied:

> . . . My trial is coming up in a few weeks, not looking forward to it, Ill just be looking forward to getting it over and done with,
>
> I spend most of time day dreaming about what could of been, I believe in destony and I believe that one way or another we would of met up sooner or later . . .

The trial was drawing near and I wanted to get as much out of him as possible. He'd entered stage three of his incarceration – the realisation he was fucked. This deflated him and his ego, so I had to write more often.

He wrote again on 6 May:

> . . . on an brighter note things are not looking to bad for my trial I could if im lucky get diminished responsibility and then it will be up to the doctors when im released, but that wont be for a long time, how are things with you, are you enjoying the weather, anyway thats all for know write back soon
>
> Love Dave.

Shortly after that letter arrived – less than a month before his trial – I got a call on my mobile. Someone claiming to be a detective with Scotland Yard's Anti-Terrorist Branch said he was standing at my front door. He wanted to speak to me. I'd been warned by Adolf that the police were rounding up Nazis and ex-Nazis in the wake of Copeland's bombings. I feared they'd now come for me. I drove home immediately. Two plain-clothes officers stood outside my home. They flashed their ID cards and asked if we could talk inside. Once inside, I offered them a seat, but remained standing myself.

One of them said, 'We've been monitoring your correspondence with David Copeland. Do you want to tell us about it?'

I explained the hoax and how I'd previously used the same ruse to extract the truth from two child-killers. They asked to see the letters. I produced my thick file, and they read through everything. They said the letters could be of great use to the prosecution in the light of Copeland's plan to plead insanity. They asked me to make a statement, which I did. Then they told me to stop writing to Copeland immediately, because I might be called as a witness. They took the letters away as possible evidence.

The trial began at the Old Bailey on 5 June 2000. I didn't take great pleasure in imagining Copeland's feelings when he discovered that 20-year-old blonde/brunette secretary Patsy was in fact 40-year-old balding ex-bouncer Bernard. I hoped I wouldn't be called as a witness. I knew my appearance would only make everything a bit more painful and embarrassing for Copeland, and I didn't relish the idea. The person Copeland thought he loved would already have been taken from him – though perhaps not in quite as cruel a way as he'd taken other people's loved ones from them.

A few days into the trial, I was told that, although I probably wouldn't be called as a witness, the prosecution did intend using the 'Patsy Scanlon' letters. I followed closely the news reports of the proceedings, waiting for the moment when Copeland would finally be made aware of the dreadful truth about Patsy.

That moment came on the tenth day of the trial: Monday 19 June. The prosecution barrister Nigel Sweeney introduced the 'Patsy Scanlon' letters during his cross-examination of a defence psychiatrist. Mr Sweeney said that, while in custody, Copeland had been in correspondence with a 'Ms Patricia Scanlon'. Moreover, the letters showed he'd fallen in love with this woman. Unfortunately for Copeland, said the prosecutor, 'Ms Scanlon' was not a woman at all. She was in fact a man with a criminal record and other aliases. Sniggers filled the court. In the dock, Copeland inhaled deeply – and bowed his head dramatically. Some people thought he might slump to the floor.

Until that point, he'd shown no emotion. In the face of descriptions of the carnage he'd caused, he'd remained unmoved. Neither stories of the lives he'd blown apart, nor the amputees haunting the gallery had provoked any response from him. Only now did the Aryan soldier crumple in shame.

The judge described my deception as 'shabby'. I'd encountered such responses before, often from journalists who'd approve of putting hidden cameras in people's houses to catch dodgy plumbers. Prosecutor Nigel Sweeney spoke of a 'low trick'. However, low as it was, he stooped down to pick it up. He read out long extracts from the letters, then asked a simple question of a defence psychiatrist: 'Where, in all these letters, is there any sign of mental illness?'

The psychiatrist – one of five for the defence – admitted he could see no such sign. He suggested perhaps Copeland hadn't wanted to appear mad to his girlfriend. Another defence psychiatrist said Copeland had grandiose delusions, arrogance and a certainty he was right, whereas the ordinary far-right activist would recognise another viewpoint. I doubted whether the psychiatrist had ever met Adolf.

The prosecutor said the letters clearly showed Copeland had set out to fool doctors by faking mental illness. Dr Philip Joseph, a consultant at St Mary's Hospital in west London, supported this view. He told the court he'd read the whole correspondence. He criticised the five defence psychiatrists for using what Copeland had told them as almost their sole basis for concluding he was mentally ill. He said the 'Patsy Scanlon' letters made him sceptical of everything Copeland had said. For Dr Joseph, Copeland had been suffering from a personality disorder which did not amount to mental illness. He'd retained sufficient choice, will-power and ability to enable him to decide whether to carry out the bombings. So, whatever weird compulsions had driven him, they hadn't in legal terms impaired his judgement. Copeland's responsibility had not been diminished. In short, he was bad, not mad. The jury could find him guilty of murder, not manslaughter.

The judge in his summing-up put it simply: did Copeland know the difference between right and wrong? Had he been able to exercise will-power and free choice? The judge said all the psychiatrists agreed that Copeland had an abnormality of mind. However, they disagreed fiercely on the key issue of whether that mental abnormality had substantially impaired his judgement. The judge told the jury that if they felt Copeland's judgement had been substantially impaired, then the verdict had to be manslaughter. If not, then murder.

The jury found him guilty of murder. Many of Copeland's surviving victims roared their approval from the gallery. The judge, the Recorder of London Michael Hyam, said:

> Anyone who has heard the facts of this case will be appalled and horrified at the atrocity of your crimes. The evidence shows you were motivated to do what you did by virulent hatred of, and pitiless contempt for, other people. On your own admission, you set out to kill, maim and cause terror in the community. And that is what you did.
>
> As a result of your wicked intentions, you have left three families bereaved and many people so severely injured by the explosions you caused that they are reminded every day, and perhaps many times every day, that you alone are accountable for ruining their lives. Nothing can excuse or justify the evil you have done, and certainly not the abhorrent views you embraced.
>
> It is only too apparent that you have no feeling for those whose lives you have affected. The public must be protected from you and must be assured that if you are ever released it will not be for a very long time.

He gave Copeland six life sentences. Spectators in the gallery clapped and cheered. Some cried, others hugged one another. As he was led away, survivors and victims' relatives shouted, 'You bastard', 'Rot in hell' and 'Nazi scum'.

The facts of Copeland's anti-social life – as revealed during and after his trial – helped explain both why he'd so quickly fallen for 'Patsy Scanlon' and why he'd become a Nazi in the first place. I'd been right about his childhood disturbance, but wrong about its source. I'd assumed that, like me and many others who drift into the far-right, he'd become a people-hater after physical or mental abuse as a child. However, no evidence of that emerged. On the surface, he seemed to have had a relatively comfortable and stable upbringing (despite his parents' divorce when he was in his teens). But, in his own eyes – so he told police – he'd had 'a horrible, bad childhood'.

To a workmate, he said, 'My family fucked me up.' His feelings originated in his undersized genitals. From birth, there'd been medical concern about the size of his testicles. At 15, his parents sent him to a special clinic for children with growth problems. Doctors there had put his equipment under the microscope. No pubic hair had remained unruffled in their quest for medical knowledge. A memory of humiliation had stuck in Copeland's mind. His small penis and testicles began to obsess him.

Consequently, he only ever had one short-lived girlfriend. He told a psychiatrist they'd had sex, but she hadn't enjoyed it because of his small penis. With 'Patsy' – for the first time in his life – he must have thought he'd become an object of fascination for a woman. No wonder he lied about his height: he was in fact only 5 ft 6 in., not 5 ft 8 in., as he'd told Patsy.

He told psychiatrists that his family – mother, father and two brothers – had often discussed his lack of girlfriends. He believed they thought him homosexual. He spoke of one episode when they sang the jaunty song of the television cartoon series, *The Flintstones*. 'Flintstones, we're the Flintstones, we're the modern stone age family . . . we'll have a zoo time, a yabadoo time, we'll have a gay old time.'

Copeland felt they kept emphasising the word 'gay' to mock him. His mother would ask if there was anything he'd like to tell her. She also said that, if he were gay, there'd be no problem. Copeland didn't appreciate her warm-hearted tolerance. His older brother, perhaps less tolerant, used to call him 'gay boy'. He told a psychiatrist he still wanted revenge against his family. He said, 'It makes me want to hurt someone.'

He told police his bombing of the mostly gay pub (in which a pregnant woman had been among the three dead) had been 'personal'. He even said he preferred blacks and Asians to gays.

Around the age of 13, he'd become fascinated with Nazism – and had dreamed of butchering, strangling and torturing his classmates. Indeed, his first ambition had been to become a serial killer or mass murderer. He told psychiatrists he'd often fantasised about being a Waffen SS commander. He'd imagined himself as tall, blond and powerful – with a harem of female sex slaves. Sometimes, he'd dream of being an SS man who'd pick a female, rape her, then shoot her dead. When he was writing to me, I flattered myself with the thought that my skill as a sympathetic penfriend was drawing him out. I know now that he'd probably have written enthusiatically to anyone who'd wanted him as a friend.

In the years leading up to the bombing, he'd been isolated and friendless. At the time he planted his bombs, he'd been living alone in a bedsit with only his pet rat 'Whizzer' for company. His deep personal unhappiness had provoked suicidal thoughts, but, he told a psychiatrist, he'd been too cowardly to take his own life. After his arrest, he told a police interviewer that life in prison didn't bother him: 'I don't care. I had no life anyway. I'd say this is freedom to me.'

He wasn't stupid. He had an IQ that put him in the top 10 per cent of the population, but he knew he was a nobody going nowhere, and that angered him, because he craved fame and notoriety. He told police, 'I wanted to be famous. I believe in what I believe in, and I took that belief to the extreme.'

Small and insignificant, he dreamt of being omnipotent, with the sort of power over life and death possessed by his dictator heroes: Hitler, Stalin and Saddam Hussein. His bombing campaign had been inspired in part by reading *The Turner Diaries* – the so-called 'fascist Bible'. This novel, written by the American Nazi William Pierce, imagines a race war against ZOG, the Jewish-controlled Zionist Occupation Government. The book has a central male character, a hero who gains immortality for himself by his violent and ruthless struggle on behalf of the white race. This book also inspired the Oklahoma bomber Timothy McVeigh.

At one stage, Copeland had wanted to go to America to join the Ku Klux Klan. Copeland hoped his bombs would provoke a race war between blacks and whites, the end result of which would be a BNP government which would repatriate all foreigners – and release him from prison as a national hero. One of his former housemates said that, apart from his dislike of blacks and Asians, Copeland had also expressed a strong aversion to people from the north of England.

Several psychiatrists diagnosed Copeland as a paranoid schizophrenic, partly because of his peculiar ideas. But Dr Joseph, the one psychiatrist who argued he could be found guilty of murder, suggested his colleagues hadn't appreciated the significance of the nail-bomber's reading material. He said Copeland had simply been repeating things he'd read in Nazi texts. He added that psychiatrists unfamiliar with such literature might think their patient delusional – but some intelligent people put forward such extreme views in all seriousness.

Copeland's father later slagged me off publicly for having hoaxed his 'mentally-ill' son in such a 'cruel' way. He called me a low-life scumbag.

After Copeland's trial, the government discussed changing the law to allow the preventive detention of dangerous psychopaths. Under the proposals, people with certain personality disorders could be detained – even if they'd committed no offence – if they presented a serious risk to others. The Home Office consultation paper listed ten characteristics of such people. They'd have to demonstrate at least six of the ten in order to be detained. I went through the list. Before his bombing campaign, Copeland would only have scored four out of ten.

To my horror, I realised that my brother Paul scored nine out of ten. The only point that didn't cover him was one relating to sexual offences. Copeland had collected photos that showed people suffering. He cut them from newspapers and magazines, then plastered them over the walls of his bedsit. The police found photos of famines, bombs, riots and atrocities. Until recently, my brother Paul used to do the same.

It's desperately painful for me to write about Paul. His story leaves me feeling sad, bleak and, worse, helpless. I can no longer reach him. His madness has swallowed him up. The violence and mayhem that's marked every step of his way through life seems about to find its end in his premature death.

And there's nothing more I can do for him.

CHAPTER 19

DEVIL DOG

AS YOUNG BOYS, PAUL AND I USED TO SHARE A DOUBLE BED IN THE FRONT ROOM of our house on the outskirts of Wolverhampton. We didn't have blankets. Instead, our mother used to cover us with heavy winter coats, the most comfy being a duffle coat with tartan-check lining that we used to fight over.

We were all terrified of our father, but Paul seemed to fear him the most. At night, Paul would lie next to me, shaking. Then he'd wet the bed. His bed-wetting got so bad that my mother took him to the doctor, who referred him to a specialist. Even at that age – I was about four, Paul two years older – I knew my brother didn't need a specialist to discover why he wet the bed. But nobody dared tell anyone that my father was beating us senseless.

I can remember Paul being admitted to a children's hospital on the Penn Road in Wolverhampton. Mum took me to see him. I think it's the only time I've ever seen him truly happy. He was driving around in a pedal car, playing with the other children. My father arrived as my mother talked to the consultant. I remember him shouting and swearing, and then we all – Paul included – headed for home on the bus.

My father's demented cruelty turned me and Paul into violent and unruly children. Like me, Paul began venting his anger and frustration on others. Years later, he used to joke, 'At school, I wanted to be a surgeon, but the teachers had me locked up when I tried operating on the other kids.' Many a true word spoken in jest.

At first, he remained content to assault only the other kids, but before long he started hitting teachers too. Aged 15, he approached a bearded English teacher who'd slapped me round the face. 'Oi, you,' said Paul. 'Did you slap my brother?'

Taken aback, the teacher said, 'Oi? Oi? Who do you think you're talking to, boy? Are you chewing gum?'

Paul confirmed he was. The teacher ordered him to remove it from his mouth. Paul did so – then rammed it into the teacher's beard, saying, 'That's for my brother, and this is for calling me "boy".' He punched him, sending him sprawling, then walked away. The headmaster expelled him later that day.

I laughed every time I saw the teacher walking around the school with bald clumps in his beard where he'd had to cut the gum out. He never bothered me again.

One of the saddest aspects of Paul's depressing story is that he was by no means the brainless yob that some saw. He was a very bright boy. He could bury his head for hours in books about warplanes, weapons and battles. By his mid-teens, he could have held his own with a military historian. He'd become fascinated by the police and military from an early age. He loved putting on uniforms and even joined the Air Training Corps. When I was in the army, he used to know more than I did about the equipment I used and the history of my regiment.

Away from school, Paul's behaviour became criminal. On the outskirts of the village was a fishing lake popular with boy anglers. Its owner, a confirmed bachelor in his 50s, lived alone in a grand house. Boys had to go there to obtain their fishing permits. Stories began to spread about the man's over-familiar behaviour.

Paul saw a money-making opportunity. He called at the man's house and gave him an ultimatum. Either the man paid him to keep his mouth shut or he'd go to the police and allege the man had been fiddling with boys. The horrified man initially paid up, but when the fee began to rise extortionately he went himself to the police, and Paul was arrested for blackmail.

For many years, violence and a bed were all Paul and I shared. Our lives mirrored one another's, they'd been formed in the same environment, but we could never talk about our grim inheritance. Most of the time, we could only communicate with our fists.

When I was ten, Paul smashed me in the mouth with a rifle butt because I'd been lippy with my mother. The dentist had to remove various nerves. To this day, I still have no feeling in some areas of my mouth.

In later years, I can remember my youngest brother Michael bringing home for the first time his new girlfriend (and future wife) Carol. He wanted to introduce her to my mother. Michael and Carol walked into a bloodbath in the sitting room. I'd smashed a dinner plate over Paul's head. His blood had then spattered the walls as we'd grappled with each other in what one of his war books would have described as bitter hand-to-hand fighting. My mother was doing her best to separate us. I can't even remember what we were fighting about. It was just another violent and bloody row.

This madness was the norm for our family, though not for Codsall, which was then a quiet, picturesque village, not some inner-city slum littered with dysfunctional families. Indeed, gangs from Wolverhampton used to visit looking for trouble, because they regarded Codsall as 'posh'.

It was one such gang that Paul attacked when he was 16. They'd come to Codsall to fight the locals, but only Paul showed willing. With a screwdriver in each hand, he stabbed three people before being beaten senseless. He was sent to Borstal. With good behaviour, he could have got out in six months, but he refused to respect the rules, which included having to wear a coloured tie. Different colours signified the different stages towards release.

From the first day, Paul said, 'Fuck your ties. I'm not wearing a poncy tie.'

They said, 'Well, then, you won't be allowed any privileges or visits.'

Paul said, 'Fuck your privileges and visits.'

They said, 'You can be out in six months or we can keep you here for two years. It's up to you.'

Paul said, 'I don't give a fuck.'

He ended up serving the full two years – with an additional two months for crimes committed while inside. He didn't receive a single visit in that time. By law, including the ones he'd broken in there, they couldn't keep him any longer. In the end, I think they had to beg him to leave.

His spell in Borstal hardened him further. It was soon after his release that he bashed my father, who, wisely, left the house next day, never to return.

Within the week, Paul had also left home with no forwarding address. He just packed a rucksack, told us he'd see us later and drove off on a motorbike. 'Later' turned out to be the best part of five years.

I'll always remember him with the big green army rucksack on his back, like a soldier going to war, trying to kick-start the motorbike. He couldn't get it going. Eventually, he ran with it. The engine bump-started with a roar and Paul zoomed off up the road. I watched him disappear round the bend of our estate. A few days later, the police called. They said they'd found Paul's bike near a small village some miles away. It had broken down. Over the next five years, he didn't phone once, let alone send a postcard. He just disappeared, like my father.

In 1981, while serving in Northern Ireland, I got three days' leave. I rang my mother to tell her I'd be home for a few days. She told me Paul had just got back in touch. He'd phoned her from London, but hadn't explained where he'd been. He'd asked her to get me to phone him.

I rang him after I arrived at Heathrow. He didn't say much. He only wanted to know about the six counties of Ulster. Had I been in any fire fights? Had I shot anyone? Had I tortured any prisoners? Could I get him a classified field book (containing mugshots of IRA suspects and the like)? Would I be able to get hold of guns and ammunition? Without needing to ask, I knew Paul was all right – being his old self, that is.

I arranged to meet him at Birmingham New Street Station next morning. Within a few minutes of our greeting each other, we were engaged in close combat on the station concourse. I don't know why. Perhaps I'd asked him why in five years he hadn't phoned our tormented mother. Perhaps I'd asked him the time. Whatever – I'd taken some diabolical liberty that merited a violent assault. After a few minutes, we stopped punching. We wiped the blood from our faces, then went to a pub round the corner where we drank a lot, argued and talked about the joys of Northern Ireland. It was our first talk as adults. The one thing we didn't talk about was 'us', our family and what we'd been through as children. I could still feel that sense of hopelessness we'd shared.

I had to squeeze in a court case during my leave, so I had limited time with Paul. However, we travelled together on the train back to London. At Euston, we jumped on a tube heading west to Heathrow. A few stations down the line, as the nameplate for Green Park flashed past our eyes, Paul said, 'This is me.' He just stood up and got off. No goodbye, no good luck, no 'we'll meet again, don't know where, don't know when'.

However, surprisingly, this time he kept in touch with my mother. When I left the army, I moved to London and began to see a bit more of him. He'd tried joining an army himself – the Spanish Army. If he'd just wanted to carry a gun and wear a uniform, he could have applied to join the Hell's Angels, like my oldest brother Jerry. But Paul wanted more. He wanted real-life adventure, the sort he'd read about in his military books. So he became a paratrooper with the Spanish Foreign Legion.

After basic training, they sent him to the 8th Airborne Battalion stationed on some forgotten piece of colonial territory somewhere in north Africa. But he kept falling foul of the petty rules and regulations. Paul, in his mind, is always right. Others know nothing. So he spent most of his time in the guardhouse. He decided to desert.

He stowed away on a holiday cruise ship bound for England – and arrived in Grays, Essex, still wearing his legionnaire's uniform. I understand the Spanish Army no longer accepts foreigners in its ranks. I think its experience with Paul may have provoked it to change its policy.

It was Paul who introduced me to Adolf. For a while, Adolf became his best friend. They'd worked together as hod-carriers at the building of a hospital in Croydon. Their boss, a King's Cross villain, asked them to work for him as 'strikebusters'. Their new job – for which their boss provided them with a Jaguar car, well-tailored suits and a licence to maim – involved their threatening, bullying and, if need be, beating union reps who visited, or tried to visit, sites run by the boss. If a strike still managed to get off the ground, then Adolf and Paul would visit striking members at their homes to point out the error of their ways. That was Paul's first taste of far-right politics. He learnt the Nazi approach to negotiation.

However, although Paul and Adolf seemed close for a while, their friendship came to a sudden end one day when Paul stabbed Adolf. I've heard both versions of what happened – and there's no disagreement about the facts. Paul had been sitting in Adolf's front room as Adolf had started arguing with his mother. Adolf's tone of voice and choice of words had displeased Paul, who said, 'Don't talk to your mother like that.'

Adolf said, 'I'll talk to my mother how I like. What are you going to do about it?' Paul jumped out of his armchair, pulled a nine-inch bayonet from somewhere and thrust it into Adolf's stomach. It came out his back.

Paul then ran off. He travelled back to our mother's house in Codsall, where he burnt his clothes in the garden. When my mother asked him what he was doing, he told her he'd killed someone.

The knife hadn't hit anything vital, so Adolf survived. He refused to tell the police what had happened, so Paul was never questioned, let alone charged. Paul did later make some sort of gesture of apology to Adolf, but their friendship never recovered. Understandably, like almost every human being who meets Paul, Adolf started avoiding him.

We had a favourite uncle called Bernie. He was one of my mother's brothers, and I was named after him. He'd lived with us briefly in Dunstable and he visited us now and again in Codsall. He was a good, decent man, but misfortune and unhappiness dogged his life. In 1985, Paul and I had to identify his body.

In the '60s, Bernie had served a short prison sentence in Ireland for assault. He came to England to start a new life. He married a woman he adored and they lived together happily. He could never bring himself to tell her about his prison sentence, because he felt ashamed. On a trip to Ireland, someone raised the subject and the marriage hit its first rock. His wife couldn't accept he'd kept his past from her. Eventually, she left him.

Bernie turned to drink. He soon lost everything else – his job, his fixed address and his hope. One evening, a security guard saw him sitting alone on a bench in a communal garden near the subways of Birmingham's Bull Ring shopping centre. He was holding an unopened bottle of Australian wine.

A few hours later, another security guard saw him lying on the ground, his face covered in blood. Bernie was semi-conscious when the guard went to help him. Before passing out, he mumbled, 'No, no. Stop it.' He died a few days later, never having regained consciousness. The bottle of wine lay unopened by his side, and he still had money in his pocket, so he hadn't been the victim of a robbery. The police put up posters and a sign appealing for witnesses to 'an incident', but none came forward.

When my mother and one of her sisters went to identify the body, they couldn't say for certain if it was his. Paul and I had seen Bernie only a few weeks earlier, so the police asked us to view the corpse. We were both living in London at the time, so we travelled to Birmingham together. I'd been working the night before the journey and felt tired. I hoped to catch a few hours' sleep on the coach. I stretched out across the back seat. Trying to relax, I took off my trainers and used my coat as a pillow. I soon fell sound asleep.

Paul had been drinking the night before. He continued drinking from a carrier bag full of beer. He woke me when we reached Birmingham two and a half hours later. I sat up, stretched and rubbed my eyes. As I bent down to put on my trainers, Paul shouted, 'No! No! Don't put them on.'

'Why not?' I said.

'Because there's no toilet on here and I had to piss in them.'

'You had to piss in my fucking trainers?'

Paul looked at me earnestly and said, 'Well, of course I did.'

I began doing my nut. He seemed sincerely confused by my anger. He said, 'What's up with you? What fucking choice did I have? I couldn't piss on the floor, could I?'

His cold logic had defeated me. The problem with this logic is that it fails to take into account other people's needs and rights. In his world, only his needs exist. They take priority over everything and everyone else. He has a coldness that puts people on edge. He almost never laughs. My father taught us as children to repress all feeling and emotion. He wanted to make us cold, hard and callous, just like him. Paul is a successful product of my father's parenting skills.

I left my urine-soaked trainers behind on the coach. Fortunately, I found a shoe shop near the station, so I didn't have to hobble too far in my socks. I bought a new pair of trainers before heading off to carry out our grisly task.

At the mortuary, an official warned us that Bernie had sustained head injuries which we might find distressing. He told us to wait while the body was 'prepared'. Eventually, he returned to lead us into a spine-tinglingly cold room divided by a large glass panel. Curtains covered the panel. The official pressed a button. The curtains opened slowly to reveal a body lying on a trolley. A sheet covered the body to its chest. I'd been hoping and praying they'd made a mistake, that the body lying there wouldn't be Bernie's, but I recognised him instantly, even though his swollen eyes were no more than slits, one of his ears was the size of my hand, and bruising covered his face and head.

When we left the room, the official told us the date of Bernie's forthcoming inquest. He said we didn't need to attend, as it would just be a formality, the most likely outcome being a verdict of accidental death.

His words shocked me. I said, 'Accidental death? You're calling that a fucking accident? Have you seen his face?'

The official said the police believed Bernie had accidentally fallen off the bench.

I couldn't believe what I was hearing. I said, 'Where was the bench he fell off? On top of the fucking Empire State Building?'

The official said he couldn't comment. He said, 'You can raise any concerns you may have at the inquest.'

The inquest went ahead. I got the impression the police hadn't spent too much time investigating 'the incident'. I also got the impression the coroner didn't give a shit about the dead 'tramp'. Despite our protests, he recorded a verdict of accidental death. I felt livid. I believe to this day that someone beat Bernie to death. If he'd been leading a 'normal' lifestyle, the police would have investigated his death fully.

One Christmas Day, I went for a lunch-time drink in

Wolverhampton with my three brothers and my friend Millie.
Everyone was in a good mood. As we stood chatting near the bar,
a middle-aged man accidentally knocked into Paul, spilling his
drink. The man, who was drunk, didn't apologise. I don't think
he even realised what he'd done. When I looked at Paul's face, I
knew that, unless I intervened quickly, the man was doomed.

Before Paul could do anything, I manoeuvred the drunk away
and gripped Paul's arm. I said, 'Leave it, Paul. Please fucking leave
it.'

He said, 'That fucking ignorant cunt's bumped into me and
he's not said a word.'

I said, 'Paul, it's Christmas Day. Forget about it.'

The man went into the toilet.

I tried to change the subject. Paul said, 'When he comes out,
he either apologises or he gets it.'

I told him again to forget about it. He said, 'Fuck "forget about
it".'

I knew the way his mind was working: if the man didn't
apologise, then he must have done it deliberately. And if he'd
done it deliberately, then he deserved punishment.

I still hoped to step in to prevent an unpleasant incident. The
man came out of the toilet and squeezed past, putting his hand
lightly on Paul's shoulder. The man didn't say anything. Without
a word, Paul grabbed the man by the throat, forced his head down
and gripped him in a head-lock. Then he picked up a pint glass,
smashed it and began shoving the jagged stump repeatedly into
the man's face. 'Ignorant cunt,' he said with each stab, 'ignorant
cunt, ignorant cunt, ignorant cunt.'

When the glass had totally disintegrated, Paul let the blood-
soaked man fall to the floor, his face cut to ribbons.

Paul neither ran nor showed any emotion. Instead, he asked for
a fresh pint. The trembling barman said, 'Sorry, mate. I can't serve
you.'

Paul sat down. I said, 'Get out of the pub, you thick cunt.'

Paul said, 'I'm going fucking nowhere.'

Millie stood there shocked and on the verge of tears. I asked her
to go outside. At the same time, I grabbed Paul and manhandled
him out into the car park. One of my brothers had called for two

taxis, which arrived quicker than the police and ambulance. I put myself and Millie in the first, then left my three brothers to get in the second.

Paul could never grasp why I'd brought our little Christmas drink to a premature end. Later, he said, 'What's your fucking problem, Bernie? He asked for it. He was an ignorant cunt.'

'Yeah, you already said,' I muttered. I didn't bother arguing. The police didn't catch up with Paul for this attack.

Paul has been scary and unpredictable for as long as I can remember. You can never relax in his company, because you don't know what's going to happen next. You're always at risk of saying or doing something that might somehow offend him. You can't really talk to him, let alone reason with him. Sometimes, after some awful and unnecessary bit of violence, I've tried to get him to reflect on what he's done and why. But he's just exploded and accused me of picking on him.

Some years later, in the late '80s, I went for a Sunday afternoon drink in south London with Paul, my brother Michael, Army Game's dad, Adolf and a few other friends. Paul started playing cards for money with two Scotsmen and a mate of mine from Codsall called Gary 'Chop' Lambeth. After a few hours of play, several hundred pounds had piled up on the table. Slowly, the Scots lost the lot. When they could play no more, having run out of cash, one of them foolishly made a grab for the money.

Paul punched him in the head. We all joined in on Paul's side. The fight only lasted a few seconds before the penniless, and now battered, Scots found themselves bundled out the door. One of them shouted, 'We'll be back for you, you English cunts.'

I saw Paul's face don its psycho mask. A minute or so later, he got up and left the pub. I could tell he had unfinished business, but I didn't want to be party to whatever hideous act he might now commit. Moments later, a woman pushing a buggy burst into the pub and screamed, 'Murder! Murder! Call the police! Someone's been murdered!'

I ran outside with Gary 'Chop' Lambeth. About a hundred yards away, we saw one of the Scots lying face-down on the pavement next to a zebra crossing. He wasn't moving. We ran over. His back, his head and the pavement were all soaked in blood.

Paul, in his rage, had left the pub, got into his Transit van and sped after the Scots. As they'd stood between a park fence and the pole of the zebra crossing, Paul had mounted the pavement and driven into them from behind. One had managed to jump out of the way – and had run off. The other had been run over – literally. A gaping v-shaped wound covered his back. His flesh had been torn off. I learned later the damage had been caused by the nut used to drain oil from the van's sump. I felt for a pulse. Although unconscious and badly injured, the Scot was still alive.

Then I heard the roar of an engine. I looked up and saw Paul's van shoot through a red light up the road outside Clapham's Cavendish Road police station. I assumed he was now making his getaway. To my surprise, the van skidded round in the road – and started tearing back down towards us. I guessed instantly he wanted another run at the motionless man, who'd surely die if I allowed that to happen. I wasn't prepared to let Paul serve a life sentence over a game of cards, if only because I knew I'd probably be the only person prepared to visit him inside.

I didn't fancy spending the next 15 years traipsing round the country once a month to sit in a prison visiting room. So I stood over the injured man, even though I didn't have much sympathy for the cheeky scumbag at my feet. As Paul hurtled towards us, I saw him waving and flailing his arms at me. From his gestures, I knew he wanted me to get out of the way. I stood my ground. For a moment, I really thought I might die. But, realising he'd have to run me over in order to squash the jock, Paul swerved at the last moment, taking out a zebra-crossing pole on the traffic island before screeching to a halt.

He jumped out of the van and ran to where I was standing. He wanted to know why I'd stopped him. What did I think I was playing at? Then he grabbed his unconscious and blood-soaked victim by the hair and began kicking him in the body, screaming, 'Dirty fucking cunt. You dirty fucking cunt.'

I'm no referee, but the jock had certainly lost this one.

I tried pulling Paul away, but he'd lost it so much he started on me. I said, 'For fuck's sake, Paul. Get in your van and disappear or you'll get nicked.'

Paul shouted, 'Fuck the police, fuck you and fuck him.' Then boot, boot. He started kicking the rag doll again. Finally, he turned, jumped in his van and disappeared.

I turned the Scot over. I thought at first he'd been glassed or stabbed in the forehead, but the mess must have been caused when his head hit the pavement. Gary and I fucked about with him for a short while. When we were happy he was breathing all right, we left him. The buggy-pushing woman who'd run into the pub screaming blue murder had been taken home by Del Boy. He'd told her he needed to take her name and address in case the police wanted to get in touch. He said, 'Don't bother calling them. They'll call you, if they think it's necessary. But I don't think it will be, because we know who did it.'

That night, Paul went round to the victim's house, kicked his door in and threatened the man's parents. He said he'd be back for them if their hospitalised son grassed him up. Paul wasn't even questioned over the incident.

I might have given the impression he gets away with a lot. That's not true. He spends his life yo-yoing back and forth through prison gates. A cell has been his home for at least half his life. He's also himself often been the victim of extreme violence.

I got a call from him once from hospital. I knew something serious must have happened, because he was laughing, which he normally doesn't do. And what had provoked this hilarity? He'd just come out of intensive care. He said he was lying in bed with plaster covering most of his body. Apparently, he'd fallen out with one of his 'friends' (his word for short-term acquaintances as weird, unstable and psychotic as he is). He'd beaten up this 'friend', who, a few days later, had invited him to return to the flat for a 'reconciliation' drink. A normal person might have been wary of the olive branch, but not Paul. His 'friend' and two others were waiting for him with baseball bats. Paul only narrowly escaped with his life.

I've let him stay with me a few times over the years. I wouldn't do that now. Once, in Deptford, I went away for a week and came back to find my motorbike had disappeared. A little agitated, I asked Paul if he knew when it had been stolen.

'Stolen?' he said. 'It wasn't stolen. I got you a very good price for it.'

I said, 'What d'you mean? Have you sold it?'

He claimed a stranger had knocked on the door and offered to buy it. 'Don't worry,' said Paul, 'I got you more than it's worth.'

Trying to come to terms with the bike's loss, and hoping to draw some consolation from the episode, I said, 'Well, how much did you get, then?'

'About three hundred quid.'

'So where's the money?'

'I've spent it.'

A few years later, he came to stay with me at a south London squat I was living in temporarily. I came home to find he'd stripped the whole house of lead and valuable metals. And not just off the roof – he'd ripped out internal pipes and appliances too. According to his logic, the stuff didn't belong to me, so he had as much right to it as I or the squat's other occupants.

It just didn't register with him that what he'd done was wrong. However hard I tried to explain things, he just couldn't see what my problem was. The truth is that Paul only understands violence. He only respects the opinions and rights of people who hurt him. And that's only till he's well enough to come back and stick something in them.

One sunny Sunday afternoon – I think it was around 1989 – I was walking with Paul through a housing estate in Battersea, south London. We'd just had a lunch-time drink in a nearby pub. The happy sound of children at play filled the summer air. People were snoozing in deckchairs or mowing their lawns or washing their cars. England was at peace. But not for long.

Tabloid newspapers had been running a campaign against dangerous dogs (by which they meant breeds like Rottweilers, American pit bull terriers and Staffordshire bull terriers). The papers had been demanding the muzzling in public places of the animals they'd branded 'Devil Dogs' after a spate of horrific attacks on children.

As Paul and I strolled down the street, a weedy little cross-bred collie dog started barking at us from the other side of a hedge. I say 'barking', but in fact it was making more of a wimpy little yapping sound than a full-throated bark. That was enough for Paul. He suddenly leapt across the hedge and attacked the dog. He struggled with it violently on the ground, apparently trying to throttle it.

The dog's male owner stood at his open front door and shouted, 'What the fuck are you doing? Leave my dog alone!' Paul lifted the dog up and gave it a punch in the head that launched it flying across the garden. It landed on its back and rolled over before scampering to the corner furthest from Paul. It didn't dare bark. It just stood there, cowering, waiting to see what the lunatic would do next.

The owner was screaming at Paul, who said, 'That's a fucking Devil Dog. It tried to attack me. It was jumping up, barking and snarling.'

The man said he was calling the police. He went inside. I told Paul we had to go, but he wouldn't listen. He'd now switched to full psycho mode. 'Let him call the fucking police,' he said. 'That's a fucking Devil Dog and it should be muzzled.'

A police car arrived swiftly. Two policemen got out and asked what was wrong. Paul said, 'That man has a Devil Dog which tried to bite me. I want it put down.' The police spoke to the owner and viewed the 'Devil Dog', which still sat cowering in the corner, shaking with fear.

The police told Paul to move on or get nicked. I tried to grab Paul by the arm, but he shrugged me off. One of the policemen said again, 'I've told you. Move on or you're nicked.'

Paul said, 'Fucking nick me, then.'

I knew what was coming. The policeman put his hand on Paul's shoulder. My brother punched him to the ground with a right-hander. The other officer jumped on Paul. He, too, ended up on the ground. They called for back-up.

I was saying, 'He's all right. He's sound. He's with me. I'll look after him.'

Paul turned on me, 'What d'you mean, I'm all right? I'm not fucking all right. I've just been attacked by a Devil Dog.'

A police van screeched to a stop beside us. The riot squad

jumped out and dived on Paul. In the struggle, they ripped off his shirt. They finally managed to handcuff him and load him into the back of the van, where he continued to writhe, kick and scream about the 'Devil Dog', which he was now claiming had bitten him.

Charged with assaulting police officers, Paul defended himself at his magistrates' court trial. He explained the danger he'd felt himself to be in from the 'Devil Dog'. The elderly magistrate told him he couldn't understand his concern if the dog had been in its own garden and not in the street.

Paul said, 'If you can't understand that, then you must be a fucking senile old cunt.'

The magistrate sent him to the cells for contempt of court. After an hour, Paul was brought back up. The magistrate told him he expected an apology. Paul said he had no intention of apologising, because facts were facts. He said, 'If you can't understand a straightforward explanation, then you must be a fucking senile old cunt. Simple as that.' The magistrate gave him three months' imprisonment for assaulting the police – and an extra seven days for contempt.

Paul's psycho behaviour can frighten anyone, but can terrify normal people, who are sometimes forced to take desperate measures to escape him. One time, Paul met a quiet and shy pianist called Jonathan in a south London pub. He invited himself back to Jonathan's flat, where he ordered him to play the piano. Jonathan had to play for hours. Over the next few months, whenever Paul wanted to hear some music he'd say, 'I'm going to Jonathan's.' He used to use him like his personal jukebox. I saw him once frogmarching a scared-looking Jonathan down the road for yet another piano session.

In the end, Jonathan just disappeared. He moved – probably to another country – without leaving a forwarding address.

For many years, Paul had no trouble finding girlfriends. At school, the girls thought him handsome and used to swarm over him. He fathered his first child in his teens. That relationship, like his other relationships, didn't last long. Subsequently, he had a child with another woman. He's had very little contact with the children. In the early '90s, he started going out with a woman in south London. They had a daughter. I think Paul looked upon his girlfriend's happiness with her daughter in much the same way that my father looked upon our happiness with our mother. It drove him insane with jealousy, which soon became anger. Paul had turned into my father.

His girlfriend, terrified by his outbursts, soon wanted nothing more to do with him. But he wouldn't leave her in peace. His odd behaviour terrified her. She could see no way out. Through experience, I know that the most dangerous person in the world is an extremely frightened one with nowhere to run.

One day, she asked Paul to collect their daughter from school. She insisted he be there punctually at 3.30 p.m. Paul agreed, but when he arrived he noticed that most parents had already left with their children. The school seemed almost empty. He walked from the main entrance to a side entrance, looking all over for the girl, but there was no sign of her. Growing more concerned, he went back to the main entrance. He called out the girl's name, but no one appeared. As he stood there, he saw three black men getting out of a car. They walked towards him. When they reached him, one said, 'Paul?'

My brother said, 'Who wants to know?' He was then stabbed four times in the body and left for dead. He recovered – and went looking for the men who'd stabbed him. He wasn't stupid. He knew his ex-girlfriend had set him up to be murdered.

I think he must have terrorised her into giving him a name. He ended up being stabbed again a month later in Hackney after trying to sever a black man's head with a shovel. He claimed to me from his hospital bed that his victim had been one of the men who'd attacked him. I wasn't convinced. However, he finally accepted that his ex-girlfriend didn't want to see him any more.

The break-up of this relationship did genuinely upset Paul, although he tried not to show it. Having for so many years seen only his cold and unfeeling front, I was surprised to detect the flickering of emotions other than anger.

Like my Uncle Bernie, he turned to drink to dull the pain. He'd always drunk a lot – we all had – but that was 'normal' drinking. Now, in the course of a year, he became a full-blown, spirits-guzzling alcoholic. His new status didn't improve his behaviour.

He began living in a tower block near the Millwall football ground on an estate the *News of the World* had once described as 'Crack City'. He became friendly with a man and woman who lived together on the floor above. Within a short while, the woman ended up in hospital after being badly beaten by Paul. As told to the police, her version of what happened differed significantly from Paul's. All I know for sure is that this attack marked the start of Paul's final downward spiral.

I'll never forget the cryptic phone call I received from an over-excited policeman. He said, 'Your brother Paul wants you to know he's been arrested and is in police custody.'

The news didn't surprise me. Paul's alcohol-induced slide during the last year had ensured he was spending more and more time in custody. I asked what he was in for this time.

'Sorry, I can't tell you,' said the policeman.

'Where's he being held?'

'Sorry, I can't tell you.'

'Can I talk to him?'

'Sorry. Not at this stage.'

Irritated, I said, 'Is there any purpose to this phone call?

'Sorry?' said the policeman.

'My brother Paul's in trouble, you can't say what for, I can't talk to him and you won't tell me where he's being held.'

'He'll be at Tower Bridge Magistrates' Court in the morning. Goodbye.'

I went to court in the morning expecting to hear about some unfortunate human being who'd been stabbed or badly beaten by Paul for some perceived misdemeanour. I sat down to wait for Paul's appearance. It wasn't the first time.

After half an hour or so, he shuffled into court in handcuffs. Screws stood near him. He looked grim. Usually, he'd glance round the court to find me, but this time he kept his head down. I felt a fluttering-butterfly sickness in my stomach. I knew something wasn't right.

The court clerk read out Paul's name, address and date of birth. Then he came to the charges. I'd guessed a shock might be on its way, but nothing had prepared me for what I heard: '. . . is charged with grievous bodily harm and rape.'

The word 'rape' twisted through my head. I felt dizzy. How could Paul, psychotic as he was, be charged with a nonce charge like rape? He could have been charged with mass murder and it wouldn't have surprised me. Perhaps it wouldn't even have bothered me. But rape? I felt every dirty emotion – and I could tell Paul knew my feelings. He was sitting there, head bowed, his eyes fixed on his cuffed hands.

The magistrate said he'd be remanded in custody to Belmarsh Prison and he gave a date for his next appearance. Then the screws led Paul away. He shuffled back out, staring at the ground.

I arranged to visit him in prison the next day. I felt I wouldn't need a jury to tell me if he was guilty as charged. I wanted only the chance to look him in the eyes. From childhood, I'd shared his nightmares, his fears, his pain, his anger, his violence. I felt sure he could neither lie to me, nor fool me. I believed I'd know in the instant our eyes met if he'd indeed added rape to his list of crimes.

CHAPTER 20

BURYING THE PAST

IN THE VISITING ROOM OF BELMARSH PRISON, MY BROTHER SAT IN A CHAIR NEAR A group of screws. Both Paul and I knew that 'nonces' had to do that for their own protection, because 'normal' prisoners viewed them as the lowest of the low and attacked them whenever possible.

As I walked towards Paul, I felt anxious in a way I hadn't experienced for a long time. My brother looked down briefly at his hands before looking back up at me. I sat down in front of him and swallowed. He said, 'Bernie, don't you fucking dare ask me if I did this.' He put his head down again.

I knew what he was saying, but I had to ask him. I had to know the truth. I said, 'Paul, look me in the face. Whatever's happened has happened. Don't mug me off.'

With his head still down, he started crying, just sobbing quietly. Tears dropped down onto his lap. The last time I'd seen him crying was as a child being beaten by my father. Each and every one of his sobs ripped through me. I felt myself becoming tearful. After a short while, he composed himself enough to talk. He lifted up his head and looked hard into my eyes. He said the rape charge disgusted him. He'd raped no one – and never would. He swore on our mother's life he was innocent.

He told me the story. He said he'd started an affair with the woman. Her partner had come home unexpectedly and found them having sex. The woman had later claimed Paul had raped her. Her partner had called the police. In his rage at being accused of rape, he'd gone berserk and beaten her badly.

I felt a surge of relief. I wasn't happy he'd assaulted the woman, but I knew for sure now that he wasn't a nonce. I believed his swearing on our mother's life guaranteed his total honesty. The mere mention of her name would have been enough. I didn't need to know any more. I'd do whatever I could to help him clear his name.

My priority now was to get him out on bail so we could fight the case. That wasn't easy. He had to stay in prison for a few months until a judge finally granted him bail. He laid down stringent conditions, one of which was that Paul had to live outside London. Without consulting my brother Michael and his partner Carol, I put forward their address in Wolverhampton as Paul's new residence.

With hindsight, I made a terrible, and almost fatal, mistake. Michael is the quiet, gentle and normal one in our family. He leads an upright life, paying his taxes, observing the law and helping old ladies cross the road. Technically, he's even an ex-public-school boy. My eldest brother Jerry, who'd started earning good money on oil rigs, paid to send him to a posh boarding school. Unfortunately, the toffs sussed he was a commoner – I think he may once have failed to use a napkin correctly – and made his life a misery.

On leave from the army, I visited him at his new school. I found his sunken eyes harrowing. You'd have found more cheer in one of South African Dougie's prisoners. Eventually, I talked my mother into freeing him and he returned gratefully to civilisation.

Paul moved in with Michael and Carol. He immediately accelerated his self-destructive slide to oblivion. He'd drink a bottle of whisky in the morning, followed by bottles of wine throughout the day. He'd shout, rant, rave and occasionally weep, because he just couldn't come to terms with the rape accusation.

Life for Michael and Carol became unbearable. After a few weeks of madness, Michael asked Paul to leave. Paul flipped out. In his shattered state, he concluded that Michael wanted to send him back to prison. I was called to the house to reason with Paul. In our family, I fulfil the role of negotiator, problem-solver and peacemaker. The others don't really talk to one another. I arranged a truce. Paul agreed to cut out the drinking. Michael and

Carol agreed to let him stay until his trial. However, they warned that if he started drinking again, he'd have to leave.

That evening, England were playing Sweden. I decided to go for a drink with Hughie and my mates at The Crown in Codsall. Just before half-time, the barmaid put the phone on the bar next to me and said, 'Bernie, it's for you. They say it's urgent.'

When I picked up the receiver, Michael said, 'Bernard, is that you?' He sounded breathless and scared, as if he'd just been crying his eyes out.

'Yes,' I said. 'What's up?'

'You'd better come quick. I've just killed Paul.'

He replaced the receiver before I could speak. I put the phone down, finished my drink in a gulp, said goodbye to my mates and drove at top speed to Michael's. On the journey, I felt cold and drained. In my mind, I accepted Paul was dead. I began thinking of ways to get rid of his body because, if Michael had killed him, I knew he'd only have done so in self-defence, and I didn't want him rotting in prison for that act. One sibling's wasted life was enough.

I was surprised to see the flashing blue lights of several police cars and an ambulance outside the house. I'd hoped Michael and Carol hadn't phoned anyone else. As I walked to the front gate, two medics began wheeling Paul out on a trolley. I noticed a drip attached to his arm, so I knew he was still alive.

They placed him in the back of the ambulance. I jumped in behind them. I could see Paul's throat had been cut, but he was not only alive, but conscious. I pushed my face close to his and said, 'If you grass Michael, I'll come up the fucking hospital and finish this job off.' Paul didn't speak. I jumped back out of the ambulance.

The house looked like the set of a horror film. In the dining room, blood had spattered the walls and even the ceiling. Carol sat in a chair sobbing. I could see no sign of Michael. The police left after saying they wanted to talk to him.

Carol told me they'd all been sitting down to dinner when Paul had gone berserk again. Both she and Michael had been terrified. Paul had moved to grab Michael, who'd lashed out with a mug which had broken. Paul's throat ended up cut. There'd been so

301

much blood that Michael was convinced he'd killed him. After phoning me, he'd run off to hide down a nearby canal towpath.

I told Carol not to speak to the police under any circumstances and not to answer the door. She should only pick up the phone if it rang, went off, then rang again. I promised her everything would be all right. Then I went looking for Michael.

I found him hiding in bushes on the towpath. His face shone with relief when I told him Paul had still been alive when they'd wheeled him out. We went back to the house so he could get rid of his bloodstained clothes and clear away any other incriminating evidence.

When two detectives called later that evening, I told them the owners wouldn't be back until the next day. I asked them to leave a number. I assured them Michael and Carol would call and, if necessary, attend a police station.

At the hospital, Paul denied he'd been the victim of an assault. He refused to answer police questions. A nurse told me later that, though critically injured, he'd started swearing at the detectives and threatening them. They'd had to restrain him in his bed. The following day, I sent Michael to the police station with a solicitor. He was arrested on suspicion of attempted murder, but refused to answer any questions. The police later released him without charge. After a few weeks, Paul recovered enough to leave hospital. He moved into a friend's house in Codsall.

Paul's trial for GBH and rape took place at the Old Bailey. On the first morning, I arranged to meet him early on the steps outside. I hadn't told him I was bringing Michael along. I wanted to get them to shake hands and put the past behind them, because I was worried that, if they didn't, Paul would turn up one day at Michael's – as he'd already threatened – and kill him. To my relief (and, I think, Michael's), Paul stretched out his hand and agreed not to mention the incident again.

Paul's trial lasted three days. Our mutual friend Ray lent him his best suit. Paul pleaded guilty to GBH, but strenuously denied rape. On the third day, a female friend of the alleged rape victim went into the dock and testified that her friend had been having an affair with Paul and she had told her that he hadn't raped her.

Paul was immediately acquitted of rape, but sentenced to 18

months' imprisonment for GBH. Ray was sitting with me in court as the screws led Paul away to begin his sentence. I thought Ray looked more devastated than Paul. I asked him why. He said, 'Because I know I'll never see that suit again.'

For me, the outcome didn't mean much, because I'd lost Paul the day they charged him with rape. I didn't recognise the broken and confused man making his way down those wooden steps to the cells.

Paul came out of prison in early 1994 and moved back to his tower-block flat in 'Crack City'. Again, he began drinking suicidally. I visited him there and tried to divert him from his kamikaze dive. He'd decorated the walls of his lounge with photos of real-life horror – a man with an axe in his head, blood-soaked murder victims, gruesome autopsies and war scenes such as HMS *Antelope* exploding in the Falklands.

He put on a video. I thought at first it was a normal boxing video. Then I realised all the boxers had Down's syndrome. In fact, he started earning money by selling so-called 'video nasties'. Some of his customers were teenagers. Some months later, this sideline brought him to the attention of the *News of the World*, which on 8 May 1994 described him as 'the Pied Piper of horror' for selling 'death videos to our kids':

> His biggest seller is a video called *Faces of Death*. It depicts sequences from real tragedies, including a parachutist landing in an alligator park and being eaten alive by reptiles. In another scene, a live monkey's head is smashed open with a hammer. Asian diners are then seen eating the whimpering creature's brains. There are also close-ups of the mangled victims of fatal car crashes, and surgeons carrying out autopsies. Yet another clip shows a woman falling to her death under a lorry.
>
> The 35-year-old monster who touts his grisly wares around the east London borough of Newham also has a video called *Being Different*. It shows sad, seriously disfigured people with growths on their heads and stunted limbs.

Paul couldn't understand the fuss. He said the same 'kids' to whom he was selling the videos carried guns and sold crack cocaine. He hardly thought he could be accused of corrupting them. 'Anyway,' he said, 'it's only real life, isn't it?'

Paul's grasp on reality continued to deteriorate. I found him harder and harder to deal with. When he wasn't drinking, you could have a semi-coherent conversation with him. But boozed-up, he became more of a nightmare than he'd ever been.

In an attempt to help him, I got him a job in early 1996 working with me for an Irish haulage company in London's King's Cross. After leaving Raquels following the death of Leah Betts and the murder of my three one-time 'business associates', I'd gone back to driving tipper lorries. Another new start. I got Paul a job labouring in the yard. Within hours of his arrival, he was chasing the foreman with a lump of angle-iron in his hand. I calmed things down and managed to convince everyone there'd been a 'misunderstanding'.

Next morning, I picked Paul up at six. By seven, he'd drunk half a bottle of whisky, neat. This led to further 'misunderstandings' at work. By ten, we'd both been sacked. As I'd done absolutely nothing wrong, I vented my anger at Paul as I drove him home in my car. At first, he shouted back, but then he stopped shouting and asked me to pull over. He went quiet. I thought he might have been feeling sick and wanted to puke. I found a space at the side of the road and parked.

For a few seconds, Paul just sat there without moving. Then he started crying, really crying, sobbing desperately. I'm not good at dealing with tears, especially men's tears. Paul had cried in Belmarsh Prison – the first time I'd seen him do so since childhood – but this was different. And my reaction was different, because I didn't know what was wrong. I suppose I felt embarrassed. I said, 'Come on, Paul. What's up?'

In a voice almost cracking with desperation, he said, 'Help me. Please help me.'

Awkwardly, I put my arm round his shoulder. I said, 'Fuck the job. I'll get another. I'll find something for you too. Don't worry.'

'I'm not on about that,' Paul said, 'I'm on about me. You don't know what it's like. You just don't know what it's like. Help me. Please help me.'

I told him I'd do anything for him, but what was it he wanted me to do? He didn't say anything. He wept a little bit more, then stopped as suddenly as he'd started. He wiped the tears from his face and sat quietly for a few seconds, staring out the windscreen. I could see he was embarrassed. He said he wanted to get the tube back to south London. He opened the door and got out. He didn't say goodbye. I watched him cross the road. For a few seconds, he bobbed in and out of view, mingling with shoppers, then he disappeared.

I began to see him very irregularly. Sometimes, I'd get a call from the police to say he'd been arrested again – and I'd have to head off to a magistrates' court. When he wasn't appearing in court, he was appearing in newspapers. On 24 March 1996, he featured once more in the *News of the World*, though not under his real name. The headline was 'Fascists target Euro '96':

> A Nazi thug is planning to bring violence to the European football championships in England this summer. He told an undercover reporter, 'There's going to be some grief.' The man and his neo-Nazi group Combat 18 plan to team up with fascists from across Europe to attack black Holland fans.

Paul had never been a member of Combat 18. Even they wouldn't have let him join. And, as far as I know, he had nothing to do with any violence at the Euro '96 championships. I think he was just talking a bit of nonsense to a reporter for a few free beers. Beyond the expression of extreme views, Paul had little understanding of politics. For instance, he also expressed support for the IRA, partly because he saw northern Catholics as an oppressed minority. Politically, British Nazis line up with the Loyalist paramilitaries. It's not really possible to be a British Nazi and an IRA supporter at the same time. Unless you're Paul.

Later that year, he got sent back to Belmarsh Prison for bashing a shopkeeper who didn't serve him fast enough. I visited him. He told me the screws had appointed him as a 'counsellor' for prisoners in danger of committing suicide. I tried not to laugh. I didn't think Paul ought to have been allowed near people thinking of topping themselves. I could only imagine him giving prisoners tips about successful exit strategies whilst eyeing their wallets. Perhaps he'd show them photos. I assumed his appointment represented a devious unofficial plan to ease prison overcrowding.

During his stay in prison, Paul met a Palestinian man. My brother had felt strongly about the Palestinian struggle for years, even though his understanding of the conflict was hardly sophisticated. Whenever anything appeared on television about Israeli incursions into Palestinian areas, he'd start ranting, really ranting: 'Look at those Jew cunts. Grown men hiding behind tanks firing bullets at small children with stones. No wonder Hitler hated the fuckers.' His support for the Palestinians, like his support for the Provos, sprang from his sympathy for a perceived 'underdog'. No doubt his immersion over the years in Nazi anti-Jew rhetoric also played its part.

Paul's new friend asked him if he could contact Palestinian prisoners on his behalf when he got out. The friend said he couldn't do so himself, because the Special Branch had him under surveillance. After his release, Paul began writing to Samar Alami, who'd been jailed for 20 years for terrorist offences. To avoid the prison censors, he tried to pass on letters to her through her celebrity lawyer Gareth Peirce, who over the years has represented countless prisoners accused of terrorist offences. His war effort ended up being reported in the *Mirror* on 25 February 1997. Paul was again using a false name. This time, he called himself 'Tom Halloran':

> A vile neo-Nazi is attempting to recruit Britain's leading lawyers to carry out his dirty work.
>
> Repulsive Tom Halloran targets lawyers to gain access to convicted terrorists who he believes will be sympathetic to his own sickening causes.
>
> He tricked crusading solicitor Gareth Peirce into thinking he was a well-wisher of her female client, Samar Alami, jailed for 20 years for plotting to blow up the Israeli Embassy and a Jewish charity.
>
> His motives, however, are far more sinister. Halloran is a

306

far-right extremist who has said, 'Adolf Hitler was too soft for our way of thinking. I'm against anyone who doesn't agree with my views.'

Halloran, an IRA sympathiser, is intent on building contacts with terrorist organisations to further his fascist and racist causes.

Following this article, the police arrested Paul under the Prevention of Terrorism Act. They took apart his flat, searching for incriminating material. I don't know what they made of his video collection. In the end, they released him because – unusually for him – he hadn't committed any offence. However, Paul soon returned to prison for other offences. His regular stays in jail had the side effect of bringing phases of stability to his life. But every time he came out, he seemed just a little bit madder.

Paul wasn't the only lunatic I had on my mind. Over the years, I'd often wondered what had happened to my father. No one had seen him, or heard anything of him, since he left the house in August 1976. Sometimes I fantasised about tracking him down. I suppose I'd have liked to ask him why he'd treated us so brutally. I suppose, too, on occasion, I'd have liked a chance to kick his head in.

But most of the time I tried to forget him and to pretend I didn't care what had become of him. However, my mother, who wanted some sort of closure on his disappearance, kept prodding me to try to find out. Every now and again over the years, I'd contact the police's Missing Persons' Bureau and the Salvation Army, always without success. Then on a whim in 2001 – the 25th anniversary of his disappearance – I asked my journalist friend Gary Jones to see if he could find him. I stayed on the line as Jones tapped my father's details into his computer. Within five minutes, as I waited on the phone, Jones said he'd found him. My father was dead. He'd died four years earlier of natural causes. Jones gave his last address as a tower block opposite the cricket ground in Edgbaston, Birmingham.

I was in a pub in London's King's Cross when Jones told me, for which I was grateful, because I needed a drink. My father was dead. And all along he'd been living just down the road from the home he'd left. I abandoned my other plans and headed instead to Birmingham. I had an irrepressible urge to see where my father had spent his last years. On the journey, I experienced a whole spectrum of feelings, including sadness, but mostly shock and rage. I felt cheated. I could never now fulfil that fantasy of confronting him.

It was strange, and a little spooky, to stand outside my father's last front door. It stood on the tenth floor of a municipal block of flats. I knocked, but no one answered. So I went next door. An elderly West Indian man, wearing an Old-Man-River trilby hat, opened his door cautiously.

I introduced myself and asked if he'd known my father. He said he had. They'd even been mates. He said my father had lived for years in an attic flat above a shop round the corner. The flat in the tower block had belonged to the old woman who'd owned the shop. She'd become ill, and my father, who'd become good friends with her, moved into her flat to keep her company. It wasn't a romantic relationship. They were merely companions. She'd then died and my father had stayed on in the flat, living alone.

He and the West Indian man used to go for a drink on Sundays to a pub round the corner. One Sunday, they had their lunch-time drink and headed home. My father, a heavy smoker, coughed most of the way along the street. They said goodbye at their doors. The man said he used to see my father, or hear him coughing, most days, so when he'd neither seen nor heard him by Tuesday, he called the police. They broke down the door and found my father dead in bed. His grave lay in a council cemetery a few miles away.

I asked if my father had ever spoken about his family. He said he had. Apparently, he'd occasionally mentioned he'd been married and had children, although he hadn't gone into details. I thanked the man for his time and left. That night, I found myself standing outside the cemetery with my brother Michael. The gates had been locked for the night. Earlier that day, I'd rung the council and had been given my father's plot number. Michael and I clambered over the big iron railings. In a few minutes, we stood in front of my father's last resting place. Neither flowers, nor headstone, nor name decorated the plot. Only a number. I broke down and cried. So did Michael. We both felt devastated.

In the past, I'd genuinely hated my father, but as I stood there over his grave, I realised I actually felt sorry for him. I'd spent so much time hating him I hadn't realised his own hatred and anger had stemmed from the fact that he'd never had much love or affection in his tormented life. He'd been buried in a pauper's grave, which an Irish-Catholic charity had supplied and paid for.

The next day, I broke the news to my mother. She took it very badly. Over the following days, we spoke together about my father in a way that brought me a bit closer to him and made me understand better why he'd become such a vicious bastard. My mother told me things she'd never told me before. She said in Ireland during the 1930s my father's unmarried mother had become pregnant after sleeping with a married man. After abuse from locals, she became so ashamed and scared she went to the 'county home' to give birth.

She abandoned my father there – and disappeared. She was never seen or heard of again. My father was at first brought up in the county home, where some staff subjected him to extreme cruelty and violence. His health and state of mind suffered badly. Eventually, his grandmother took him out and reared him herself. He worshipped his grandmother, but grew to hate 'normal' people, because he'd been deprived of the most basic normality (that is, the affection, care and protection of a mother and father).

My mother said he'd been a good singer, so much so that he was known in pubs and clubs as 'Danny Boy' after his favourite song of the same name. The song in its original form had been an Irish republican anthem. He'd especially enjoyed singing it at the Royal British Legion Club in Codsall. He'd laugh to himself, because he knew the clapping audience hadn't understood the significance of the song's words.

When my mother lay desperately ill in hospital after the birth of Michael, she'd confided in a consultant about my father's violence. The consultant suggested that in my father's mind he wasn't beating us, he was beating his own mother. He thought my father hated the fact that we had a mother who loved us. This conversation sounded a bit like the final scene from Hitchcock's classic film *Psycho*, where the psychiatrist gives an explanation of why the now straitjacketed lunatic of the title murdered all those people and kept his mother's mummified body in the cellar.

Paul travelled to Birmingham when I told him about our father. I drove him and my mother to the cemetery, but he refused to get out of the car. He told my mother he wouldn't stand over my father's grave unless pissing on it.

I phoned my oldest brother Jerry on the other side of the world to break the news. He didn't say much. He lives in Brazil, still working on oil rigs. He puts most of his earnings towards a home for Rio's street children. He's lived all over the world. I think he's tried to get as far away from everything that returns him to, or reminds him of, our dismal past. He doesn't really have much to do with us. He no longer speaks to Paul or Michael, and he only speaks to me if I happen to call at my mother's when he's there on one of his flying visits. He takes what happened to us very hard, but he keeps his feelings to himself. He's been married four times. He never seems happy within himself.

A few months after our phone call, he came to England. I took him to the cemetery, but, like Paul, he didn't want to get out of the car. Eventually, I persuaded him to come with me. We walked together towards the grave, but he stopped about ten yards away and refused to go any further. I could feel his anger.

Afterwards, we went for a drink in a pub near the huge Rover car plant. Neither of us said much. Jerry's eyes welled up with tears. I started to cry, went to the toilet, composed myself and went back to sit with him. That was it. We didn't mention our father again. We talked about work, our mother's health and the weather. Then, two hours after we'd met, he was gone.

Some years earlier, I'd stolen a blank headstone, which I'd stored in my garage. I'd intended it for use on my own grave. Living the life I've led, a stolen headstone over my grave struck me as fitting and amusing. Headstones are ridiculously expensive, and I'd also been hoping to save my loved ones a few bob when the time came. I decided to use this headstone for my father's grave. I had it engraved with his dates and the words 'Patrick "Danny Boy" O'Mahoney. Rest in Peace.'

Dealing with the dead was a lot easier than dealing with the living who happened to have a death wish. After yet another violent incident, my brother Paul was sectioned under the Mental Health Act.

He was released some months later, on medication, but was now a registered lunatic, with card, T-shirt and free travel on the tube. He'd been a violent madman since his teens. Now it was official.

He took to wearing army fatigues and cycling shorts. I'd see him very irregularly, but when we met he'd talk as if we'd only seen each other ten minutes earlier. Then he'd say something like, 'I can't hang around,' and he'd be off. He believed he'd successfully outwitted the doctors by pretending to be mad in order to get free travel on public transport and lighter sentences in court.

I couldn't help but laugh whenever I met Paul. He told me he'd started stalking one of his carers. He'd say to me, 'Followed that fucking cunt again. Thinks I'm mad.'

Until a few years ago, if you didn't know him, he could still give an impression of lucidity. He continued to form friendships with nutters from all over the world – former hangmen, South African mercenaries, ex-prisoners – cranks and weirdos just like himself. But, in the end, no one remained in contact with him for long. Stranded alone in a desert, he'd fall out with himself.

Paul's couldn't-care-less attitude did bring him into contact with countless dubious individuals, some of whom worked for newspapers. I suppose to a stranger he could appear as a useful, though brainless, thug. But Paul has never been brainless. He used to exploit and use anyone he encountered, regardless of how untouchable they thought they might be. He got involved with a Russian mafia scam to find British husbands for eastern European 'dancers' and call girls. He 'married' one 'dancer' himself, for which he was paid three thousand pounds.

Then, to make some more money, he went to the *News of the World* and gave the story to their legendary undercover reporter Mazher Mahmood. Mazher specialises in dressing up as an Arab sheikh to get famous people to do drug deals or betray secrets. His most famous scoop came when he fooled the Countess of Wessex into talking indiscreetly about the Royal Family. On

3 March 2002, with information supplied by Paul, Mazher exposed the 'mafia bosses' behind the marriage scam. However, for some reason, Paul felt misused by the one-time 'Reporter of the Year' and decided to get his own back.

His chance came when Mazher asked him for help in exposing a story about two racist policemen. The officers worked at a station in London's West End. Apparently, they would arrest black people, then take bets on who'd be the first to get the prisoners to call them 'master' and beg for food. Mazher wanted Paul to wear a special denim jacket fitted with a hidden camera and voice recorder, so he could tape the officers boasting of their deeds. Paul agreed.

Mazher met up with Paul in a café. He gave him the jacket to try on. Mazher boasted it was state of the art and worth about £30,000. Paul put it on – then ran off down the road with it.

Mazher got my number and rang me. He sounded desperate. He begged me to help him get the jacket back. He said he'd have to go to the police if Paul didn't return it. I rang Paul, who said, 'I'm not giving that cunt anything. He ripped me off.'

I said Mazher would have to go to the police. Paul said he didn't give a fuck. He'd already sold the jacket for five hundred pounds to some West Indians.

I asked Paul if Mazher might be able to buy it back. Paul agreed to take him to the shop in Hackney where he'd fenced the jacket. Sadly, the trip wasn't successful. Mazher ended up being set upon by the West Indians. Paul was arrested for theft. He told the police that Mazher had been trying to expose two of their colleagues. He said he hadn't been prepared to help, because he felt the police did a wonderful job. Paul wasn't prosecuted and, so far as I know, Mazher never got his jacket back.

I'd been worried for years by Paul's mental health. I'd also become worried by our mutual friend Ray's physical health. Over the years, he'd destroyed himself by drinking vast amounts of alcohol with Paul. When I saw him at the beginning of 2002, he looked horribly skinny. He'd been fitted with a colostomy bag because of kidney trouble. Only a decade earlier, Ray had been a healthy, happy hooligan for his beloved Millwall. Now he looked desperately ill, like a man twice his age.

In the spring of 2002, I flew to New York with my partner Emma and my son Vinney. On the flight home, I found myself overcome with a crushing sense of doom. I'd never before experienced anything like it. I told Emma and Vinney I thought something terrible had happened. I felt sure someone had died – either Paul or Ray. I'm not a believer in the supernatural, so I felt a bit uncomfortable in my new role as the reincarnation of Doris Stokes. However, as soon as we landed, I switched on my mobile to discover lots of messages. Adolf's was the first. He just told me to ring him urgently.

I rang him straightaway without listening to the other messages. He said, 'Ray's dead.' Adolf had spoken to Ray's father, with whom Ray had been staying. On his last night, Ray had stretched out on the sofa to watch the football on telly. His father went to bed. In the morning, he got up to find Ray still on the sofa with the telly on. He realised his son was dead.

I'd once been very close to Ray. His loss at such an early age – he was only 37 – hit me hard. I contacted Paul, whom I hadn't seen since the previous year when he'd refused to visit my father's grave. We arranged to go to Ray's funeral together with my brother Michael, who'd also known and liked Ray.

I met Paul at King's Cross. His appearance shocked me. It wasn't just his cream trousers, which I suggested were unsuitable for a funeral. He was thin and gaunt and looked ten years older. Mentally, too, he was just shot to pieces. It was hard to get a coherent word out of him. Emma took a photo of us three brothers together. When I showed it later to my mother, she cried because she thought Paul looked so frail.

I offered to buy Paul some black trousers, but he declined. We took a taxi to Dulwich, where Ray had been living with his partner Lorna and their children. I had to laugh at the name of the road – Marcus Garvey Mews, named after a black nationalist leader.

The whole gang turned out for the funeral. Seeing them standing there together made Ray's death real for the first time. I couldn't speak. I tried talking to Ray's dad, but no words came out. He, too, was speechless. The poor man looked totally destroyed, totally. I felt for him throughout the day.

It was strangely comforting when the hearse carrying Ray

pulled up outside the house. He was back among the boys and his family. The Catholic church was already packed by the time we arrived. At the front near the altar stood four black women. Adolf asked if they were 'Martha Reeves and the Vandellas'. But no one was in the mood for humour.

The service started. It was led by an Irish priest. Adolf didn't like the cut of his jib. He whispered to me that he looked like 'a red'. He began muttering about 'conspirators' in the ranks, but no one paid any attention.

Several of Ray's black friends turned up. In truth, Ray had never been much of a Nazi. He just loved the excitement of anti-social behaviour. In fact, Adolf had viewed Ray with suspicion for some years. Among other things, he regarded Ray's skin as a trifle too sallow for him to be a kosher Aryan. Of course, Ray was as white as any of us; he just took a good suntan.

This sort of conjecture isn't unusual for Adolf. Even your choice of holiday destination can arouse his suspicions about your 'true' racial origins or political leanings. Too many trips to 'unsound' countries (that is, most of the world) may lead to your inclusion in his mental list of those marked down for arrest, imprisonment, torture and possible execution when the National Socialists come to power.

Adolf had begun hunting for proof of Ray's impure blood and believed he'd found it when he discovered Ray's father had been born in Canada. It's one of Adolf's fixed ideas that Canada is full of Jews. To make everything even more murky for Adolf, he was told that Ray's father, the son of British expatriates, had spent part of his childhood in India, where his father's work had taken him. This led Adolf to speculate that Ray might actually be a 'shopkeeper' (his favourite word for Asians).

During the service, the congregation sang enthusiastically the stirring song 'Jerusalem', written by the poet William Blake around two centuries earlier in the heyday of the British Empire. I later discovered that the song is normally associated with the Church of England, not the Church of Rome. But even among Anglicans, there's been a controversy about whether 'Jerusalem' is really a hymn or merely a sort of national anthem. The song's last verse shook the church:

I will not cease from Mental Fight,
Nor shall my Sword sleep in my hand,
Till we have built Jerusalem,
In England's green and pleasant Land.

Outside the church, Adolf said to me bitterly, 'Did you see that Provo bastard?'

I said, 'Which Provo bastard?'

'That so-called "priest", Father Fucking Fenian.'

'What about him?'

'He didn't sing along to "Jerusalem", the IRA scum. I watched him closely. His lips didn't move.'

'Perhaps he didn't know the words.'

'No, he did it deliberate. A coldly planned provocation. Fucking republican.'

I couldn't see how a failure to sing 'Jerusalem' – even if that had indeed been the case – could be interpreted as support for the provisional wing of the Irish Republican Army. The priest had struck me as a very nice man who was about as likely to go on a rampage with Millwall fans as support the Provos. He'd conducted a moving service. The many normal members of the congregation would have been horrified to hear Adolf's rant, but they didn't know him like we did. If Ray had been around, he would have laughed. It was only fitting that Adolf behaved entirely in character for our friend's farewell.

We drove to the crematorium. Lots of flowers had been made into blue-and-white footballs or Millwall shields. I stepped forward and laid my hand on his coffin. I said my goodbyes. All of a sudden, the sound of grinding hydraulic machinery snapped everyone out of their personal misery. Ray's coffin began slowly to disappear on its last, short journey. It was awful.

As we left the crematorium, Ray's dad could speak to me for the first time. He said, 'He won't be getting in any more trouble, will he, Bernie?'

I couldn't answer. We all went back to a club which Lorna had hired. Adolf stood on the table and asked everyone to raise their glasses in memory of our friend Ray. None of us will ever forget him. He was, as they say in south London, 'proper'.

Later, we went to one of 'our' pubs, The Brockwell Tavern, near Ray's house. A couple of men sat down at a table near our group. Adolf soon became convinced they were Special Branch officers, there to keep us under surveillance. At first, we all laughed at him, but his paranoia became infectious. After several drinks, one of our group told the 'Special Branch' men that they'd been sussed. He ordered them to leave quietly and immediately – or be dealt with violently. The men denied vehemently they were police officers, but left hurriedly anyway, thus confirming Adolf's suspicions. We found out later that the men were in fact well-known regulars who had nothing to do with the police.

As the evening wore on, Paul became convinced the barman was stealing money from us. I could see in his eyes that without my intervention the dispute would end in violence. I talked him into leaving the pub. I called a taxi, paid the driver to take him wherever he wanted and gave Paul a few quid on top. I haven't seen him since.

Over the following months, he rang me to say he'd been evicted from his flat and was living on the streets. On Christmas Eve 2003, he rang me. I told him to meet me at Barnet tube station. I brought along three sets of new clothes and five hundred quid in cash. I wanted to take him home to my mother, who hadn't seen her four sons stand in the same room together for 20 years.

At nine in the morning, Paul rang to say he was at the Embankment and would be with me in half an hour. I sat waiting for three hours. He never showed. Since then, he hasn't rung me – or anyone else in the family.

A few months ago, I got a call from Adolf. He said he'd found Paul lying in a sleeping bag at the Elephant and Castle in south London. He'd hardly recognised my brother, who'd grown a long beard and looked like a last-gasp wino. Adolf said he'd tried talking to him, but Paul hadn't appeared to recognise him. He'd just mumbled something incoherently to himself.

Now, when I'm lying in bed, listening to the driving rain outside, I feel overcome with guilt, because I know Paul's out there. My conscience screams at me. Bernie, who's always tried to pick up the pieces and make things right, should get out of bed, drive to London, pick his brother up off the street and bring him to shelter.

I'd do it now, if I could, but I know I can't help a man who won't help himself. I can't help a man who doesn't want my help. Like my uncle Bernie before him, Paul has simply given up on life. He's just waiting for his time to come.

And that breaks my heart.

CHAPTER 21

NAZIS AREN'T US

ADOLF'S MEETING WITH PAUL AT THE ELEPHANT AND CASTLE STRUCK ME AS ONE of those startling little accidents of fate. It reminded me of a spooky incident some weeks after the death of Adrian 'Army Game' Boreham. A group of us decided to head off in an old white Transit van up the M1 motorway to Codsall for a 'jolly up'.

The van belonged to Paul. I think it was the one he'd used to run over the Scots who'd tried cheating at his card game. The van's main deficiency was the leak in the brake-fluid compartment. The reservoir had to be topped up every few hours. Even then, the driver had to pump the brake-pedal manically to get the van to slow.

We wouldn't allow Paul himself to drive, because he was too appallingly drunk. I was the only other person with a full licence, but I felt too slaughtered to manage the motorway. Ray volunteered. He was also pissed, but still in possession of many of his faculties. The main drawback with using him as driver was that he'd never driven before.

We reached a compromise. I'd tackle the difficult stage (that is, from south London to the M1 at Brent Cross) and non-driver Ray would steer the van up the motorway. We felt the M1 offered a suitable learning environment for him, because he needed only to drive straight ahead. He wouldn't have to worry about turning left or right or manoeuvring down narrow side streets.

At Brent Cross, we picked up a young hitch-hiker, who turned out to be a soldier on leave. He'd looked reluctant to get into a van packed with Paul, Ray, Tony, Benny, Colin, Larry, me and two crates of beer. But Benny had cunningly held out a can and said, 'D'you want a beer, mate?' The man looked nervously at Ray's co-pilot, Colin, who was wearing a crash helmet. He glanced at the beer and got in.

Ray got off to a spluttering, van-hopping start. I had to keep explaining which pedal did which and Colin had to grab the steering wheel occasionally. Along the way, our guest expressed some anxiety about Ray's driving skills. He said he'd become a bit more nervous on the road since three of his roommates had been killed in a car accident in Germany. Benny asked if one of his dead mates came from south London. He said yes. Benny said, 'What was his name?' The hitch-hiker said, 'Adrian Boreham.'

If I were Doris Stokes, I'd conclude that the ghost of Adrian had sent his mate to warn us of the dangers of a man with no experience driving a van with no brakes up the M1 while drunk. However, perhaps under Army Game's ghostly protection, we reached our destination alive and uninjured.

It seemed fitting that Adolf of all people should have met Paul at the Elephant and Castle in the way he did. It had, after all, been Paul who'd first introduced me to Adolf and the whole south London gang. Though I'd long moved away from 'the Movement', I'd still kept in touch with Adolf over the years. I wasn't always sure why. Nor, I suppose, was he. We were mates, bonded by blood, albeit other people's. We went back a long way, but we'd certainly grown apart – in our views, at least. He regarded me as a turncoat and a lackey of ZOG. I regarded him as a dangerous and deluded lunatic, though that's never stopped me liking someone. In truth, Adolf's never really had friends – just people who put up with him. He won't let anyone get too close, because he trusts no one fully. Everyone's an actual or potential agent of ZOG. Everyone. Consequently, he's always at war with those around him.

But, for all that, he's likeable and he's loyal. He'll do anything for you. In his own way, he's a very kind and generous person. He has his own code of behaviour, which is sometimes difficult to decipher. Weirdly, like many Nazis, he's always had a few black, Asian and Jewish mates. I think he turns them into honorary Aryans for the duration of their friendship.

He was never involved in football hooliganism, and Millwall was never his team. He supports Tottenham Hotspur, nicknamed 'the Yids' (apparently because so many of their supporters are Jewish). In fact, for many years he used to go to their games with a Jewish-Asian solicitor from Brighton. He's got a lot of respect for Muslims. Indeed, Islam is fast becoming the religion of choice among Britain's Nazis. In particular, he admires the American 'Nation of Islam', which, like the Klan, believes in racial separatism.

On the British far-right scene, he's always been in the engine room of things. He knows personally all the main faces, past and present, although he's never joined any party, assuming they're all infiltrated by ZOG. I was talking to him once on the phone when he said proudly, 'Ah, I've just got an e-mail from David Irving.' Irving is the writer of history who believes that no systematic murder of Jews took place in Nazi Germany, that there were no gas chambers at Auschwitz and that Hitler should be exonerated from the atrocities committed in his name. In 2000, Irving lost the libel action he took against a writer published by Penguin Books who'd described him as a 'Holocaust denier'. He refuses to use the word 'Holocaust', seeing it as vague, imprecise and unscientific.

Adolf has also met the former US Nazi party officer William Pierce, who's better known as the author of *The Turner Diaries*, that infamous novel about a violent Aryan uprising. After one trip to the States, Adolf came back to say he'd seen a video which, if made public, would cause Pierce a lot of embarrassment. He wouldn't tell me what the video contained, because, since I'd done work against 'the Movement' for the tabloid representatives of ZOG, I was no longer to be trusted. I kept pressing him to tell me. At first, he refused, but then he said that, compared to the contents of the Pierce video, a film showing Mrs Thatcher having unnatural relations with a goat would be quite mild. This aroused my curiosity even more, but Adolf wouldn't go into details. He adopted instead his usual 'protective adult' pose, saying he couldn't tell me in any case, because the description would only irreparably disturb an innocent young 'northern' lad such as myself. All he'd divulge was that the video showed some sort of extreme homosexual activity between Pierce and various males. William Pierce went to join the immortal heroes of the Aryan race on 23 July 2002, when he died of cancer.

Adolf went out with a nice girl from Liverpool for a few years. She had no interest in his Nazi activities. For a while, there seemed a chance he might settle down and become semi-normal. But the relationship came under strain, partly because of his constant sniping at northerners. His girlfriend's city of origin came in for particular stick as the home of 'whinging, unemployed, Militant Tendency, red Scouse bastards'. He used to mimic a Liverpool accent to tell jokes like, 'A dog isn't just for Christmas. You should be able to squeeze a few sandwiches out of it on Boxing Day, too.'

When he went to meet her parents in 'the Third World' (as he calls Liverpool and the north generally), he took not only his own water, but also a crisp fifty-pound note. He wanted to show the inhabitants what one looked like, because he believed they'd never have seen one before. He told me he put it in the charity bottle on the bar of her local pub just to fuck off the natives.

The cultural divide became a chasm. In a last-ditch effort to keep them together, he paid for a Christmas holiday to America. He promised her a big surprise. She began dreaming of Yuletide romance in the snow. He took her to a Klan rally. The relationship ended shortly afterwards.

Copeland's bombing spree in London had a huge effect on the far-right in the United Kingdom. A lot of the smaller, crankier Nutzi groups had already been wobbling, riven as usual by splits and squabbles. The intense police focus killed off several of these groups – and made would-be mainstream 'nationalists' like the BNP shout themselves hoarse trying to convince people of their new commitment to democracy and the rule of law.

Adolf declared glumly to me on the phone one day that National Socialism in the UK was dead. He said, 'How can I build a movement with beer-swilling football hooligans?' He seemed to have forgotten that almost every one of his friends was once a beer-swilling football hooligan. But he refused to abandon his dedication to the cause. Instead, he fixed his fanatical Hitlerian gaze across the Irish Sea. He believed that any hope of a white man's heaven in Europe now lay in Ireland – land of one branch of his forefathers. Racism had become an increasingly touchy subject in Ireland since the beginning of the '90s when refugees, asylum-seekers and foreign workers began for the first time to arrive in large numbers in the overwhelmingly white, Roman Catholic country.

Adolf saw the influx of foreigners – particularly black African foreigners – and the natives' sometimes violent and vocal resistance to them as an opportunity to fan the flames of racial hatred. He wanted to start a forest fire of animosity towards foreigners in Ireland. He hoped the flames might then jump across the water, both to the UK and to the rest of Europe.

He helped form a group named 'National Socialists Are Us' (NSRUS). He took part in organising an anti-immigration march in Dublin, which was modestly attended, then he started canvassing in the city of Limerick in the run-up to elections there. He kept the message simple and found his 'Say No to a Black Ireland' slogan going down very well in the city's white, working-class housing estates.

He decided to help start up an Internet site to promote the 'Say No to a Black Ireland' message. The NSRUS editorial talked about parasitical invaders 'raping and pillaging their way across sacred Ireland'. It lamented 'the destruction of a monoracial society and its replacement by a multiracial experiment'. And it called upon the Irish to draw their inspiration for resistance from Adolf Hitler ('the leader and guide sent to us by Providence'). NSRUS set up links between its site and those of the mainstream Irish political parties, the Irish army and University College Dublin. These activities provoked a storm of outrage in the Irish media.

Adolf sent me an e-mail of a story published by CNN on 24 August 2001:

> Irish police are investigating racist Internet sites calling on Ireland to remain 'white for ever'.
>
> The websites promote messages such as 'Say No to a Black Ireland', 'Ireland is under Attack', and 'Savages Stalk the Land'.

'I can confirm we are aware of them and are investigating,' said police spokeswoman Lynne Nolan.

'We are trying to track down the people concerned,' she added, saying that the case was being handled by the National Bureau of Criminal Investigations.

Irish police said all of the websites appear to be based outside the country, with at least one of them in Britain.

The websites have already caused embarrassment to the Irish political establishment by including links to mainstream Irish political parties.

Adolf's NSRUS site also attracted the attention of the BNP's leader, Nick Griffin, who was disturbed that it might set back the cause of racial nationalism in Ireland. He sent an e-mail, which Adolf later sent me. It read:

What are you playing at?

If you are not state *agents provocateurs*, for God's sake drop the outdated NS tag before you set back the construction of a credible and acceptable racial nationalist movement in Ireland for years. Hundreds of thousands of Irishmen volunteered to fight against Hitler and for Britain in the last war and, regardless of the rights and wrongs of that conflict, that has left a political and psychological legacy that you cannot overcome.

How on earth do you think that you can sell an ideology of dictatorship to the section of the European race that is probably the most individualistic and bloody-minded of all? . . . In fact, the idea is so ridiculous that it's odds on that you are indeed yet another state-sponsored pseudo-gang on the C18 model. If so, damn you to hell. If not, wake up and look at the model presented by people like . . . Le Pen [leader of the French National Front] . . . A movement like [that] could save Ireland, and we will do what we can to help build it if asked. A crank group modelled on Hollywood will be just another nail in the coffin.

Adolf was furious at Griffin's suggestion that NSRUS might be agents of ZOG. He mentioned sneeringly some allegations about Griffin's private life which had been printed in the anti-fascist magazine *Searchlight*. He said, 'And that fucker talks to me about being a member of a fucking crank group.'

He also found himself being pursued by lawyers for the Irish political parties whose websites had been abused. And the British police received a request from the Irish police to track down the NSRUS site's owners. All of this made Adolf even more twitchily paranoid than usual. He was convinced everyone was after him. I'd speak to him every few months, but he'd only ring me from call boxes – and he wouldn't tell me his location. He sounded hunted. ZOG was everywhere.

Eventually, the Internet provider removed the website.

In fact, the NSRUS campaign became so popular that Adolf attracted the attention of Irish republicans. On one of his visits to Limerick, Adolf found himself invited to a meeting with Sinn Fein, who sent a car to pick him up from his hotel. The car contained three men. One sat on either side of him in the back. Adolf told me it 'didn't feel right'. He said none of the men wanted to talk as the car set off on its journey.

They arrived eventually at a grey housing estate. The car circled the block a few times before stopping outside an end-of-terrace house with drawn curtains. Adolf said that when he entered the house he realised no one actually lived there, because he could see very little furniture and no 'personal effects'.

One of his minders led him into the front room. No one switched on the light – and not just to save on electricity. As his eyes acquainted themselves to the darkness, he could make out what appeared to be aluminium foil covering the walls and ceiling. He asked why. One of his hosts said it prevented listening devices picking up conversations. Or screams.

Everyone sat together in the darkness. A senior Sinn Fein man arrived. He spoke politely, but firmly, to Adolf. He explained that a new political party, however admirable in its aims, was not welcome in the urban working-class territory that Sinn Fein regarded as its own. He said the grass-roots support for Adolf's anti-immigration campaign looked like taking votes off the republicans – and that was unacceptable. He added that people who caused harm to the republican movement would be dealt with firmly. He asked Adolf if he'd got the message.

Adolf had got the message loud and clear. He decided that Ireland, for all its charm, wasn't worth dying for. He ceased his canvassing activities immediately and NSRUS withdrew from the election campaign. Later, he said to me, 'Sinn Fein? They're just the fucking Irish National Front, aren't they?'

The next time I heard from Adolf, I discovered he'd moved to Philadelphia in the United States after linking up with a White Power female activist through the Internet. I prayed she wasn't Breeze or any of the other Manson groupies who'd written to me. Around a year later, he returned to London. 'The Yanks,' he declared, 'are fucking cranks.' These days, Adolf lives in west London and sells 'erotic art' (statues mainly) at exhibitions both here and abroad. A south London villain introduced him to this lucrative sideline.

Where are the others? 'Benny the Jew' is married, has children, lives in Kent and works in the building industry; Del Boy runs an old people's home; Larry 'The Slash' is single and lives in London (no one knows what he does: the last I heard he was either working for, or was an exhibit in, a museum); Ray's brother Tony lives with his partner in south London. He's got children and works in the building industry. Unlike the other surviving members of our gang, Adolf hasn't calmed down or mellowed in the intervening years. He probably never will. The rage still dwells within.

Recently, I got an e-mail from someone claiming to be an organiser of the BNP in 'the Black Country' (as parts of the West Midlands are called). He'd read a blurb on my website mentioning *Hateland* as one of my future books. I think I'd touched on my encounters with the BNP and its former leader, John Tyndall.

> Sir, what a pathetic and deluded man you are. Is it not about time you actually took a look around you, and updated your information? The BNP has a totally different leadership now, including me in the Black Country, who is from the 'old left' . . . You are presumably part of the ANL

325

[Anti-Nazi League]/*Searchlight* brigade, who are now being seen for what they are – pre-Zionist hard-left has-beens, and users and abusers of our white youth . . . You and your kind are in for a terrible shock soon, as millions of white, proud and browbeaten people from all walks of life will totally destroy the pretend 'democracy' that Blair and Co have used and hijacked.

He said he'd recruited 230 new BNP members in his area alone in the previous two years. His meetings, on premises supplied free of charge by local businessmen, attracted up to 90 people, including an 85-year-old woman who'd given 40 years' service to the Labour Party. Prime Minister 'Phoney Tony' Blair himself had acknowledged her sterling work. He'd sent her his signature on a yellow 'Post-it note', which she'd since burnt in protest at his policies.

My ranting correspondent added that even his own mother – supposedly a lifelong Labour supporter – had now gone over to the BNP:

> Having been in a post office when a couple of Negroes held up the terrified young girl at gun-point, even my mom can't ignore the perils of 'downtown Kingston-cum Britain' that you two-faced Liberals have created, while of course living in your elitist ivory towers. Why are you not taking your families to Harlsden for instance? I hear it is really 'diverse' there. Obviously I jest, because like every other black run town, it is a filthy cess pit of aids riven rapists, gun gangs, and typical low brow third world morons.

He said the BNP under its 'young, vibrant and intellectually superior political leader Mr Nick Griffin' was smashing all the 'limp-wristed Liberal arguments' put forward by people like me. He drew my attention to the fact that the 'late, great Enoch Powell' had just been put forward as a candidate in a poll for the 'top 100 Greatest Britons'. He said everything had turned out exactly as Powell had predicted it would.

I didn't like the turd's tone. I don't take kindly to being called a pathetic, limp-wristed user and abuser of white youth. I sent back an immediate reply:

> You WILL regret calling me pathetic, you sad sex case. Call me. Let's meet. Let's see who is pathetic. Check out who you are gobbing off to with your pal Lecomber/Wells in London. He will advise you that you have fucked up. See you soon, dickhead.

My uninvited correspondent also responded immediately:

> I have advised my Lawyer to allow the Police to take a look at your intimidating reply. It is obvious you were offended by my email, but it would have made a good piece of political banter and on/off communication between two opposite thinkers, but you are not the type to be light-hearted with . . . I apologise for offending you, Sir.

At that point, our correspondence ceased.

I planned to marry Emma Turner on 16 July 2004 in Peterborough Cathedral. It was to be another of my many new beginnings, my umpteenth new start. I decided to have my stag night in Dublin the weekend before. Around 20 of us flew there to celebrate the passing of my bachelor status.

One of our group got very drunk and began pinching women's bottoms. I've never liked that sort of noncey behaviour. I asked him to refrain from doing it in my company. He refused to comply with my polite request and called me an arsehole into the bargain. Later that night, the bottom-pincher was found lying in the street, unconscious and with severe head injuries. Doctors at the hospital diagnosed a fractured skull and two blood clots on the brain. They placed him under intensive care when he failed to regain consciousness.

The Irish police arrested 16 of the men in my stag group and told them the injured man might die. He underwent surgery and spent the next six days fighting for his life. His family flew out from England to be at his bedside. Everyone feared that, even if he pulled through, he might still be brain-damaged. Perhaps he'd start talking like Larry Grayson and take to the stage with a poodle act.

The day before my wedding, I was informed that the man had regained consciousness and would be discharged from hospital shortly, though not in time to attend the wedding, which in any case he might well have opted to avoid. He didn't appear to have suffered any brain damage, which came as a relief to his family, friends and show business.

The wedding went ahead as planned. I had difficulty choosing just one 'best man'. So I chose four – one to represent each of the four main phases of my life. My schoolfriend Hughie would represent my youth in the Black Country, Adolf my life in London after the army, Gavin from Raquels my life in Essex after my escape from South Africa and Rashed (someone I've become good friends with since moving to Peterborough) my new life after Essex. Prior to the service in Peterborough's Church of England cathedral, we played Sinead O'Connor's version of the uncensored, raw republican 'Danny Boy' in remembrance of my father, Emma's parents, Ray and 'Army Game'. I'm not sure the Archbishop of Canterbury – to whom we had to apply for our marriage licence – would have approved of the song's call to God to help set Ireland free.

As Sinead's haunting vocals filled the cathedral, I scanned the faces of the 250-odd (very odd) guests. Prejudice and hatred had dominated my life and the lives of many of my friends. Yet now, at the age of 44, to my left stood Gavin, an Asian, and to my right stood Rashed, also an Asian. Nearby were two of Emma's beautiful bridesmaids – her mixed-race nieces.

In the congregation stood Glen, my future brother-in-law, who's black, and my good friend Bobby from Peterborough, who's also black. Then, also from Peterborough, were my friends Jimmy (from the former Yugoslavia), John (from Italy), Taff, Whizz and Shane (all travellers) and Assad (Asian).

A few of my invitees couldn't attend. I was especially disappointed that my mate Fazbul from Codsall had to decline. He's the owner of the Rajput Tandoori restaurant, whose maharajah statue I'd helped vandalise more than a quarter of a century ago. Fazbul had also been the owner back then. He'd never known the identity of the yobs who'd kidnapped, hacked at and finally torched his Indian prince. Over the years, on my regular trips back to the village to visit my mother and friends, I've frequently ended up at his restaurant after a night out. We've often chatted and had a laugh.

A few years ago, Fazbul witnessed an altercation outside his restaurant between me and members of the local constabulary. Blows had been exchanged. Fazbul, who's a real gentleman, very civilised and fair-minded, hadn't liked what he'd seen. He told me he was prepared to act as a witness for me in my pending court case arising from the incident.

Being familiar with the often astonishing petty-mindedness of the upholders of the law, I turned down his offer, because I knew that, if he went into the witness box against the police, they'd find some way of giving him grief in the future. I went alone to court, defended myself and was acquitted of breaching the peace, but convicted of assaulting an officer.

Sitting in Fazbul's restaurant late at night, chomping my poppadams while waiting for my next pint of Tiger lager, I've often felt guilty about my part in vandalising the maharajah. I've sometimes felt the urge to confess all to Fazbul as an act of apology, but I've always bottled out at the last moment. I don't know why, really. It's not that I've feared ending up in a curry. It's more that I've feared being crushed by Fazbul's look of disappointment. In many ways, I've written this book to apologise to Fazbul and lots of other people too numerous to mention.

There's no happy ending to this book. My story isn't over. Who knows how things will end? Life has taught me that, however strong your beliefs, events can and will change them. I thank God that my experiences have changed some of my abhorrent views. All I can do is look back on my past, learn from my mistakes and try to become a better person. Only those who know me will be able to judge if I've been successful.

I'm not sure if I'm qualified to offer advice, but if you're some fucking little hard man reading this book, and you think you know better than I do, then think again, because you're wrong. Unclench your fist, fool, and respect yourself and those around you. You're better than no man – and no man is better than you. Rise above those who've caused your misery. Or else your hatred may destroy you, your children and your children's children.

AFTERWORD

This book wasn't meant to have an Afterword, because I thought I'd said everything I wanted to say. But on Thursday, 2 December 2004, just as the editor had finished his work and the manuscript sat ready for the printer's, my wife Emma died in my arms at the age of 26. Not even five months had passed since our wedding.

Around ten days earlier, Emma had fallen ill with flu-like symptoms. She was normally one of those annoyingly healthy people, so her illness left me a little surprised and, I suppose, a little worried. I asked her not to go to work, but she insisted she wasn't sick enough to stay at home. She also wanted to work overtime to earn a bit extra for Christmas.

She worked hard, and late, all that week. The symptoms didn't seem to get any worse, though they didn't disappear either. On the Saturday of her last weekend alive, we had a wild party night, a real mad one. On Sunday, we stayed in bed to recover. On Monday, we both got up and went to work. At home later that evening, Emma told me she felt really ill. We agreed she wouldn't go to work the next day.

In the morning, she didn't seem that bad. We even made love. Afterwards, we laughed about possible excuses I could give when I rang in sick for her. In the past, I hadn't always conveyed accurately the details we'd agreed. On one occasion – after she'd instructed me to say she had a bad cold – I'd rung her work with the excuse she sat stranded 100 km away. I'd said that, after visiting her sister Siobhan, she'd gone to drive home only to discover that someone had stolen her car's wheels. I neglected to tell Emma I'd altered the story slightly. Sitting at her work desk next day, with fake cough and theatrical sniffles, she'd been stumped by her boss asking sympathetically if the police had found her wheels.

I jokingly called her a skiver as I made up the bed before leaving home. I left fruit-juice, books, magazines and the television's remote-control at her fingertips. At 9 a.m., I rang in sick for her. At ten, I phoned home. She said she felt awful, so I rang the doctor's surgery which stands almost on our doorstep. Thanks to a cancellation, the doctor could see her in just over an hour. I phoned Emma back to tell her to walk the 30 paces to the doctor's. In a weak voice, she replied she couldn't make the appointment because she couldn't get out of bed. I felt so alarmed I left work immediately and headed home.

The doctor agreed to come to Emma. I sat on the edge of the bed holding her hand and talking to her until he arrived. Then I left the room and waited downstairs till he'd finished. He diagnosed 'inflamed lungs', and prescribed anti-inflammatories and antibiotics. I went straight across the road to the chemist, who told me to bin the prescription because I could buy the same medication more cheaply off the shelf.

I brought the tablets back to Emma, who started taking them. She seemed to pep up a bit, so I returned to work for a few hours. When I got home later that Tuesday, Emma told me she felt worse. She looked pale and poorly. I wanted to take her to hospital, but she thought I was overreacting. She insisted she didn't feel bad enough to merit a trip to casualty. I'll never forget her words, 'Stop worrying, Bernie. It's only a cold.'

On Wednesday morning, I said I wanted to stay at home with her, but she ordered me to go to work, insisting she'd survive without me. I spoke to her on the phone during the day. When I got back late afternoon, she asked me, as she often did, to lie in bed with her and Brumble, her beloved teddy bear and almost inseparable companion. She loved watching TV in bed, snuggled up with me and Brumble rather than sitting in front of the screen downstairs. That Wednesday night, we hardly slept at all. She kept saying how awful she felt. I sat up in bed most of the night, holding her hand and stroking her hair.

At five in the morning, I kissed her goodbye and told her I'd finish work early to be with her. She said, 'Don't be long, Bernie.' During the day, I rang home to check on her condition. She said she felt a bit better, and we talked about poxy curtains. At four, I finished work and went home to find her sitting on the sofa in the front room downstairs. She looked strange. She seemed scared, like she'd seen a ghost. I asked if she was all right. She said, 'I love you, Bernie.' I knew then that something was desperately wrong. She seemed to know that, too. She said again, 'I love you, Bernie,' and added, 'Help me.'

I said, 'Don't fuck about, woman. You're scaring me.'

She laughed, which came as a relief, but then she repeated the words, 'I love you, Bernie.'

I sat next to her with my arm around her, holding one of her hands. My 17-year-old son Vinney popped his head round the door to ask if everything was all right. Over the next few hours, Emma's condition deteriorated rapidly. I kept wanting to make her a cup of tea, but every time I tried leaving the room, she'd beg me to stay. I made another attempt to get to the kitchen. She said then what I later realised had been her last words, 'Please don't leave me, Bernie. Stay here with me. Don't go now. I love you, Bernie.' Her pleading tone filled me with fear. I guessed something dreadful might be about to happen – and I felt powerless to stop it. I picked her up in my arms, like you'd pick up a child, and held her, trying to reassure her. Suddenly, her eyes rolled in her head. Gripped by a desperate panic, I laid her down gently, then rang the doctor's and implored them to send someone immediately. By now, Vinney had joined us in the front room.

I put the phone down, and again held Emma in my arms. All of a sudden, she leant forward. Her upper body stiffened, as if she were having a convulsion or even a heart attack. She seemed to stop breathing. Sick with shock and fear, I rang 999 and told the operator my wife had stopped breathing, though I could still feel a pulse in her neck. I begged for help. The operator instructed me on how to give the kiss of life – and promised an ambulance would soon be there.

Vinney helped me lay Emma on the floor. He held her head as I tried desperately to breathe life into her. The 999 operator had stayed on the line. Vinney picked up the phone and began describing what was happening. Then he started passing on further instructions from the operator to me. I felt Emma's heart stop. I shouted at Vinney, 'Tell them her heart's stopped! Tell them her heart's stopped!' The operator told me via Vinney to try to restart her heart by pushing her chest down with the palm of my hand. I did as instructed, crying the whole time, pleading with her to wake up, but I knew my Emma had just died. Sobbing and shouting, I continued doing everything to get her breathing again. But she'd gone.

The paramedics arrived swiftly. They set to work urgently, but I could see no response from Emma. I slammed the door shut. I said no one could leave until they'd saved my Emmie. They fought for more than an hour to revive her. It was too late. They pronounced her dead at '2024 hrs'.

The next day, a pathologist performed an autopsy. I can't bear to think of what he had to do to my beautiful Emma's body, but his work meant he could tell me why she'd died. He said a common flu virus had attacked her heart. Normally, this virus just travels round the bloodstream till it's zapped either by antibiotics or the body's own defences. But sometimes, rarely and unpredictably, it attacks the heart. The pathologist told me he'd only ever come across one other case. The victim then had also been a woman in her 20s. He told me that, once the virus had started attacking Emma's heart, nothing could have saved her. She could have been on antibiotics in the best hospital in the world, but she'd still have died.

One day short of five months since our marriage, and only ten days before Christmas, I buried my wife in her wedding dress. More than 100 people followed the horse-drawn carriage containing her coffin. At the cemetery in Codsall, my four best men – Rashed, Gavin, Adolf and Hughie – together with my sons Adrian and Vinney and my brother Michael helped me carry Emma to her grave.

We made our way through the cemetery at a solemn snail's pace. Each step brought me closer to the moment when Emma's body would disappear for ever. My sense of dread filled my feet with lead. The coffin, too, grew heavier with every second. I felt a stab of pain as I saw ahead of me the mounds of freshly dug earth that would soon cover my beloved Emmie. Slowly, we reached our grim destination. One day it'll be my grave too, but, as I helped lower Emma into the ground, I wished that day had come and I could have joined her.

Less than halfway down, the coffin came to a sudden stop. It wouldn't go any further. We realised the grave was too small. The funeral director blushed with embarrassment. Adolf said, 'Lift the coffin back up, boys.' The funeral director said he'd fetch a 'grave attendant' (which I believe is the new term for 'gravedigger'). But before he could do so, Adolf stepped forward and said, 'Forget it. It's not a good idea to bring us the fool who dug this.' Then he picked up one of the long-handled shovels lying on the ground and said, 'One of you grab that one.' Emma's uncle Jerry reached for the other shovel. He and Adolf took turns in digging away the excess earth on the grave's walls. Huffing, puffing and ranting inaudibly, Adolf looked up at me at one point and said, 'Typical O'Mahoney. She won't do what she's told.' After Adolf and Jerry had exerted themselves for ten minutes, the grave could finally receive my Emma. This mishap managed somehow to make bearable what otherwise could have been an unbearable moment.

All day, I had to tell myself to stay strong, not just for myself, but for my mother, my children and Emma's sister, Siobhan. I knew too that Emma wouldn't have wanted me to go to pieces in public. All day, I stifled my tears. The priest had warned me I'd find difficult the task of reading a tribute to my wife during the service. But I had to do it, because I felt that's what she'd have wanted.

After the burial, everyone went to the Royal British Legion Club near my mother's house. One of my Irish uncles, Paul from Sligo, stood on the same stage my father had stood on 30 years earlier and raised a toast to Emma. Then he sang a shatteringly moving version of my father's favourite, 'Danny Boy', the song we'd played at our wedding in memory of Emma's parents, my father and dead friends.

Only when everyone had gone home that night did I allow

myself to break down. I walked crying through Codsall's empty streets and made my way back to the cemetery. In the darkness, I found Emma's grave and lay down on the thick carpet of flowers that covered her final resting place. Alone again with my Emma, I let my tears fall until I cried myself to sleep. My uncle Paul found me there at four in the morning. He lifted me to my feet, put his arm round my shoulder and helped me walk back to my mother's.

This grief is too deep for tears. The pain is physical, like somebody has punched a hole in my chest and is twisting and squeezing my heart. I've never felt so alone in my life. Emma was more than my wife. I loved and trusted her completely. She was my best adviser, my best barrister, my best psychiatrist, my best protector and, above all, my best mate. We went everywhere, and did everything, together.

Just a few weeks ago, when I finished *Hateland*, I felt like I'd brought to an end a whole rotten chapter of my life. I looked with optimism to the future – my future with Emma. And now that future is gone. I don't know how I'm ever going to get over this loss.

I'm not sure why I'm writing these words. I don't know if I should be sharing my despair with strangers. But if you've got this far in the book, then you've been living for a few hours in my world. Perhaps I just want to say: when you go back to your world, be kind to the people you love, because you never know when you're going to lose them.

Now I'm faced with another new start, another new beginning, but this time it's one I'm not sure I can make.